Eastern Europe in Children's Literature

Eastern Europe in Children's Literature

An Annotated Bibliography of English-language Books

Frances F. Povsic

Bibliographies and Indexes in World Literature, Number 8

GREENWOOD PRESS
New York • Westport, Connecticut • London

Library of Congress Cataloging-in-Publication Data

Povsic, Frances F., 1923-
  Eastern Europe in children's literature.

  (Bibliographies and indexes in world literature,
ISSN 0742-6801 ; no. 8)
  Includes indexes.
  1. Children's literature—Bibliography. 2. Europe,
Eastern, in literature—Bibliography. 3. East
Europeans in literature—Bibliography. 4. Europe,
Eastern—Bibliography. 5. East Europeans—Bibliography.
I. Title. II. Series.
Z1037.P875 1986 [PN1009.A1] 016.82′08′03247 86-3104
ISBN 0-313-23777-8 (lib. bdg. : alk. paper)

Library of Congress Catalog Card Number: 86-3104
ISBN: 0-313-23777-8
ISSN: 0742-6801

First published in 1986

Greenwood Press, Inc.
88 Post Road West, Westport, Connecticut 06881

Printed in the United States of America

The paper used in this book complies with the
Permanent Paper Standard issued by the National
Information Standards Organization (Z39.48-1984).

10 9 8 7 6 5 4 3 2 1

Copyright Acknowledgment

The frontispiece is an illustration by Trina Schart Hyman to "The Shepherd's Nosegay,"
reprinted, by kind permission of Little, Brown and Company, from *Favorite Fairy Tales
Told in Czechoslovakia*, retold by Virginia Haviland. Copyright 1966 by Trina Schart
Hyman.

To the children of the world
and the parents, teachers,
and librarians who introduce books to them.

The head does not hear until the heart has listened, and
what the heart knows today the head will understand
tomorrow.

--James Stephens, <u>The Crock of Gold</u>

Contents

x   Contents

Foreword

A sense of place is one of those vague, mysterious elements of style that is frequently mentioned in literary criticism, yet rarely defined in specific terms. That is, many critics have pointed out the sensation one can get of "being there" while reading certain books set in real or imaginary places, but they are often hard-pressed to describe precisely what it is that gives us such sensations.

Mere detail in description on the part of the author is not enough. The actions of the characters must fit in with their surroundings and situations as satisfyingly as the pieces of a jigsaw puzzle come together and form a whole picture.

Why this happens in some books that are written with settings in other places (or translated from the works of writers from those places), and does not happen in other books with similar settings, can be one of the delightful and enlightening discoveries one makes in real life.

Upon seeing a first glimpse of a remote Swiss mountain village, who among us has not been thrilled to recognize many a scene in <u>Heidi</u>, in spite of the fact that the book was written more than a hundred years ago? Yet the numerous dry descriptions we were forced to read in some geography texts are not likely to be recalled when we finally get to see the sites at first hand.

I remember so well reading Louise Rankin's <u>Daughter of the Mountains</u> and being captivated by the descriptions of the Himalayan Mountains, the people, and, most of all, the whole aura of Buddhism that pervades the book. Prayer was very much a part of my daily life, especially prayer that had to be repeated over and over. How fantastic to think one could turn a wheel or spin a metal cylinder and automatically have the prayer repeated a hundred or a thousand times (depending upon how many times they were

written over and over again on the paper)! A setting
further away from my Wisconsin farm home could hardly be
imagined, yet I did not look upon it as farfetched. It was
very real to me, because of the author's success in
conveying so well the sense of place. And I was not at all
disappointed, years later, when I experienced firsthand some
of the things she wrote about.

Another book that gave me the same deep-down feeling of
knowing it was "just like that" was <u>The Good Master</u> by Kate
Seredy, which is annotated in the Hungary section of this
bibliography. Kate and Jansci were so real to me, I felt I
could reach out and touch them if I caressed their lovely
portraits on the front pages. In fact, I think I even
kissed them!

It would have been wonderful had I had similar reading
experiences using books with settings in the Polish homeland
of my ancestors, but such books were not available in my
childhood, and few are to be found even now. Nor are there
many describing the variety of immigrant experience that
such families as those of my great-grandparents might have
lived through. It was one of my reasons for writing about
them.

It is good to have this bibliography to indicate what
has been published for children that reflects the lives and
culture of immigrants from the East European countries.
There is much that is good in the old stories, especially if
they can be interpreted by someone who has lived a life
enriched by these treasures, firsthand.

But I hope that the bibliography will also serve to
show what great gaps we still have in our children's
literature, especially our modern stories depicting the ways
in which these cultures have been passed on to present-day
American children. In the U.S. today, there are over 14
million persons (as indicated by the 1980 census) who
describe themselves as ethnic immigrants, or descendants of
immigrants, from the countries included in these lists. A
large number of the families have been here three or four
generations, but there are also many who have arrived since
the end of World War II. But their experiences are hard to
find in the mainstream of children's literature.

My challenge to the user of this bibliography,
therefore, is twofold. Select from these pages the stories,
biographies, folktales, and other literature that appeals,
and use it with children of many different backgrounds and
tastes. Whenever you meet a person from one of the
countries covered in this bibliography, and that person has
an interesting story to tell, encourage him or her to work
at the difficult (but not impossible) task of getting it
down in print.

--Anne Pellowski

Preface

Yes, children's books keep alive a sense of
nationality; but they also keep alive a sense of
humanity. They describe their native land
lovingly, but they also describe faraway lands
where unknown brothers live. They understand the
essential quality of their own race; but each of
them is a messenger that goes beyond mountains and
rivers, beyond the seas, to the very ends of the
world in search of the world, in search of new
friendships. Every country gives and every
country receives, innumerable are exchanges.[1]

Since Paul Hazard's classic work <u>Books, Children and Men</u> was
first published in 1944, numerous works pertaining to
children's literature have appeared in print. These works
overwhelmingly support the centuries-old belief that
literature has the power not only to delight and inform, but
also to influence people's attitudes and values.

Although in its scientific form bibliotherapy is a
product of the twentieth century, the idea of using books in
preventing and solving emotional problems, in building a
positive self-concept, and in gaining insight into confusing
situations is as old as books themselves. Studies on
bibliotherapy frequently mention the fact that the door of
the library at Thebes in ancient Greece bore the
inscription, "Healing place of the soul," and that the
Romans frequently recommended those having psychological
problems to spend time reading orations. During the last
twenty years some promoters of bibliotherapy for children
have centered their research studies on the topic of
attitudes toward ethnic and anthropological groups and have
concluded that the reading of good literature produced
positive attitudinal changes. It has also been pointed out
that when group discussion followed the reading of the
stories, attitude changes were even more prominent.[2] This

was especially true when fiction was used, as children tend to identify with characters and respond to their experiences.

Walt Whitman wrote in <u>Leaves of Grass</u>: "I hear America singing, its varied carols I hear." Over a hundred years ago, when Whitman wrote about his America and heard the diverse strains of its cultural symphony, the predominant social idea among Americans was the "melting pot," a term created by the English author Israel Zangwill in 1909 in his play by this title. For too many years most of the nation was deaf to the melody of Whitman's words, and it was not until the middle of this century that an awakening of ethnic consciousness appeared. During the 1960s and 1970s, decades of social change, there was a resurgence of ethnic activities on national, state, and local levels. Sociologists, educators, and, consequently, publishers of educational materials began to emphasize national and cultural diversity as a basis for unity of the American populace, rejecting both the approach of assimilation as well as the notion of separatism. Educational organizations, such as the American Association of Colleges for Teacher Education, the Association for Supervision and Curriculum Development, the National Council for Social Studies, and others adopted the principle that the recognition and strengthening of cultural pluralism should become an essential element of educational processes on every level. The statements of these organizations pointed out that creating a curriculum reflecting the multicultural nature of American society is a democratic and professional responsibility. The education guidelines they prepared were based on the concept that multicultural education would aid students in understanding and appreciating their own culture, leading to a fuller acceptance and deeper respect for other cultures. It was pointed out that especially for those who have cultural roots outside the country of their adoption, the understanding and developing of their cultural heritage is a necessity.[3]

Moreover, in 1978, the United States Congress established an Ethnic Heritage Studies Program through which financial assistance was provided to public and private institutions to develop educational materials and design projects that would help American students learn more about their own cultural roots and about the cultural heritage of other ethnic groups in the nation.[4]

In 1978 and again in 1980, while serving on the consultant panel to the International Education Division of the HEW's Office of Education, evaluating proposals submitted to the Ethnic Heritage Studies for funding, and a year later, while participating in the Social Science Education Consortium's evaluation of materials produced with the support of the program, I became aware of the scope and wealth of activities prevalent among ethnic groups across the nation. At the same time I noted the gaps that

existed in the information available for young people
regarding Slavic and other East European ethnic groups in
the United States. I was not able to find much material
written in English relating to the traditions and general
culture of East European groups and their contributions to
the American heritage that could be used in elementary and
secondary schools or educational institutions of higher
education. Most available guides to literature with ethnic
and pluralistic concepts deal largely with America's most
prominent ethnic groups. One notable exception is Buttlar
and Wynar's guide for school media centers and public
libraries, <u>Building Ethnic Collections</u>, published in 1977
(see Sources listed in the Introduction). The coverage,
however, is limited to selected materials available for
purchase.

Even before awareness of a multicultural society began
to be manifested in the literature, there already existed an
effort to promote internationalism in children's books. The
tragic consequences of World War II had strengthened the
conviction that an understanding, tolerance, and
appreciation for the differences among the peoples of the
world as well as an affirmation of a common humanity are
absolutely necessary if relations among nations are to be
improved and world peace is to be achieved and maintained.
The belief that the exchange of children's books from one
country to another could be instrumental in fostering
international cooperation has been frequently expressed in
writings dealing with children's literature.

One of the strongest promoters of this idea was Jella
Lepman. As a young journalist, she escaped in 1936 from her
native Germany to London, where she worked during the war
for the British Broadcasting Company as well as for the
American Broadcasting Station in Europe. Only three years
after the war she established the International Youth
Library in Munich, which is currently housed in the
impressive castle Blutenburg and contains nearly half a
million children's books in more than one hundred
languages.[5] Five years later (in 1953), striving to
establish a common ground on which to bring together
individuals and agencies involved in writing, illustrating,
producing, distributing, promoting, and interpreting
children's books, Lepman established the International Board
on Books for Young People (IBBY) in Zurich, Switzerland.
Since then IBBY has systematically and significantly
contributed to the promotion of international cooperation
through several projects and activities, among them:
biennial congresses; international exhibitions of children's
books; presentation of awards to outstanding authors and
illustrators, especially the Hans Christian Andersen Award
and the Janus Korczak Award; designation of International
Children's Book Day (April 2, the birthday of H. C.
Andersen); and the creation of its voice, the journal
<u>Bookbird</u>. More of IBBY's work is done through its national
sections, currently located in over forty countries. The

United States Board on Books for Young People (formerly Friends of IBBY) is especially active.

In addition to IBBY's untiring efforts, other projects sprang up in support of intercultural exchange in children's literature. Anne Pellowski, an established writer and storyteller and a widely recognized authority on internationalism in children's books, established the Information Center on Children's Culture (supported by the U. S. Committee for UNICEF) in New York and directed it for several years. Attempting to "introduce children to the children of other lands and other cultures"[6] the Center contains materials in English about children of the world as well as books and other media in the languages of the countries where they originated. The extensive collections of foreign language children's books at the Children's Division of the Library of Congress should also be mentioned.

Moreover, the American Library Association (ALA) through its division, the Association for Library Services to Children (ALSC), and the division's committees on the Selection of Children's Books from Various Cultures, and the International Relations Committee also focus their attention on promoting literature as tools in achieving international understanding. These groups prepare bibliographies of books from other countries, of books reflecting immigrant experiences in the United States, and of books published in America that are of international interest. Most of these lists are published in the ALA journal Booklist and/or separately in pamphlets and books. In a special effort to bring good children's books published in other countries into the hands of American children, the ALSC has annually granted the Mildred L. Batchelder Award to an American company that publishes the most outstanding translation.

Other organizations, such as the United Nations Educational Scientific and Cultural Organization (UNESCO), the Children's Book Council, the Association for Childhood Education International, and especially the International Reading Association (IRA) prepare and publish bibliographies that provide the readership with materials supporting the idea of global understanding. Examples of such lists include ten short bibliographies prepared by this author and published in the IRA journals The Reading Teacher and Journal of Reading from 1980 until 1982. In fact, it was because of the numerous positive responses received from the readers of the two journals regarding these bibliographies that I decided to expand the work originally done for the IRA and prepare a comprehensive book-length bibliography describing books and stories with East European themes that have been published since the turn of the century.

The project of gathering together works for children written in English or translated into English was undertaken to make researchers, elementary and secondary teachers, and librarians aware of the literature concerned with multiculturalism and internationalism as they relate to the Slavic and East European nationalities. In the belief that fiction is especially effective in portraying other people's cultures and in giving insight into other people's way of life, it was decided that the book should present mostly fiction. It has been widely recognized by the promoters of children's literature that fiction is a most powerful medium in helping people comprehend a point of view different from their own and in helping people understand attitudes and problems remote in time, place, and social positions. Good stories not only inform, but help the readers, especially young readers, to experience other persons' joys and sorrows, fears, disappointments, inner hurts, hopes, defeats, and victories. Literature rooted in other cultures and other countries allows the young person to experience what would otherwise be undreamt of in a single life span. Through literature, young people share in the experiences of others, learn their words, understand their thoughts, and above all feel their heartbeats. Good stories not only make children aware, but help them comprehend and feel that, in spite of the differences among people, there is one world, and that people of this world share in a common humanity.

Because stories involve not only the reader's intellectual powers but also his or her emotions, they tend to leave much stronger and longer lasting impressions, rather than to impart purely rational information. When, in my early teens, I read Harriet Beecher Stowe's story <u>Uncle Tom's Cabin</u> (in a Slovenian translation), the plight of the black slaves made an unforgettable impression on me, although at that time I had never personally met a black person. Arriving after the war as a refugee to the United States from my native Slovenia and working in an orphanage with ethnically mixed children, I could not help feeling closer to the black children there. Through my reading of <u>Uncle Tom's Cabin</u>, I had become sensitized to the tragedy of bigotry early in my life. Similarly, ever since I read an absorbing story about a Czech immigrant and his longing for his homeland (the story is not available in English translation, but I still remember the title of the song in which he expressed his feelings), anything Czech - the Czech people, their country, their literature, their folklore - is especially dear to me. Young readers also have the potential to gradually respond to good stories and new experiences with positive concepts about other people or with changed and transformed attitudes. Without a doubt, this is what the divided, polarized world needs most today: to understand better, to feel more deeply, and to respond with tolerance, good will, and compassion. The Tin Woodsman also had some brain. What he wanted the Wizard of Oz to grant him was a heart. It is hoped that the books described in this volume, if introduced and made available, will have an enduring influence on young people's minds and hearts. I feel that by presenting the book <u>Eastern Europe in Chil-</u>

dren's Literature, I am joining hands with thousands of others, who are working within the aforementioned groups and organizations to achieve these goals.

NOTES

1. Paul   Hazard,   Books, Children and Men,   trans. Marguerite Mitchell (Boston: The Horn Book, 1944), 146.

2. Joanne E. Bernstein, Books to Help Children Cope with Separation and Loss (New York: Bowker, 1983), 24-25.

3. American Association of Colleges for Teacher Education, Commission on Multicultural Education, "No One Model American," Journal of Teacher Education (Winter 1973): 264-5.

4. "Ethnic Heritage Studies Program" (P.L. 95-561, 1 Nov. 1978).

5. Eileen Tway, "The International Youth Library: Schloss Blutenburg," Newsletter of the United States Board on Books for Young People, Inc. (Fall 1985): 6.

6. The Information Center on Children's Culture (New York: U.S. Committee for UNICEF, n.d.), no page no.

Acknowledgments

Appreciation for assistance in the preparation of this work is due to the following institutions and individuals: to the Bowling Green State University Research Committee for a grant to help defray expenses; to the administration of the Bowling Green State University Libraries, Dr. Dwight Burlingame, Dr. William Miller and Dr. Sharon Rogers for their support and understanding; to Kausalya Padmarayan of the Bowling Green State University Library for the generous interlibrary loan services; to the staff of the Curriculum Resource Center: Kathleen Aufderhaar, Sara Bushong, Linda Funk, Gaynelle Predmore, and student assistants for various kinds of aid; to the publishers of children's books for supplying review copies; to the libraries across the nation for sending out-of-print books; to Thomas Povsic and Rebecca Rupert for critically reading the manuscript; to John Rice and Wally Vogel for assistance in preparing indexes; to Anne Pellowski for invaluable advice and writing the Foreword; to Lorene Malanowski for typing the manuscript; to Marilyn Brownstein, the acquisition editor at Greenwood Press, for her unabated patience; to my family, Slavko, Thomas, and Maria, for their overall support and good will.

Introduction

SCOPE, CRITERIA, AND METHODOLOGY

The book <u>Eastern Europe in Children's Literature</u> contains titles of works written originally in English or originally written in another language and subsequently translated into English, that reflect the lives of East European immigrants in the United States as well as the lives of these peoples in their homelands. The following seven nationalities and countries are represented: Albania, Bulgaria, Czechoslovakia, Hungary, Poland, Romania and Yugoslavia. (Russia and the Soviet Union, including the Baltic countries, the Ukraine, Byelorussia and the Asian Soviet nationalities, will be represented in a separate volume now in preparation.) Most of the books written originally in English were published in the United States, though some were first published in Britain and Canada.

This bibliography includes traditional stories; single title books; collections of folk and fairy tales, ballads, myths, and legends; collections of national proverbs; and selected collections of poetry. Although traditional stories were not originally created and written for children, they have been enjoyed by children because of the simplicity of their construction, their uncomplicated characters, and their uncondescending style. Their themes seem to be the most universal in literature. They contain the accumulated experiences of each nation and each nation's understanding of the meaning of life, of life's values, virtues, and vices. They reflect the people's perceptions of the supernatural world and their explanations for natural phenomena. In summary, traditional literature contains the spirit of the nation. It is no wonder that, along with a renewed cultural consciousness and international awareness, there is a renewed interest in making folk literature available to the young through translations, retellings, adaptations, and new editions of old treasures. Out of three hundred fifteen titles described in the book, one hun-

dred six represent traditional literature: one title is
Albanian, three are Bulgarian, twenty-three are Czech,
twenty-four Hungarian, twenty-seven Polish, twelve Romanian,
and sixteen titles originated in the various Yugoslav
nationalities.

The second type of literature gathered in the book is
historical fiction, biography, and autobiography. I find it
necessary to emphasize that for the purpose of this book,
the term "historical fiction" was interpreted in its
broadest sense. Generally, books portraying the lives of
people and historical events taking place in their native
countries or in the countries of their adoption up to the
immediate post World War II period are included in this
group, even though some of these books, at the time they
were written, were not intended to be historical fiction.
Such factors as the intent of the author and the accurate
portrayal of times and places have been taken into
consideration. Some of the examples are Petershams' story
Miki (117), Seredy's stories The Chestry Oak (120), The Good
Master (121) and The Singing Tree (122), and even Sawyer's
The Christmas Anna Angel (119). Biography and autobiography
complement and reinforce historical fiction. Biographies
show the young that history is made up of people, from their
relationship to others, and from their failures and their
achievements. Reading and discussing stories grouped under
historical fiction, biography, and autobiography should
enable young people to understand historical periods and
historical personages more comprehensively and should add
dimension and life to their perception of the past. A
special group of stories within this category are those that
deal with World War II in general and specifically with The
Jewish Holocaust. They are especially valuable as they
create a strong aversion to war and to international hatred
on one hand and an admiration for the strength of the human
spirit and of human endurance on the other. The subject
index should be consulted in order to locate these entries
in the bibliography.

The remaining books are grouped under "Other Fiction,"
which comprises modern fiction and modern fantasy, neither
genre numerous enough for separate classification. In the
modern fiction category are stories that have the potential
to entertain but that also underscore the social values of
the people belonging to each nationality, their family
lives, and the problems and joys of their personal
relationships. Most of the fanciful tales are humorous,
merely fun to read. Youthful human characters assume
supernatural forms and strengths (as in the story of Deborah
the Dybbuk, 132). Animals talk, inanimate objects come to
life, and both possess extraordinary powers. It seems that
science fiction, with its glimpse into a future where
technology governs all aspects of life, as well as adventurous stories of traveling into the universe and of
interactions with aliens, reflects particularly well the
concepts different nationalities hold of the future of the

world and the way these nationalities perceive and struggle against evil powers.

In all, <u>Eastern Europe in Children's Literature</u> contains descriptions of three hundred fifteen titles. These are arranged under the name of the country and, within each country, under three types of literature: traditional literature; historial fiction, biography and autobiography; and other fiction. If there were not enough titles to justify the use of all three headings, the groupings were combined, as is the case with Albanian literature.

It should also be pointed out that in the case of literature representing smaller nations, e.g., Albania and Bulgaria, where not many works in English were located, I searched for and included individual stories that appear in various collections. One example of this type of entry is the story of Albanian immigrants in the United States, "Vasil Discovers America" from the collection <u>Told Under the Stars and Stripes</u> (2). Moreover, in the case of Bulgarian literature, I included the four stories, mostly animal tales, written and illustrated by Ivan Gantschev, a Bulgarian-born artist now living and publishing in Austria, which, in my mind, still reflect the spirit of the Bulgarian people (13, 14, 15, 16).

A serious attempt was made to list all available and appropriate titles for children and young adults through the junior high school level. Materials suitable for senior high school reading were included only if they could also be read and enjoyed by junior high school students. Excluded were those adult titles which, in the opinion of competent reviewers, are also suitable for older high school students. Thus, in spite of the fact that many of the listed titles are used by senior high school students, it was not my intent to give a complete coverage for this group. In determining what to include and what to exclude, I kept in mind not only the theme of the book but also the reading level and the amount of historical knowledge necessary to understand the story fully. The probable reading and use levels are indicated with the bibliographical information for each title.

All books listed were read, but not all that were read were selected. They were excluded if they did not fit the acceptable literary standards for their genres. A good number of titles, however, that do not possess the literary elegance one would wish them to have, were included if they could be valuable in other respects. The annotations and evaluative comments should help the user of the book decide whether a particular title is worth acquiring for his or her needs.

Obviously, not all titles listed are available in print, but all are available in various libraries and can be obtained through interlibrary loan services. It was my intent to bring together all suitable stories published from the beginning of the century until the end of 1984 that, in different times and different styles, portray the peoples of Albania, Bulgaria, Czechoslovakia, Hungary, Poland, Romania, and Yugoslavia either in their homelands or as immigrants in the new world.

I wish to stress that the proper names in titles and annotations listed are spelled as they appear in the books described. Thus, one name may vary from title to title. In the subject index, however, the most common spelling is used. Diacritical marks are implemented exactly as used by the original authors. They are omitted if the authors did not use them.

INDEXES

Three separate indexes are provided. The first is the author, translator, and illustrator index. It should be noted that all individuals who appear as compilers of collections or retellers of stories are included, as are original collectors of folk tales when their names appear in the books described. This index is followed by the title and subject indexes. In preparing the subject index, the needs of potential users were kept in mind. As the intent of this annotated guide is to present relevant titles portraying East European nationalities, no attempt was made to analyze the literature as such (e.g., to list folklore motifs or characters contained in traditional literature); but every effort was made to list various aspects of people's lives (e.g., family life, customs, and traditions) historical periods, historical personages, and major historical events, where these are reflected in the works cited. For easier identification, life dates are included with proper names. Because different historical sources vary slightly in regard to these dates, the three-volume historical guide Rulers and Governments of the World, (Bowker, 1978) was used as the authority. The numerous national and international literary and illustration awards granted to many of the annotated titles are also indexed. All listings in the three indexes refer the user to the item number assigned to each title, not to the page number.

SOURCES

Among the numerous sources consulted in compiling the titles in this book are the bibliographies and selection tools listed below. Although various editions of these guides were used, only the most recent ones are cited for the sake of brevity.

Books

Books from Other Countries. Ed. Anne McConnell. Rev. ed.
  Chicago, Ill.: American Association of School Librarians,
  1978.

Buttlar, Lois and Lubomyr R. Wynar. Building Ethnic
  Collections: An Annotated Guide for School Media Centers
  and Public Libraries. Littleton, Colo.: Libraries
  Unlimited, 1977.

Chase, Judith Wragg. Books to Build World Friendship: An
  Annotated Bibliography of Children's Books from Pre-School
  to 8th Grade: Europe. Dobbs Ferry, N.Y.: Oceana, 1964.

Children's Books of International Interest. Ed. Barbara
  Elleman. 3rd ed. Chicago, Ill.: American Library
  Association, 1984.

Children's Catalog. 14th ed. and supplements. New York:
  H. W. Wilson, 1981, 1982-85.

Cianciolo, Patricia J. Picture Books for Children. 2nd ed.
  Chicago, Ill.: American Library Association, 1981.

Dreyer, Sharon Spredemann. The Bookfinder. Circle Pines,
  Minn.: American Guidance Service, 1985.

Eakin, Mary K. Good Books for Children: A Selection of
  Outstanding Children's Books. 3rd ed. Chicago, Ill.:
  University of Chicago Press, 1966.

The Elementary School Library Collection: A Guide to
  Books and Other Media, Phases 1-2-3. 15th ed.
  Williamsport, Pa.: Brodart, 1986.

Gillespie, John Thomas. Best Books for Children, Preschool
  Through the Middle Grades. 3rd ed. New York: Bowker,
  1985.

Hotchkiss, Jeanette. European Historical Fiction and
  Biography for Children and Young People. 2nd ed.
  Metuchen, N.J: Scarecrow, 1972.

Junior High School Library Catalog. 4th ed. and supplements. New York: H. W. Wilson, 1980; 1981-84.

Lima, Carolyn W. A to Zoo: Subject Access to Children's
  Picture Books. 2nd ed. New York: Bowker, 1985.

MacDonald, Margaret Read. The Storyteller's Sourcebook: A
  A Subject, Title, and Motif Index to Folklore Collections
  for Children. Detroit, Mich.: Neal-Schuman, 1982.

Metzner, Seymour. <u>World History in Juvenile Books: A</u>
  <u>Geographical and Chronological Guide</u>. Bronx, N.Y.: H. W.
  Wilson, 1973.

National Council of Teachers of English. Committee on the
  Elementary School Booklist. <u>Adventuring with Books: A</u>
  <u>Booklist for Pre-K - Grade 6</u>. New ed. Urbana, Ill.: The
  Council, 1985.

<u>Reading Ladders for Human Relations</u>. 6th ed. Washington:
  American Council on Education, 1981.

<u>Senior High School Library Catalog</u>. 12th ed. and supple-
  ments. New York: H. W. Wilson, 1982; 1983-85.

Sutherland, Zena. <u>The Best in Children's Books: The Uni-</u>
  <u>versity of Chicago Guide to Children's Literature</u>.
  Chicago, Ill.: University of Chicago Press, 1980.

Sutherland, Zena. <u>Children and Books</u>. 7th ed. Glenview,
  Ill.: Scott Foresman, 1986.

Sutherland, Zena. <u>History in Children's Books: An Annota-</u>
  <u>ted Bibliography for Schools and Libraries</u>. Booklawn,
  N.J., McKinley, 1967.

<u>Subject Guide to Children's Books in Print</u>. New York:
  Bowker, 1984.

Journals

<u>Booklist</u>. Chicago: American Library Association, 1905-.

<u>Bulletin of the Center for Children's Books</u>. Chicago, Ill.:
  University of Chicago, 1947-.

<u>Journal of Reading</u>. Newark, Del.: International Reading
  Association, 1957-.

<u>Kirkus Reviews</u>. New York: The Kirkus Service, 1932-.

<u>School Library Journal</u>. New York: Bowker, 1954-.

<u>The Horn Book Magazine</u>. Boston: The Horn Book, 1924-.

<u>The Reading Teacher</u>. Newark, Del.: International Reading
  Association, 1948-.

Eastern
Europe
in
Children's
Literature

Albania

TRADITIONAL LITERATURE

001. Wheeler, Post. <u>Albanian Wonder Tales</u>. Illus. Maud and Miska Petersham. Garden City, N.Y.: Doubleday, Doran, 1936. 282 p. Grades 5-9.
   A rich and intriguing collection, these ten ancient tales possess the strong characters fostered by the rugged Albanian countryside. There are giants of great strength, wild witches, and fearful monsters, who seem to personify the destructive forces of nature, also half-human birds, flying men, and talking animals and plants. Most of the tales are about young men: a boy who takes a letter to where the dead live, a boy who visits nightingale, a man who understands the speech of animals, and a man who goes to find an angel. Only two stories are about girls: one about a girl who takes a snake for a husband and one about a princess with a silver tooth. In both of these a king has three daughters, the youngest being the loveliest, wisest, bravest, and most virtuous. These vigorous stories contain many typical Albanian proverbs expressing the people's everyday wisdom, which has preserved their heritage through the centuries. The tales, translated both from original Albanian and German sources, are accompanied by attractive drawings, an introduction, and an explanation of foreign words.

FICTION, BIOGRAPHY, AND AUTOBIOGRAPHY

002. Association for Childhood Education. <u>Told Under the Stars and Stripes</u>. Illus. Nedda Walker. New York: Macmillan, 1959. 347 p. Grades 4-8.
   A collection of twenty-seven stories dealing with the acculturation of children from various national and racial backgrounds to the American way of life. Maintaining that people from each national group have contributed significantly to the rich heritage and

quality of life in America, the authors have selected the stories that strengthen the reader's understanding of the differences between people and that encourage the reader to accept these differences with a generosity of spirit. The story "Vasil Discovers America," written by Leslie G. Cameron and printed originally in <u>American Junior Red Cross News</u>, is about an Albanian boy, Vasil Tsilta, who has lived in the United States with his parents for two years. Vasil is especially fond of his new friend, Nikola Novan, also an Albanian from Pogdanoc, whose family moved to their town recently. Vasil is deeply saddened when he finds out from his parents that Nikola's family has had a long feud with his family, that uncles and cousins on each side have been killed because of it, and that the feud between the two families must continue between him and Nikola. The two boys realize how foolish the feud is and how necessary changes in their ancestral ways are when Vasil is chosen to lead the singing of the "Star Spangled Banner" and "America the Beautiful" and Nikola is to recite a patriotic poem at a school celebration of Columbus Day. When Nikola whistles a special call used by Albanian mountaineers to save Vasil from a traffic accident, Vasil vows to take the first step toward a new life in a new land: a life of peace and freedom for both families.

003.   Cleaver, Elizabeth Cleveland.   <u>Pran of Albania</u>. Illus. Maud and Miska Petersham. New York: Doubleday, Doran, 1929. 257 p. Grades 6-9.
Pran, a girl of fourteen, her mother, Lukja, her father, Ndrek, and her twin brothers, Gjon and Nikola, are of the Maltsar tribe living in the northern Albanian village of Thethi, a two day walk from Skodra, at the beginning of the twentieth century. The story, centered around Pran and her family, contains vivid descriptions of the life of the mountain people, their unwavering courage, their patriotism, their traditions, beliefs, their strong sense of belonging to one another, their hospitality, and their care for one another. Pran emerges as an intelligent girl, a loving daughter and sister, a courageous young lady, and an eloquent spokeswoman for the ideas of peace, a new life, and a change that has to take place if they are to live free of the old and evil bloody feuds. At a young age, Pran shares in the household responsibilities of a grown woman. In a cradle tied to her back, she takes the sick baby of a family friend to a doctor in Skodra and returns after four days of hiking with news of signal fires burning in the north, warning the Albanians of approaching strikes from the neighboring Slavs. When her country is at war, she carries food from the refugee camp to her father, who is fighting with the other men. There is no room for fear in her heart when she returns to the fighting grounds with information concerning the planned enemy attack, which she has overheard while

hiding from a group of spies. Unlike other young women, for whom husbands are selected at an early age by their parents, Pran marries the man she loves. The absorbing story contains much action, suspense, and even a bit of mystery.

004. Greene, Carol. <u>Mother Teresa: Friend of the Friend-less</u>. Picture-Story Biographies. Chicago: Childrens, 1983. 31 p. Grades 2-4.
This biography of Mother Teresa emphasizes her work among the world's poor. Born in 1910 in Skopje, Yugoslavia, to Albanian parents, she was given the name of Agnes. At the age of eighteen, she joined the religious order of the Sisters of Our Lady of Loreto and was assigned to missionary work in India. After the completion of her studies, Agnes, now Sister Teresa, was sent to Calcutta to teach in one of the Sisters' high schools and soon became the school's principal. Her calling, however, led her elsewhere. Realizing that many poor people in the Calcutta slums were ill, had no homes, no food, and no one to love them, she decided to study health-care in order to be able to help them. The unwanted children were her first charges. When more women began to join Sister Teresa in her work, she established a new order, the Missionaries of Charity, which was charged with the task of serving the poorest of the poor. For her extraordinary love of and dedication to the needy of the world, Mother Teresa received many awards and prizes, including the Nobel Peace Prize in 1979. A simply written biography, the book is printed in large type and accompanied by numerous high quality photographs and drawings.

005. Miller, Elizabeth Cleveland. <u>Children of the Mountain Eagle</u>. Illus. Maud and Miska Petersham. New York: Doubleday, Doran, 1936. 328 p. Grades 5-8.
The mountain villages in the northern Albania at the turn of the century are the setting for the story. A loosely structured plot is centered around the coming of age of the girl, Bor, and around a somewhat older boy, Marash, who lives in another mountain village. When Bor was a baby, her mother straped her tightly to a cradle hewn out of soft wood by her father, Gjok. Because of this, Bor grew into a fine, straight young girl. At a tender age Bor takes care of her baby brother and brings firewood and water from a stream down the hill. She soon becomes a shepherdess, climbing up the rocks after the goats and leading the sheep to the pasture grounds. Bor meets Marash at the Komarra celebration for her baby brother. Together they explore the city shops while attending the bazaar at Skodra. Unlike most of the mountain children, Bor and Marash attend the Friar's school. It is Marash's desire to know what lies beyond the Red Mountain that draws him to the top of this highest peak. Here he is entrusted with a man's task, to carry a secret message to the other Albanian tribes

warning them of the possible danger from outside and
encouraging them to unite. A slow moving story, it
richly portrays the simple wisdom and courage of the
people of Albania.

006. Zaimi, Nexhmie. <u>Daughter of the Eagle: The Autobiography of an Albanian Girl</u>. New York: Washburn, 1937. 271
p. Grades 5 and up.
Nexhmie, the youngest of four children, was born during
World War I. When she was two years old, her family
settled in Valona, a town along the southern Albanian
coast of the Adriatic Sea. Nexhmie's early childhood
recollections, however, concern events which took place
in Krip, a small coastal settlement. With warmth and
affection she remembers the evenings when the children
waited for the village shepherd, Sadik, to return with
his flock from the green hillsides and to share with
them the warm goat milk. She recalls the excitement
felt upon the arrival of the Sarakacans, who came with a
cavalcade of horses to gather and to transport salt from
Krip to the towns along the northwestern borders. Most
vividly, however, Nexhmie recalls the manner in which
her sister's fiance came to their house to meet her
parents for the first time. The bride, who had never
met her future husband, was not supposed to know
anything of her marriage plans and was not to take part
in the welcoming ceremony. Wearing a black veil
concealing her young figure as a sign of her ripening
womanhood, she had to stay in hiding, while her spunky
six-year-old sister Nexhmie spied at the window to the
horror of her parents. This autobiography offers a
fascinating portrayal of the hard life in Albania
between the two World Wars, the devotion these people
had for one another, their superstitions, their strict
adherence to the old customs, the discouragingly low
position of women in the Albanian society, and the
changes and modernization that inevitably followed.
Written with remarkable skill, attention to detail, and
perceptive insight, the story describes Nexhmie's life
from the time she was six years old until she decided to
immigrate to America at the age of nineteen.

Bulgaria

TRADITIONAL LITERATURE

007. Pelin, Elin. <u>Bag-Boys</u>. Trans. Petroushka Tomova.
Illus. Elie Danova. Bulgaria: Sofia, 1975. (Distributed
by Imported Publications.) N. pag. Grades 2-4.
   Being constantly scolded by his wife because of their
   poverty or for some other trivial reason, a poor old man
   goes to the river to ask a golden fish for advice and
   help. Instead of the fish, however, he catches a crane,
   who begs him to let him go. In exchange for his freedom
   the crane gives the old man a magical bag. When given
   the proper command two boys jump out of it, set a table
   with golden plates and goblets and begin to serve
   delicious delicacies. On the way home, darkness
   overcomes him, and the old man decides to spend the
   night at his goddaughter's house in a nearby villge.
   Amazed at the magical powers of the bag, his goddaughter
   takes the man's bag and puts a new bag, which she and
   her two girls have sowed over night, in its place.
   Disappointed that the bag produces none of the expected
   results when he returns home, and beaten by his wife who
   thinks he is trying to make a fool out of her, the old
   man returns to the river to plead with the crane for
   help. The grateful bird understands his situation and
   gives the man another unusual bag, also containing two
   youths, who, at his command, beat the women thieves and
   make them return the stolen property. The folktale is
   printed in a slim paper cover format with full-page
   brightly colored illustrations.

008. Pridham, Radost. <u>A Gift from the Heart</u>. Illus.
Pauline Baynes. Cleveland, Ohio: World, 1967. 156 p.
Grades 4-12.
   The book contains twenty delightful folk tales from
   Bulgaria, originally collected by Angel Karalyichev, now
   skillfully translated and retold by an expert on
   Bulgarian literary traditions. The title story, "A Gift

from the Heart," tells about the youngest of three brothers, who, unlike the older two, chooses three walnuts instead of a large sum of money for his wages because they are a gift from the heart. His choice proves to be wiser than that of his brothers, who boast of their bagfuls of golden coins. The walnuts that looked quite ordinary have magic powers. Upon cracking them, a flock of sheep, two young bullocks hitched to a cart with an iron plow, and a beautiful maiden appear before the young man. He has everything he needs to remain happy for his entire life. Other magic objects appear in the other stories. A magic pipe brings forth music as sweet as honey that makes every living creature around dance. A magic stone brings happiness to Grandfather Pavel. The theme of three brothers or three sisters, the youngest being the wisest, is repeated in "The Spring of Youth" and in the "Silver Leaves." Animal characters abound, and there are numerous beings with supernatural powers.

009. Stanchev, Luchezar. Is Fried Fish Good?. Trans. P. Tomova. Illus. Peter Chouklev. Bulgaria: Sofia, 1974. (Distributed by Imported Publications) N. pag. Grades 2-3.
A comic story about the only son of a king and his poor eating habits. The boy is as thin as a rail and has the most unsuitable name; he is called Fatty. Worried about him, the King calls on all his Wise Men for advice, but they cannot come up with a good solution to the problem. Finally, the King decides to send his son to the seaside. He is taken to the palace by the sea in a golden chariot, accompanied by more than one hundred servants, cooks, and wise men to watch over him. He has nothing to do there: no work and no tasks to perform. Although there is plenty of food in the palace, Fatty does not feel like eating. One day when the council of Wise Men again discusses Fatty's inability to gain weight, the Prince himself has an idea. Sneaking out of his room through a window, he takes a stroll along the shore all by himself. He meets the son of a nearby fisherman, a boy of his age. Without hesitation, the prince joins him in his games in the water and on the beach and helps him carry the basketfuls of fish the boy's grandfather has caught. Returning home in the evening Fatty is, as expected, famished, and for once the wise men have joyous news for the King. After a serious inquiry into the reversal of these important events, the King orders that Fatty is to play and run and carry the fisherman's baskets during his stay at the seaside. Comical, cartoonish illustrations are a very important part of this folktale.

HISTORICAL FICTION

010. Christowe, Stoyan. This is My Country. Illus. Edward Shenton. New York: Carrick and Evans, 1938. 320 p.

Grades 6 and up.
At the age of thirteen, Stoyan Christowe is the youngest in a group of five men departing from a small Macedonian village for America. The villagers accompany the group along the steep path to the plateau on the top of the mountain. There they part. Since he is too young to drink, the women stuff walnuts into his pockets; the men give him coins, but first they rub them against their beards, wishing him to earn as many coins in the new country as there were hairs in their beards. His father weeps, upbraiding himself for having yielded to Stoyan's adventurous spirit. Insisting that every flower grows best in its own soil, he pleads with Stoyan to return to the village soon. Stoyan's destination is St. Louis, where his uncle lives. Twelve men live in a two-room flat, six of them working days and six nights, sharing their beds, without sheets and covered with blankets filthy with coal dust and grease. Like most newcomers, Stoyan is offered a job in a carshop, where he is expected to work with the rivet boys at the mouth of the roaring ovens. Confused and frightened, Stoyan flees from the inferno. Luckily for him, soon afterwards he is given work in a leather factory, ten hours a day, six days a week. For five years he works in various places in the American industrial jungle. Then Stoyan begins his second journey to America, to the world of learning and the rare opportunity that American offers him. This part of the autobiography is a most respected tribute to Christowe's personal achievement in the land of opportunity. An unforgetable narrative written in a simple, lucid style and told with rare sensitivity and power.

011. Dichev, Stefan. Rali. Trans. Margaret Roberts. Illus. Liljana Dicheva. Harrisburg, PA: Stackpole, 1968. 224 p. Grades 6 and up.
The second Bulgarian empire, established in the twelfth century, was conquered by the Ottoman Turks in the fourteenth century and was controlled by them for about 500 years. When the oppressive Ottoman empire began to crumble, the captive nations of Eastern Europe became increasingly more rebellious. In 1876 the Bulgarians revolted. Their uprising was crushed under the extreme barbarity of the Turks. In that year, Rali, who lived with his family in the town of Panagyurishte, just turns fourteen. While Turkish battalions are advancing on all sides Rali, with his faithful dog Balyn, escapes into the woods. His father is one of the first to fall. His mother, grandmother, and his sister perish in the fire. His older brother Lukan is imprisoned with the other rebel leaders at Plavdiv, a city on the Maritsa River. Given a horse from a villager and accompanied by Bolyn, Rali sets out for Plavdiv prison. Rali discovers that Lukan has been sentenced to life imprisonment in Diyarbakir, a wild part of Asia Minor. On horseback to Adrianople, by boat to Samsun, and finally by camel

caravan, exposed to many dangers and struggling with starvation, Rali reaches the terrible prison and finds his brother in one of its dungeons. Pursued by search parties, wounded, betrayed by a companion, and almost dying of thirst, Rali and his brother Lukan return to Bulgaria where they sign up as volunteers in the Bulgarian brigade. Here they fight on the side of the Russians against their old enemy. Expressive ink drawings, a map of Rali's wanderings, and a dictionary of foreign words accompany the enthralling historical narrative, which was first written and published in Bulgaria in 1961 by the award winning author.

012.   Winslow, Clara Vostrovsky. Our Little Bulgarian Cousin. Illus. Ivan Doseff. The Little Cousin Series. Boston: Page, 1913. 114 p. Grades 3-6.
Through colorful vignettes centered around ten-year-old Ljuben and his friend, Donka, and their families, the author gives a picturesque view of life in southern Bulgaria just before World War I. Life in a typical village home is vividly described. Most of the people in the village lived in one-story houses with white walls and red projecting roofs. There were no big estates, and the people whom Ljuben knew lived in a kind of rude comfort. With the crops and sheep they raised, they produced most of their own food, and with the money they earned by picking and selling blossoms from the fields of damask roses, they purchased the other necessities in the town of Plovdiv, which was reached after a day's travel by cart and oxen. When Ljuben and his father make a trip to the city much information is given regarding the geography of the countryside, life in the city with its shops and markets, and important historical events. The school which Ljuben and his friends attend is especially interesting. The schoolmaster, a graduate of Robert College, which was founded by the Americans in Constantinople, Turkey, is an ardent patriot who, in addition to book lessons, spends time discussing with his pupils various progressive ideas concerning new methodology in farming and exchanging stories with them concerning the marvels of the natural world. The book also contains a description of the Bulgarian national customs and familial religious observances. The stories end with persistent rumors of war quickly spreading among the people and with an editor's note explaining the historical context and the role played by the Bulgarians in the two Balkan Wars.

OTHER FICTION

013.   Gantschev, Ivan. Journey of the Storks. Illus. author. Salzburg, Austria: Neugebauer, 1983. (Distributed by Alphabet Press.) 28 p. Grades 1-4.
Originally published in Salzburg under the title Jakob.

der Storch, this picture book was created by a Bulgarian
artist and writer educated in Sophia and now living in
Frankfurt, Germany. The story tells of the inhabitants
of a little northern town who are anxiously waiting for
the storks to return. Most of all, however, it portrays
in words and in lush watercolors the life of the welcome
birds, as one couple arrives, begins nesting, and has a
child Jacob. The story continues with their long flight
to the South until they reach their destination, where
again the sun shines warmly on their wings. The beauty
of the world as seen by the storks during their journey
is deftly captured in superb double-spread paintings. A
sign on one of the buildings along the sea adds an
authentic Bulgarian touch to the story.

014.   Gantschev, Ivan.   The Moon Lake.   Trans.   Oliver
Gadsby. Illus. the author. Salzburg, Austria: Neugebauer
Press, 1981. (Distributed by Alphabet Press.)   26 p.
Grades 2-6.
Among the rocky slopes high in the mountains, there is a
crystal clear lake. When the moon comes to visit the
earth, it bathes in the lake's waters and then, before
it leaves, it showers its banks with gold dust, silver,
and precious jewels. Many people disappear in the rock
wilderness searching for the moon lake. While seeking a
lost sheep, a young shepherd, Peter, discovers the
glistening lake with its jewel-covered banks. On the
advice of a silver fox with whom Peter shares his bread,
cheese, and onions, he leaves the lakeshore with only a
few gems before sunrise, a sunrise that would have
blinded him, had he stayed.   This misfortune later
strikes a group of greedy townsmen who insist that Peter
lead them to the silver lake in a search of precious
jewels and who disregard his warning. Weighed down by
their heavy sacks of dazzling stones and not able to see
because of the bright light, they plummet, one by one,
into a deep ravine. Gantschev's mostly full-page rich
watercolors visually extend the charm and wonder of the
story's folktale themes. This distinguished picture book
was first published in Salzburg. In 1982 it received
the Austrian State award for best illustrated children's
book.

015. Gantschev, Ivan. RumpRump. Illus. author. Salzburg,
Austria: Neugebauer, 1984.   (Distributed by Alphabet
Press.) N. pag. Grades Preschool-2.
This brief tale is a lively account of a single day in
the life of a bear, RumpRump. In spite of his greatest
fault, his inability to find food, RumpRump seems to be
happy with himself. He relishes the world around him.
He enjoys the early mornings, the crisp fresh air, and
the sweet songs of the birds.   He appreciates the
crickets' evening lullaby, the pale light of the moon,
and the safety of his den. Most of all, however,
RumpRump loves his friends, who help him to find food.

Alfie, the bird, tells him of a beehive in the woods and warns him of the danger inherent in the hornet's nest. Skipper, the rabbit, leads him to the house of a young woman, who provides him with some tasty pears and delicious apples. This does not at all mean that his day is just honey and roses. On the contrary! Searching for a beehive, he falls off a tree; following his nose to a basket of food in the forest, he barely escapes a hunter's gun, and while trying to catch a fish or two in the river, to quiet his grumping insides, he finds that they are quicker than his paws, and he leaves wet, tired, and hungry. Although the narrative is modest and not written with great skill, the imaginative watercolor paintings, some of which are small sketches, others full-page and double-spreads, are most memorable in portraying the quiet beauty of the natural world and the good and bad luck of the wacky little bear.

016.   Gantschev, Ivan.   The Volcano.   Illus.   author. Salzburg, Austria: Neugebauer,   1981   (Distributed   by Alphabet Press).   28 pp.   Grades 1-3.
First published in Salzburg in 1980 under the title Ivan, der Vulkan, this richly illustrated story is about Brok, the ominous giant crab, and his hostile attitude toward everything on the beautiful island far out in the sea.   Brok hates plants and animals, but most of all he hates the volcano and decides to destroy it.   He persuades the river to bore into its center and extinguish its fire, but the volcano proves to be stronger than the power of the river.   The terrible explosion which results not only completely changes the island, but eliminates it of the evil crab, which is lost in the limitless sea.   Distinguished watercolor illustrations admirably portray the serene beauty of the island, the evil character of Brok, and the violent explosion of the volcano.   In Austria, the book was chosen as one of the twelve best picture books of the year 1980.

017.   Karaliichev, Angel.   The Little White Lamb; The Little Miser.   Trans. Elena Mladenova.   Illus. Nikolay Stoyanov. Bulgaria: Sofia, n.d.   N. pag.   Grades 2-4.
Two stories in a paper covered oversized picture book, evidently each written with the purpose of teaching good citizenship, especially obedience.   Within the story of a newborn lamb there is a shorter story about a naughty little lamb who refuses to obey its mother; he breaks away from the flock, gets lost, and is seized and devoured by an old wolf.   The wolf eats the lamb, but leaves its bell untouched.   Ever since that incident, the bell sounds somewhat hoarse and very sad, regardless of which lamb it is tied to.   "The Little Miser" refers to a boy, Peter, who, after he hears the story told by Old Podju about a cottage in a deep woods made of chocolate bricks, wants to run into the forest to find it.   In order to get there, however, Peter has to cross

a river via a bridge made of tiny hair. If he has been
a good boy, the bridge is supposed to hold him up; if
not, it is to break. In the morning, Peter puts his
primer and a loaf of bread into his bag and, instead of
going to school, sets out for the forest. Worse than
this, on his way he refuses to share his bread with a
starving little girl, telling her that he has a stone in
his knapsack. As expected, the hair bridge breaks under
him, and Peter is swallowed by a gigantic cheat-fish and
is kept under lock in captivity in an underwater dungeon
for a hundred years. Both stories are written in a
folkloric style and richly illustrated with expressive
watercolors, but are extremely severe in their endings.
There is no place in them which expresses the
forgiveness of faults and mistakes often made by young
children.

018. Petroff, Boris G. Son of the Danube. Illus. Hans
Alexander Mueller. New York: Viking Press, 1940. 277 p.
Grades 5-10.
Fourteen-year-old Mitko, his older friend Stoyan, and
younger friend Boyan enjoy their summer vacation
together in the small town of Radovo on the hilly banks
of the mighty Danube. Across the mile-wide river that
rushes from the Black Forest to the Black Sea lies
another country, Romania. Told in the first person by
Mitko, the story vividly portrays the daring adventures
of the three friends beginning with their Danubian way
of fishing - without bait, tackle, or net. Using every
moment of freedom afforded by their vacation as
thoroughly as possible, the boys visit the exciting
annual fair at Dolni Grad, a village seven miles to the
south. As a stowaway, Mitko hides on a cargo steamboat
trying to go to Vienna. The boys' most exciting
adventure proves to be a visit to the weatherbeaten
walls of Nikul Tower, the ruins of an old Roman castle
built by the Emperor Trajan. Guided by a university
student, Ivan, the trio dig from under its ruins several
valuable amphoras, numerous artifacts, and a large
collection of gold, silver, and copper coins. Overnight
the boys become national celebrities. When the somber
days of autumn return Stoyan and Boyan leave for school
in Sofia. The reopening of school cuts down their
playtime considerably; nonetheless, Mitko and his new
schoolmate Yordan find plenty of opportunity for
adventurous undertakings. They ride the millwheel in
the river, cross the frozen Danube to Romania, and
participate in an urgent community effort to keep the
Danube from flooding the village. The vigorous story
contains a wealth of information about life in Bulgaria
between the two world wars and is illustrated by
fourteen woodcuts which give the story an authentic
background.

019. Shannon, Monica. Dobry. Illus. Atanas Katchamakoff.
New York: Viking, 1934. 176 p. Grades 5-9.

The charming, perceptive story concerns a Bulgarian peasant boy Dobry, his mother Roda, his wise and spirited grandfather, their neighbor Hristu, and his daughter Neda. Dobry loves the idyllic life of his native village and is fond of his family, but he yearns to go away to study art and become a sculptor. His artistic skill is revealed early in his drawings. His charcoal picture for his kite of a crudely drawn stork looks completely alive, and his carvings of the animals that Noah forgot seem life-like. Finally, Dobry's carving of the Nativity scene out of glittering new snow convinces his mother that he possessed unusual talents. She finally agrees with the grandfather that Dobry should attend the art school in Sofia. More than a story of a growing boy, Dobry is a lyrical illustration of the Bulgarian country life at the turn of the century, of the rituals and rich meaningful Bulgarian customs, of the fierce attachment between the Bulgarians and the land that they tilled, of the love those people felt for simple things, and of their ability to be happy with essentials and without frills. Eloquent portraits and uncluttered pencil illustrations by the distinguished Bulgarian sculptor highlight the events of the heart-warming story. The book was awarded the Newbery Medal in 1935. The 1982 printing was its sixteenth.

Czechoslovakia

TRADITIONAL LITERATURE: COLLECTIONS

020. Baudis, Josef. <u>Czech Folk Tales</u>. Illus. Joseph
Manes, E. Stanek and Aleš Mikuláš. 1917. New York: Kraus
Rpt., 1971. 196 p. Grades 4-10.
   Twenty-three stories selected and translated by a
professor of philology at Prague University. The
stories are taken from the most known collectors of
Czech, Slovak and Moravian folklore: Božena Němcová,
Josef Kubin, V. Vondrak, V. Tille, and B.M. Kulda. In
the first story "The Twelve Months", the poor girl
Marusa is sent by her stepmother and stepsister to the
forest in the middle of January to pick sweet-smelling
violets, and not the snowdrops or strawberries which
appear in several later versions of the same story.
Magic objects and beings with magical powers abound in
the other stories. There is a magic horse that can fly,
the water of life that cures all bodily ills, golden
apples that make people well, a magic ring that brings
one the strength of a hundred men, a pair of boots that
cover ten miles per stride, a cloak that enables its
owner to fly, and a hat that makes its wearer invisible.
As in other folkloric collections, the tales gathered
here reflect the Czech national spirit, as well as the
values held dear by most of the other nations of the
world. With much humor, and a bit of satire, they
portray the folly of the world and the weaknesses of
human beings. Through the centuries they seem to have
provided the common folk a dream of a better world where
bravery and gallantry always pay off and where truth and
justice prevail. Masterfully illustrated with eight
black and white pen drawings.

021. Burg, Marie. <u>Tales from Czechoslovakia</u>. Illus.
Laszlo Acs. London: U London P, 1965. 125 p. Grades 4
and up.
   Fourteen stories originally written down by the most

known Czech folklorists, Božena Němcová and Erben, and by the Slovak collector of folklore, Dobšinský. These Czech tales include the story of Kate, a dreadful gossiper, who, at the age of forty, is still without a husband in spite of the fact that she owns a cottage, a garden, and even has a bit of money. Desperate, she is ready to marry anyone, even the devil himself - except that even the devil runs away from her. Other Czech tales also contain strong and gentle female characters. Princess Krasomila marries the handsome Prince Miroslav after she learns to be thoughtful and considerate. A poor but clever goose girl marries a judge and takes over his job to the delight of the poor people in the district. A poor and gentle hearted girl, Maruska, receives miraculous aid from the Twelve Months when she is sent to the forest in the middle of winter to bring flowers, strawberries, and apples. The Slovak tales contain a variety of magic objects, such as a purse that produces as many ducates as anyone desires, a whistle that summons an entire army of soldiers, a girdle that carries a person to whatever place desired, and three golden pears that cause a wild forest to disappear and transform into a new, fresh, joyous country. The collection is illustrated with delightful pen drawings which accentuate the humor and vigor of the tales.

022. Fillmore, Parker. Czechoslovak Fairy Tales. Illus. Jan Matulka. New York: Harcourt, Brace and Howe, 1919. 239 p. Grades 4-8.
The book contains fifteen stories - translated, adapted, and retold. Originally they were found in the collections of Czech, Slovakian, and Moravian writers such as Erben, Němcová, Dobšinský, Rimavsky, Beneš-Trebizsky, and Kulda. The first story, "Longshanks, Girth, and Keen" is about three wonderful trusty servants who help a young prince deliver a beautiful princess and the entire castle from the enchantment of a wicked wizard. In other translations, this same story is called "Long, Broad, and Sharp-eye." "The Three Golden Hairs," the story of a charcoal-burner's son who marries a princess, has variants in other Slavic as well as in German speaking countries. Another outstanding story in the collection is "Prince Bayaya" with several captivating plots. With the help of a magic horse, a young prince saves three princesses from the threat of three terrible dragons, wins a war for their father, the king, gains the king's youngest daughter in marriage, and finally succeeds his father to the throne. Other tales include "Grandfather's Eyes," the story of three wicked witches who are outsmarted by a poor goatherd. "Two Wood Maiden" is the story of a little girl Betushka and two golden birch leaves which help her and her mother out of their poverty. The story "The Golden Spinning Wheel" tells about the good-hearted girl Dobrunka, who becomes a bride to the good king Dobromil. The delightful

collection is accompanied by black and white mostly symbolic drawings.

023. Fillmore, Parker. The Shepherd's Nosegay: Stories from Finland and Czechoslovakia. Illus. Enrico Arno. New York: Harcourt, Brace and World, 1958. 192 p. Grades 4-8.
   Twelve of 18 stories in this collection are Czech folktales. They are favorites with children in Czechoslovakia and should also be loved in this smooth English translation and free retelling. The title story tells how a clever, beauty-loving shepherd wins the hand of a princess who always says "Please" and "My dear Yanichko," even to her own husband. The little boy Budulinek disobeys his old granny by repeatedly opening the door to Lishka, the fox, while the grandmother is at work. Each time, the sly old thing comes into the room, gobbles up Budulinek's dinner, and finally on her last visit she carries him to her den. In the end the fox gets his punishment, the boy is rescued, and he never disobeys Granny again. The story about Longshanks, Girth, and Keen, the three extraordinary serving men, who aid a young Prince in rescuing a most beautiful maiden from the power of an evil black magician is found in many other collections in slightly different versions and under different titles. In the funny story "A Gullible World," a poor farm laborer goes out into the world to see if he can find anyone as foolish as his wife. To his chagrin, and to his wife's satisfaction, he finds that the earth is full of people who are even more gullible than she is. The simply written stories possess dramatic quality, humor, magic, wit, cleverness, and much human kindness. Illustrated with amusing black and white drawings.

024. Fillmore, Parker. The Shoemaker's Apron: Czechoslovak Folk and Fairy Tales. Illus. Jan Matulka. New York: Harcourt, Brace, 1920. 280 p. Grades 4-8.
   "The Shoemaker's Apron: The Story of the Man Who Sits Near the Golden Gate" is the last story in this collection of twenty tales. It tells about a shoemaker who is so poor that his wife and children are constantly hungry. In desperation he sells his soul to the devil, who promises him happiness and prosperity. One night, Christ and St. Peter stop at the shoemaker's cottage and ask for lodging. In their hospitality the shoemaker and his wife offer their guests five meals and give them their own bed to sleep on, while they themselves sleep on straw in the garret. Because of their kindness, the Lord rewards the Shoemaker by granting him three wishes. With them he is able to free himself from the powers of the devil and secure himself after his death a place near the heavenly gate. The fairy tales, the nursery tales, and the devil tales in this collection are either of Czech, Moravian or Slovak origin. Taken and retold from the original collectors such as Erben and Němcová, the stories are a good representation of the creative

genius of the people who live in today's Czechoslovakia. They are written in a light, witty style and are charmingly illustrated with black and white drawings. This is the author's second collection of Czech folktales.

025. Haviland, Virginia. <u>Favorite Fairy Tales Told in Czechoslovakia</u>. Illus. Trina Schart Hyman. Boston: Little, Brown, 1966. 90 p. Grades K-6.
The book contains five delightful tales gathered from out-of-print primary and secondary sources and originally written by Boźena Němcová, Karel Erben, Aleksandr Borejko Chodzko, and Parker Fillmore. The tales are retold in simple, direct style and contain much action, humor, wonder, and joy. In the story of the Twelve Months, the good-hearted and beautiful girl, Marushka, is sent by her evil stepmother and stepsister in the middle of winter up to the mountain to gather fresh, sweet-scented violets. Also included is the story about a shepherd who courts a beautiful princess with a nosegay of lovely flowers; and there are others: the story of three golden hairs in which a king overhears three old women, three Fates, prophecy that the charcoal-burner's newly born baby will become the husband of the princess, the tale about the Wood Fairy who dances with a poor girl Betushka to the music of birds sitting in the birch trees, and the story of Kuratko the Terrible, an ungrateful chick who gets his punishment because of his greediness. Drawn with delicate precision, alternately black and white, accented with color in the lovely costume details, the illustrations suit the tales admirably and transmit a feeling for the country and its people.

026. Lee, James and James T. Carey. <u>Silesian Folk Tales: The Book of Rübezahl</u>. New York: American Book, 1915. 180 p. Grades 3-5.
Most of the seventeen stories presented in this book originated in the Silesian part of Czechoslovakia. Since Bohemia was still under the control of the Habsburgs in the year the book was published, most of the geographical names, as well as the names of fairy folks having parts in stories, are in German. The most prominent creature in the tales is Rübezahl, a gnome, a spirit prince with authority over all other gnomes in the Silesian mountains. No one really knows what he looks like for he is able to assume the appearance of dazzling beauty or change himself into the form of the ugliest creature. Moreover, he has the power to change his character at will. After Silesia becomes inhabited by Slavs, Rübezahl stops fighting wild bears by inciting them over the steep mountain cliffs into deep valleys below. When he notices that the Slavs change the inpenetrable forests into fruitful fields he decides to become acquainted with these men. Thus the stories in

this collection present his better side. One tale shows Rubezahl in the form of a peasant, and everything he undertakes prospers. When he assumes the form of a a hired hand to a shepherd, the sheep thrive under his care. He also becomes an aid to a judge and becomes a terror to criminals. In each of these instances, however, he leaves his employers because of their corruption. In other stories Rübezahl shows himself to be a master of the merriest pranks and tricks. This unique collection, the first of Rübezahl stories in English, is illustrated with detailed pen-and-ink drawings impressingly depicting the episodes of the stories.

027. Michael, Maurice and Pamela. <u>Fairy Tales from Bohemia</u>. Fairy Tales of the World Series. Illus. John Lathey. London: Muller, 1966. 182 p. Grades 5-8.
A collection of nineteen stories retold for American audiences. Some are old favorites that appear repeatedly in other collections. The story of the twelve months has been published individually as well as with other stories. "The Iron Castle" is another version of the marvelous deeds of three unusual fellows, Long, Broad, and Sharp Eyes, who break a spell and bring to life an enchanted princess and with her the entire castle. The majority of the stories are set in great castles in the mountains of Bohemia, with such characters as queens and kings, counts and young knights, and some good and some bad rulers, who usually have everything that anyone could wish for, but are discontented for one reason or another. One wishes to possess a gift no other mortal has; another wants to understand the language of the animals. Still another has an only daughter, a beautiful princess, and goes about absurd lengths to keep her from harm. There is a prince with three handsome young sons, whom he wants to do only princely things. He thus drives his youngest out of his kingdom because the boy wants to become a forester and nothing else. Fortunately, there are also simple, but clever shepherds; poor, but smart peasants; brave and beautiful maidens, and legendary beings like witches, flying horses, giants, and dragons that intervene with and facilitate the deserved outcomes of the dramatic happenings. Appropriately illustrated in black-and-white drawings.

028. Němcová, Božena. <u>The Disobedient Kids and Other Czecho-Slovak Fairy Tales</u>. Trans. William H. Tolman and V. Smetanka. Illus. Artuš Scheiner. Prague, Czechoslovakia: Koci, 1921. N. pag. Grades 3-5.
A collection of ten delightful tales written and translated with fluency and charm and illustrated with graceful pen drawings as well as with richly colored paintings. The story about disobedient kids resembles the Grimms' story about the wolf and the seven kids as well as the story about the wolf and the seven goslings.

In this story a mother goat, who has to go to the
pasture, forbids her four little ones to open the door
to anyone who knocks until they hear her voice. When
the fox comes, however, and calls to them in the
thinnest possible voice, the kids cannot tell the
difference, and think that it might be their mother's
voice. Unable to agree with each other, they begin to
fight and accidently push the door open right into the
path of the hungry fox. Other stories include a tale
without an end, in which one has to wait to find out
what happens after a large herd of sheep crosses a brook
on a narrow plank, one at a time; a story about the
stars of gold in which an orphan girl Bozena gives her
only piece of bread to a hungry beggar, her shawl and
her skirt to the other little girls shivering with cold,
and receives an apron full of gold pieces in return; and
a cumulative tale featuring a cock and a hen, in which
the cock learns to keep his promise. A distinctive
collection of stories reflecting the humor and
tenderness of the people among whom they originated.

029. Němcová, Božena. <u>The Shepherd and the Dragon: Fairy
Tales from the Czech</u>. Trans. Eleanor E. Ledbetter. Illus.
William Siegel. New York: McBride, 1930. 206 p. Grades 5
and up.
One day, while he is tending his sheep high in the
mountains, the shepherd Baca notices a multitude of
snakes coming to a rock in front of him, tapping the
rock with a special herb they pick up and one by one
disappearing into the rock which opens before them.
Curious to see where the snakes vanish, he too picks up
the strange herb, knocks the rock with it, and finds
himself in a cave which shines with silver and gold and
is filled with sleeping serpents everywhere. To his
dismay, though, his curiosity is satisfied, and the
shepherd is not allowed to leave the cave until he
swears a triple oath to the gigantic old serpent on the
golden table never to tell where he was and how he got
into the cave. He is determined to keep his word until
he is tricked by the mighty three-eyed wizard of the
mountains. When the old snake changes himself into a
monstrous dragon, and threatens to destroy him, Baca is
saved by a prayer to the Father in Heaven. This and the
other twenty-three stories first written by the famous
collector, Bozena Nemcova, appear here in an excellent
translation and are illustrated with energetic black and
white drawings.

030. Quinn, Zdenka and John Paul Quinn. <u>The Water Sprite
of Golden Town: Folktales of Bohemia</u>. Illus. Deborah Ray.
Philadelphia: Smith, 1971. 159 p. Grades 3-8.
The eight Bohemian folktales contained in this
collection were originally written in Czech by the two
folklorists, Karel J. Erben and Bozena Nemcova, in the
nineteenth century. The stories are eloquently retold
in rich yet simple language and in a spirit of

admiration and fondness for the ancient Bohemian folklore themes. The title story is about a curious creature, Water Sprite, who lived with his wife Sara in the river Vltava in the golden city of Prague before it became a great town. He had long straight hair the color of the green looking river, and his eyes and mouth resembled a frog. He wore red boots and a coat with tails and brightly colored ribbons on its lapels. His appearance meant good luck to the people selling vegetables in the Horse Market, or to the cobblers who liked to ask him if they could fix his red boots. In one of the longest stories, "Our Grandfather's Wisdom," an old woman called Fate, who appears at the birth of a poor colier's son, not only foretells his glorious future, but in the most critical moments of his life also helps him to attain his unexpected fortune. Delicate ink drawings underscore the motifs of the stories.

031. Wood, Ruzena. The Palace of the Moon and Other Tales from Czechoslovakia. Illus. Krystyna Turska. London: Andre Deutsch, 1981. (Distributed by Elsevier-Dutton.) 128 p. Grades 3-10.

A collection of twelve stories translated from Czech originals and illustrated in pen and ink drawings. The title story is about Prince Silomil, who, in the absence of his parents, the king and queen, gives his three sisters away in marriage, the eldest to the King of the Sun, the second to the King of the Moon, and the youngest to the King of the Wind. When the time comes for Silomil to go out into the world to look for a wife, his three famous brothers-in-law first help him to snatch the fastest horse in the world from the evil witch, and then to rescue the princess, with whom Silomil has fallen in love, from the King of the Fire. In the story, "King Miroslav and the Proud Princess," the good king who wants to marry Princess Krasomila ingeniously puts an end to her haughtiness before he lovingly welcomes her into his kingdom. A poor farmer outsmarts a rich count and countess, whom he found more foolish than his own wife, in the story, "Who Was the Stupidest?" In other stories familiar folktale motifs abound. The youngest princess is able to prove to her father her love for him, a poor farmer becomes rich by fulfilling the king's requests, and a cobbler who is so poor that he cannot buy leather and sells his soul to the devil ends up inside the door of heaven. The sources for all of these stories are not given. The illustrations strongly augment the humor and the charm of the stories.

TRADITIONAL LITERATURE: SINGLE EDITIONS

032. De Regniers, Beatrice Schenk. Little Sister and the Month Brothers. Illus. Margot Tomes. New York: Seabury,

N. pag.   Grades K-3.
   In this delightful version of the Czech folktale (which
the author heard as a child from her mother) the
orphaned girl, who is the heroine of the story, does not
have a name such as Katya and Marushka (as she does in
other versions).   She is merely called Little Sister,
and so is more closely associated with the Month
Brothers.   The story recounts that both of Little
Sister's parents are dead.   Because of her loveliness,
gaiety, and skill at work, her stepmother and stepsister
are jealous of her.   Trying to get rid of her, they
decide to send her to look first for fresh violets and
later for fresh strawberries in the middle of the
bitterly cold winter.   Both times, Little Sister becomes
so cold and tired that she thinks that she cannot take
another step, but then she notices a light coming from
the top of a huge rock.   This is the fire of the twelve
Month Brothers.   Her kindness and her despair move the
men's hearts.   By passing their magic staff from January
to April, May, and June, the seasons suddenly change,
and Little Sister is able to gather first the
sweet-smelling violets and, the second time around, the
delicious strawberries.   When the greedy stepsister sets
out on a trip to see the Month Brothers for herself, she
perishes in a snowstorm, as does the stepmother.   This
charming, simply written tale is highlighted by
imaginative, witty illustrations in gentle colors.   The
captions accompanying various scenes on each page add
humor and unusual freshness to the story.   The book
received the 1977 Children's Book Showcase Award.

033.   Gág, Wanda.   Gone Is Gone; or, The Story of a Man Who
Wanted to Do Housework.   Illus. author.   New York: Coward-
McCann, 1935.   N. pag.   Grades K-3.
   This funny folktale is about a man named Fritzl, who
believes that his job is harder than his wife's.   After
exchanging duties with her for a day, he causes all
kinds of calamities with his awkwardness.   While Fritzl
is in the cellar getting a mug of cider, a dog steals
the sausages from the stove.   While he is chasing the
dog, the cider runs out of the barrel and floods the
cellar.   While he feeds the cow, the baby tips the
butter churn and spills the cream.   Gathering vegetables
from the garden, he leaves the garden gate open behind
him, and the pigs and the goats and the geese devour all
of the potatoes and onions, carrots and cabbages, and
everything else.   After a few even more disastrous
incidents take place, Fritzl realizes that his wife's
work is none too easy and begs her to do the housework
from now on and to allow him to go back into the fields.
Most expressive and humorous pen-and-ink drawings
complement the humor and the silliness of the story.

034.   Junne, K.I.   Long, Broad, and Sharpsight: A Slovak
Folktale.   Illus.   Sylvie   Selig.   Garden   City,   NY:
Doubleday, 1971.   N. pag.   Grades 1-3.

A version of a familiar tale about the magic powers of
three men, Long, Broad, and Sharpsight, who travel
together far and wide in search of lords and kings who
have a need for their services. Long has the power to
stretch himself higher than any other tree in the
forest. Broad can make himself wider than any valley or
plain and can gulp down the waters of the sea.
Sharpsight can see into the bottom of the ocean and into
the thicket of the darkest forest. If he looks sharply
upon something without his blindfolds it burns and
shatters into pieces. In their search for adventure the
three comrades meet a sad young prince riding in the
forest and discover his difficult task - the freeing of
a beautiful princess from a prison in an iron castle
where she is constantly watched by a wicked wizard, and
they decide immediately to help him. In ingenious ways
they assist the noble prince in the rescue of his
captive bride, and once and for all they put an end to
the wickedness of the wizard. Written in a simple
natural style and illustrated in rich watercolors.

035. McDermott, Beverly Brodsky. The Golem: A Jewish
Legend. Illus. author. New York: Lippincott, 1976. N.
pag. Grades 2-6.
As directed in his sleep by a mysterious voice, the
beloved Rabbi Yehuda Lev ben Bezalel of Prague molds a
lump of clay into the form of a man, the Golem. By
stretching himself over the clay figure he gives it the
breath of life and places the name of God into his
mouth. The Rabbi intends the Golem to guard the ghetto
and warn its people of any trouble, but as danger
encroaches upon the ghetto, the Golem grows into a
giant. He crushes the angry mob advancing against the
Jews and proceeds to destroy the ghetto surroundings.
In his dismay over the Golem's disastrous deeds, the
Rabbi commands the holy name to leave the giant. The
Golem crumbles into dust. As was done by those before
him, Rabbi Lev places the pieces of the sacred clay once
more under the prayer books in the synagogue. The
awesome watercolor, in full and double-page spreads,
effectively evoke the mystery and the power of the
legend. For her masterpiece, the author-illustrator
received a Caldecott Honor Award in 1977.

036. Marshak, Samuel. The Month-Brothers: A Slavic Tale.
Trans. Thomas P. Whitney. Illus. Diane Stanley. New York:
Morrow Junior Books, 1983. Grades 1-4.
The story of the month-brothers, or of the twelve months
as it is called in the original Czech collections, first
written down by Božena Němcová, is presented in a
slightly different version. A little girl, the
step-daughter of a wicked woman, is sent out into the
snowy woods in the middle of a harsh winter to pick up
snowdrops for her stepsister's birthday. Bewildered and
weeping, she obeys and does not get lost in the woods or
die in the snowdrifts. As she enters the forest, a

light from the twelve months' bonfire attracts her
attention and guides her to them. Her plight moves the
hearts of the twelve men, dressed in gold, silver, and
velvety green. With the help of January, February, and
March the snowdrifts vanish, and the wonders of an early
spring appear. She hurriedly gathers a basketful and an
apronful of snowdrops. In her greediness and envy, the
little girl's stepsister sets out into the forest to get
fresh fruit from the twelve months, but she freezes in
the deep snow, as does her mother, who has gone to
search for her. The story, written by Samuel Marshsak,
one of Russia's best known authors of children's books,
is based upon the author's play, "The Twelve Months," as
well as on Czech folkloric material. Exquisitely and
meticulously composed illustrations are a perfect
accompaniment for the tale.

037. Ness, Evaline. Long, Broad and Quickeye. Illus.
author. New York: Scribner's, 1969. N. pag. Grades K-3.
     A superbly illustrated adaptation of a Bohemian folk
tale based on the ancient theme of the prince who falls
in love with the most beautiful princess in the world
but has to rescue her from the enchantment of a wicked
wizard who lives in an iron castle thousands of miles
away. All of the young men who have tried before to
save her before him have failed to do so. One by one,
the old wizard turned them to stone, and none has ever
come back. The same fate would certainly have been his
had the young prince not taken into his service three
fellows with extraordinary powers who offer their help
to him. A tall man by the name of Long, who can
lengthen his body at will to the height of the clouds in
the sky; his friend, Broad, who can inflate himself to
the size of the largest plain; and their comrade,
Quickeye, who can see the smallest objects hundreds of
miles away, play essential roles in putting an end to
the wizard and his powers. With his destruction, the
princess is restored to life and the entire court of the
Iron castle completely changes. The marble figures and
the stone knights become men once more and are invited
to the wedding ceremony.

038. Newland, Mary Reed. Good King Wenceslas: A Legend in
Music and Pictures. Illus. author. New York: Seabury,
1980. N. pag. Grades 1-5.
     This is the story of the traditional Christmas carol
written in 1853 by John Mason Neale, the famous English
hymnologist. He set it to music based on an old
folksong. Each verse, printed in beautiful calligraphy
by Anita Karl, is perfectly complemented by an exquisite
illustration in black and white. The theme of the carol
concerns St. Wenceslas, a tenth century duke in Bohemia
and the first ruler who based his political actions on
the Christian beliefs of love and peace. The verses and
pictures portray the wintery journey of St. Wenceslas

and his young page to the cottage of a poor peasant with gifts of wine, meat, and firewood. When the page feels he can go no further because of icy winds, the good St. Wenceslas tells him to follow in his foosteps in the snow. To his surprise, the boy begins to feel warmth coming from the imprints of the saint's feet. A page of music for guitar, recorder, or piano, as well as historical notes about St. Wenceslas, are appended.

039. Singer, Isaac Bashevis. The Golem. Illus. Uri Shulevitz. New York: Farrar, Straus, Giroux, 1982. 85 p. Grades 5 and up.
   First published in the Jewish Daily Forward in 1969, this is a masterfully retold version of the legend of the Golem, the clay giant who helped the Jews living in Prague in their tribulations. According to the heavenly messenger who appeared to Rabbi Leib during his midnight prayers, whenever God's name is engraved on the clay man's forehead, the Golem would live for the time needed to complete his mission. He is to be brought to life only to help the Jews in their greatest need, for a single purpose, and the holy name should never be invoked for selfish reasons. During the reign of Emperor Rudolf II, when the Jews were under a great deal of stress, there lived in Prague a squire by the name of Jan Bratislawski, who lost his immense riches in gambling. In order to get money from the capable and hard working Jewish businessman, Reb Eliezer Polner, the count unjustly and wickedly accused him of murdering his daughter, Haneka. During a sham trial, the Golem exposes Bratislawski's treachery and saves Reb and other Jews from execution. As instructed by the heavenly messenger, the holy name is then erased from the Golem's forehead, and he returns to the form of a lifeless clay figure. When the rabbi concedes to his wife's insistent pleas, however, to use the Golem for the removal of a huge rock under which a treasure has been hidden, the rabbi loses his power over the Golem. It is an innocent orphan girl, Miriam, who, with the power of her love, is finally able to aid the rabbi in erasing the holy name from the Golem's forehead, thus ending the Golem's wild misdeeds in the Jewish community. The accompanying black and white illustrations fully support the simply told yet thematically complex story.

040. Szalatnay, Rafael D. The Cock and the Hen: A Czechoslovak Folk Tale. Illus. Rudolf Mates. New York: Czechoslovak Art and Craft, 1925. N. pag. Grades 2-4.
   A charming cumulative tale about a cock and a hen who go for a walk in the woods to pick strawberries. They decide to divide equally whatever they should find. When the little hen finds a nice ripe strawberry, she immediately gives half of it to the cock. When the cock finds one, however, he attempts to swallow it quickly, so that the little hen will not notice. The hen would not have noticed, had the strawberry not become stuck in

the cock's throat and forced him to ask for water. The
little hen runs to the brook, but the brook is unwilling
to give water until the sky gives water to the meadow,
the meadow gives grass to the farmer's wife, who gives
milk to the threshers, who give corn to the pig, who
gives bristles to the shoemaker who gives a pair of
shoes to the dressmaker, and who gives a kerchief to the
linden tree, who gives a leaf to the brook. The brook
finally gives some water to the hen who takes it to the
cock. The cock stops choking and promises never to be
selfish again. Authentic folkloric borders grace each
page of the book. The illustrations in rich watercolors
match the story superbly in its content and in its
light-hearted spirit.

041. Weil, Lisl. _The Golden Spinning Wheel_. Illus.
author. New York: Macmillan, 1969. N. pag. Grades K-3.
    A new version of an old Bohemian folk tale accompanied
by Dvořák's musical composition and adapted by David
Shapiro. Boldly illustrated in shades of gray, pink,
and green, the story tells of a king who, on his way to
the battle through a dense forest, falls in love with a
young girl whom he finds in the center of a clearing
humming and singing while spinning at her golden
spinning wheel. Her name is Dornischka. She lives with
her stepmother and her stepsister in a cottage nearby.
The king asks her stepmother for Dornischka's hand in
marriage. They wish to marry as soon as the king
returns from the battle. On the wedding day, however,
the stepmother ties Dornischka to the spinning wheel and
sends her own daughter, with her face covered under a
heavy veil, to the castle to be married. While the
wedding festivities are getting under way, Dornischka's
spinning wheel changes in the dark forest into a golden
bird that carries her to her beloved. Dornischka and
the king are married at once, while the stepmother and
her daughter are thrown into a prison. Dvorak's music
for the story is taken from the famous cycle of musical
poems composed in 1896.

042. Zavřel, Štěpán. _Vodnik_. Illus. author. New York:
Scroll, 1970. N. pag. Grades K-3.
    At the bottom of a deep lake in the middle of a dense
forest lives a monster named Vodnik (Waterman). He
catches people that come to the edge of the lake,
changes their bodies into fish, seals their souls into
jars, and keeps them well guarded on shelves in his
cave. More than anything else, Vodnik wants with him a
beautiful girl, Manya, who lives in an old mill on the
shores of the lake. His opportunity comes when Manya
and Honza, the young man she loves, row across the lake
to the village where their wedding is to take place.
Vodnik causes the boat to turn over, drags Honza and
Manya to the bottom of the lake, changes Honza into a
two-headed fish, marries Manya, and orders her to
perform such tasks as to take lazy fish for a swim and

to search for pearls. Eventually, clever Manya outwits Vodnik with the help of a magic scarf, a magic piece of string, and some magic ashes that were given to her by an old woman as a reward for being kind and helpful to her. Not only does she save herself and Honza, but Manya also gets rid of Vodnik - forever. Colorful water paintings strongly and dramatically support the theme of the story.

HISTORICAL FICTION, BIOGRAPHY, AND AUTOBIOGRAPHY

043. Baer, Frank. <u>Max's Gang</u>. Trans. Ivanka Roberts. Boston: Little, Brown, 1979. 298 p. Grades 6-10.
Extremely fast-paced, the novel concerns a group of five children, who, after four years in an evacuation camp in Czechoslovakia, are separated from their comrades and must find their own way home. The start of the novel is slow, as the children are forced to walk from village to village. They find refuge in a church and later a farm, where they are allowed to work for their living. Their desire to return home to Berlin, however, drives them to escape from their work, and to slowly make their way eastward. There are many adventures; Max is hit in the head trying to steal potatoes, and Peter and Max together earn 450 marks by siphoning gasoline from American Jeeps. Throughout the book the action continues to build, as the children's desire to be at home increases. Their anxiety is heightened when, while staying in the home of some of their relatives, one of the boys is told that his parents have been killed and that he is better off remaining with his aunt. The thought of reaching Berlin only to find an empty house is shattering. The characters in the book are remarkably well developed, and the reader truly feels their respect for and commitment to one another. Their difficulties are also brought out well, and the characters never seem flat. The book is well written, and the story is made even more touching by the fact that it is based upon true events. It gives a good portrayal of the poor condition Europe was in after the World War II.

044. Bartusek, Libushka. <u>Happy Times in Czechoslovakia</u>. Illus. Yarka Bures. New York: Knopf, 1940. 62 p. Grades 2-5.
Eleanor Roosevelt, who wrote the foreword for this book, says that it is "a cheerful and charming picture of the life and experiences of childhood in Czechoslovakia." In a warmly written story the author traces the life of the Horak family, as well as the national life of the country before the German occupation. The national traditions around the holidays and seasons of the year are described in a fresh story-telling manner. There are special celebrations to mark the end of winter time when a sack-cloth figure, called Morana, representing

Old Woman Winter, is tossed into the swiftly flowing stream amid joyful singing celebrating the coming spring. There are special Holy Week celebrations, and different meaningful rituals for every day of the week. "The Ride of the Kings," taking place on Whitsunday, and the Harvest rites are especially well portrayed. There is, of course, the coming of Saint Nicholas and his companions, angels and devils, and the observance of Christmas. Authentic, colorful illustrations with much elaborate detail add lovely touches to the narrative.

045. Beatty, John L. and Patricia Beatty. <u>Witch Dog</u>. New York: Morrow, 1968. 254 p. Grades 7-10.
The novel is set in seventeenth century Europe and primarily involves England, but also includes Bohemia, Austria, and the Netherlands. The story is centered around Rupert, the Prince of Bohemia, who is the nephew of the English King Charles I, and on his constant companion, a large white poodle named Boye. Prince Rupert fights in his uncle's army as a cavalry commander. During the reign of Charles I (who wanted to rule England as an absolute monarch) the Parliament frequently disputed the King's policies. Consequently, the King denied the Parliament its right to meet, and civil war broke out in 1642. The supporters of the Parliament, also called the Roundheads, under the leadership of Oliver Cromwell, are in constant pursuit of Prince Rupert and Boye, who, because of their fearlessness, are known to the enemy as the Devil and his Witch Dog. Boye becomes the object of terrible anxieties to the Roundheads, and an object of tremendous jealousy among the Prince Rupert's closest associates. The adventurous novel introduces many historical personages, and portrays Prince Rupert's military feats, as well as the superstitions, hatred, jealousy, strong convictions, and bravery among its characters. It seems to offer an authentic recreation of the terrible conflict which occured during this historic period, and its completeness is enhanced by the detailed author's notes.

046. Behfel, Tages. <u>I Never Saw Another Butterfly</u>. New York: McGraw-Hill, [1976]. 80 p. Grades 3-12.
Terezin, located about 30 miles from Prague, was founded by the Austro-Hungarian Emperor Joseph II in the eighteenth century and named after his mother, Maria Teresa, who ruled the country before him. It was intended to be, and served as a model for, an army garrison. During World War II it became a Jewish ghetto, a stopping place to which Jews from all over Europe were temporarily gathered on their way to various death camps. Included among the hundreds of thousands of adults who came to Terezin were 15,000 children under the age of 14, of whom only 100 lived to see liberation. The children were occasionally permitted to play outdoors. Secretly, they studied, drew pictures, acted

out stories, and wrote poems. The poems contained in
this anthology were written between the years 1942 and
1944. Naturally, they express the sad fate of the
prisoners and their yearnings for a return to their
homes. In addition, they contain expressions and
reactions to the beauty which the children saw beyond
the barbed wire fence: the green meadows, the trees,
the birds, and the butterflies. The poems are
accompanied by full-color children's illustrations. An
extensive introduction, a series of biographical
sketches of the children whose poems or paintings appear
in the anthology, including the dates of their arrival
to the camp and the dates of their deaths or their
departure to gas chambers, as well as a timetable of
major events in the Terezin ghetto are appended. This
anthology, a powerful testimony to the tragic events
which occurred in Terezin, was originally published for
the State Jewish Museum in Prague in 1971.

047. Bezděková, Zdeňka. <u>They Called Me Leni</u>. Trans.
Stuart R. Amor. Illus. Eva Bednářová. New York:
Bobbs-Merrill, 1973. 83 p. Grades 3-5.
    First published in Czechoslovakia in 1959 as a story for
adults, and in 1967 in a simplified version for
children, this story is the moving personal account told
by Leni Freiwald, a nine-year-old German girl from the
town of Herrnstadt. Although Nazi Germany lost the war,
Mrs. Freiwald still adheres to the ideas of Nazism and
wants Leni and her older brother Raul, a former member
of Hitler's Youth, to be proud of the fact that their
father gave his life for his country. Only Granny seems
to have a deeper understanding of things. Frequently
Leni turns to her, especially on occasions when episodes
from her earliest years flash before her eyes. She
vaguely recalls a woman holding her lovingly and singing
to her. This is not her Mommy; Leni has never heard
Mommy sing. She also remembers soldiers coming to take
Daddy away, and the great commotion when they searched
the house, but the man that appears to Leni in this
picture does not seem to look like Daddy. Then, every
once in a while, thoughts of a little peasant doll come
to Leni, and in her thoughts she holds her close and
hugs her. When Leni overhears a conversation between
Mommy and Uncle Otto, and finds an old suitcase
supposedly belonging to her, she becomes convinced that
she is not one of the Freiwalds. Assisted by her
teacher, her Jewish friends, and an American soldier at
the United Nations Child Welfare Department, Leni finds
her real mother and her real home in Czechoslovakia,
where she was abducted to be "reeducated." A touching
story, illustrated with distinctive artwork which
captures Leni's experiences with sensitivity and power.

048. Cather, Willa. <u>My Antonia</u>. Illus. W.T. Benda. New
York: Houghton Mifflin, 1918. 419 p. Grades 7 and up.
    Based on the personal experiences of the author and on

the written memoirs of her childhood friend, Jim Burden, this is the story of a Bohemian immigrant family, centered around Antonia, a beautiful, spirited, and intelligent girl. Told in the first person by Jim, now a legal counsel in New York, he relates how, more than any other person in his life, Antonia remains the most impressionable individual, the heart of his adventurous childhood. While still in Bohemia, her family had bought some land in the middle of a Nebraska prairie from a fellow-countryman. They had not known that the soil was poor and of little value for farming and that their "house" was merely a sod dugout with a grass-thatched roof. For the father, who was in the old country, a musician and weaver by trade, the struggle on the untamed land becomes too much of a burden, and he gives up. Antonia becomes the one person in the family who possesses the strength of spirit and the sensitivity of heart necessary for the family to survive and to contribute to the richness and the creation of a new life. Aiding her mother and her older, frequently insensitive brother in the difficult tasks she assumes, although still a teenage girl, she takes on more than a man's responsibility on the farm. Later she becomes a hired girl, a servant to a Norwegian family, has an unfortunate experience with a man who deserts her before her baby is born; eventually she marries a Bohemian farmer. In spite of her age and the many burdens of her past, Antonia retains her inner strength and her undaunted spirit. A superbly written portrayal of a most sympathetic immigrant girl and woman.

049. Chase, Mary Ellen. Windswept. New York: Macmillan, 1918. 440 p. Grades 6 and up.
Philip Marston comes from an old family of shipmasters and shipowners. Owning a part in a marine engineers firm, he had seen much of the world. Due to his contact with people and the cultures of other lands, he is a man, who, contrary to most of his contemporaries, believes in the positive contributions of European immigrants to the thought and diversity of the American way of life. In 1871 on shipboard, Philip meets Jan Pisek and Anton Karel, boys of sixteen and seventeen, from Bohemia. Under the guardianship of a Bohemian priest, they are on their way to a Czech colony in Milwaukee. Before the ship lands in New York, however, the priest dies and Philip takes the two heartbroken boys to his home. Jan and Anton soon become an important part of the Marston family. They become an essential part of the life of John Marston, then Philip's five-year-old son. In 1880, upon the death of his father, John inherits hundreds of acres of spacious, uncultured land, miles of the rocky coast in eastern Maine, on which a few years later a house, named Windswept, is built. Windswept becomes the most treasured center of the life of the Marstons and of the

life of their friends and relatives, to which Jan and
Anton with their rich talents contribute immeasurably.
This is a skillfully drawn and a genuinely warm story of
the Marston family, as well as a richly human story of
two immigrants from Bohemia portrayed against the
robustly beautiful background of the coast of Maine.

050. Demetz, Hana. The House on Prague Street. Trans.
author. New York: St. Martin's, 1970. 186 p. Grades
6-12.
Helene Richter's ancestors come from the family of the
famous Rabbi Low. Soon after the Jews are permitted to
move out of the ghettos, her great-great grandfather
leaves Prague and establishes a small coal transporting
business in a smaller town. Helen's great-grandfather
built the house on Prague Street, intending it to house
not only his own family, but many generations to come.
As a child, Helen spends her summer vacations with her
grandparents. She loves the large kitchen and the
gardens with their blooming roses and phlox, the currant
bushes, and the silver firs at the gate. Most of all,
however, she is fond of the attic with its ancient
treasures: the rocking horse, the armoire with the old
photographs, and her great-great grandfather's handcart
with which he began his transporting business. Then the
war comes. One by one her beloved Jewish relatives and
friends disappear; some are shot, some are imprisoned,
others are put into a transport. In Prague her mother
dies for lack of medical help. Before the war ends,
Helen falls in love with a German soldier who admires
her world of love and innocence. When the Americans do
not come to Prague at the end of the war, Helen looses
her German born father. Finally she finds out that her
young man is reported missing. When, after the war she
visits the house on Prague Street she hardly recognizes
it. The story contains none of the hatred found in many
other war novels, but portrays a true adolescent's life
among tragedies, sadness, and devastation.

051. Dolan, F. Edward, Jr. and Richard, B. Lyttle. Martina
Navratilova: The Tennis Star Who Chose Freedom. New York:
Doubleday, 1977. 79 p. Grades 4-8.
A biography of one of the best women tennis players in
the world, the story covers her childhood, her first
attempts at playing tennis, her rapid rise to success,
her defection to the United States, and the first two
years of her professional playing. Born in 1956 in a
Czechoslovak skiing center in the Krkonose Mountains to
parents avidly interested in athletics, Martina begins
to ski soon after she learns to walk. When the family
moves to a new home in Revnice, a small town near
Prague, her parents begin to play tennis in a local club
and to compete in tournaments. Martina immediately
displays a natural talent and a liking for the sport.
Coached by her strict father, Martina enters her first
tournament at the age of eight where she plays with the

girls under age twelve who are much taller and stronger than she. In a remarkable performance she reaches the semi-finals. From now on Martina knows that she has to get better and better. She does. In 1971 she wins the junior championship for girls under fourteen years of age. Two years later she goes after the Czech women's national championship and wins it for three years in a row. Moreover, during this time Martina receives a note from the Czechoslovak Tennis Federation, a government agency, which controls all tennis matches in the country, that she is to be sent to the United States to play in a series of tournaments. This seems to be one of the most important events in her life. It opens the door to a career in tennis in which she can play in freedom whenever and wherever she wishes. Black and white photographs add much interest to the easy-to-read biography of a young tennis player in the making.

052. Grosman, Ladislav. **The Bride**. Trans. Iris Urwin. New York: Doubleday, 1970. 113 p. Grades 6 and up.
The setting of this engrossing novel is a small Jewish town in eastern Slovakia in the year 1942. The story is centered around Liza, a twenty-two-year-old seamstress and one of the seven daughters of Jonah, the village baker, and his wife Golda. In the opinion of her aunts and uncles and according to the gossip of numerous neighbors, something needs to be done because Liza is getting on in years and is not yet married. The girl's mother complains to Jonah that he is not doing all he should about it, but the baker is taking a milder attitude toward the worrisome problem. He does not want to upset his daughter, who has put her foot down about the grooms offered her and maintains that she has had enough with the long line of marriage brokers who have come with their proposals over the last nine years. Liza becomes even more of a worry when it is proclaimed from the front of the town hall that all unmarried Jewish girls sixteen years and older must register. The announcement hits the village hard. Counseled by his friend, the baker finds a way out of a difficult situation. Liza, with sixteen other girls from the village, is married in a make-believe wedding ceremony. Unlike the other girls, however, Liza takes the ceremony seriously. This could be the fulfillment of her dreams, if the Nazis were not so determined to execute their destructive plan. Although the story portrays admiringly the suffocating atmosphere in which the Jewish community lived during World War II, the strength of this story is mostly in the distinctive characterization of the villagers, especially of Liza. She emerges as a woman of courage, individuality, sagacity, and endurance.

053. Ish-Kishor, Sulamith. **A Boy of Old Prague**. Illus. Ben Shahn. New York: Pantheon, 1963. 90 p. Grades 5-8.
Told in the first person by an intelligent and sensitive

peasant boy, Tomas, this is a most captivating story about sixteenth century feudal Bohemia and the Jewish ghetto in Prague. As a child Tomas works with his mother and father four days a week in the fields of their Bohemian lord and on their own small piece of land the other three days. Tomas describes the harsh life of his family in serfdom and the gross prejudices which he and other peasants, as well as the nobility, held against the Jews. In spite of his harshness, he adores the handsome Lord Rainier of the manor. When Tomas rescues the Lord's dog from a thorny bush the lord promises that he can become his page, and the jealous Monsieur Lucien begins his secret war against him. Eventually Tomas is delivered to an old Jew of the ghetto to be his servant, which is considered to be the most shameful thing that could happen to anyone. The climax of the story involves a complete change in Tomas' attitude toward Jews, as he lives among them and experiences their kindness toward each other, toward their servants, and towards strangers. The endpapers of the book represent a reproduction of a sixteenth century map of Prague. Pen-and-ink drawings washed in gray most effectively portray the harshness of the life of the serfs, the dark ghetto scenes, as well as events in the story. The book received the Jewish Book Council Award for the year.

054. Ish-Kishor, Sulamith. The Master of Miracle: A New Novel of the Golem. Illus. Arnold Lobel. New York: Harper and Row, 1971. 108 p. Grades 5-10.

In sixteenth century Prague many Jews are forced to suffer a persecution at the hands of some of their countrymen. In their desire to make peace, the good King Rudolf himself, as well as some of his wise men, and the cardinal from Prague, Johann Sylvester, come to consult with the High Rabbi in the ghetto. Because of his deep devotion, his immense knowledge, and his inspired wisdom, the High Rabbi, Judah Lowe, is respected in the highest places. In fact, he is called the Master of Miracle. His contact with the Eternal makes all things possible for him. This time, however, the wise men are not able to make peace. When the enemies of goodwill, especially the dreaded Count Batislav, are at work again, a deep grief and weariness sets in the ghetto, and the High Rabbi makes a momentous decision. With the assistance of three holy men and a young orphan boy, he enacts the ancient ritual through which a human body made of clay receives life and special powers to help the Jews out of dangerous situations. The story, told in the voice of a young boy, the orphan who plays a major role in the awesome mission, has depth and conviction and contains the gentleness and strength of young love. It reflects the attitude some of the Bohemian nobles had toward their Jewish countrymen and the manner in which civil and church authorities interpreted the Jewish position. The imaginative black and white drawings enhance the somber tone of the story. In 1971 the book received the Jewish Book Council Award.

055. Judson,   Clara.   The Lost Violin: They Came from Bohemia.   Illus. Margaret Bradfield.   Boston: Houghton Mifflin, 1947. 204 p. Grades 5-8.

This story belongs to Judson's series on the lives of immigrants in America. It centers around a Bohemian family which arrives in Chicago during the late nineteenth century. Mama and her three children, Jan and Anna, who are teenagers, and the youngest, eight-year-old Rosie Kovec, are at the end of their journey anxiously waiting to meet Papa. Josef Kovec came to America to find work and to prepare a place for his family earlier in the year. Bohemia at that time was under the rule of the Habsburgs, and the freedom-loving Josef did not want his son to serve the emperor in European wars. Papa is especially happy when he hears that while still in Prague, Anna was taking violin lessons from a famous violinist and that she is eager to continue with her studies in America. He is totally surprised when Anna reveals to him that she has brought with her the family heirloom, the Mittenwald violin, a rare old instrument which was her Grandfather's farewell gift to her. When Anna wants to play for Papa, however, she cannot find the violin with the rest of the luggage. The absorbing plot of the story revolves around the mystery of the missing violin and ends with Anna's playing "The Star-Spangled Banner" on her precious instrument to the visiting Bohemian composer Antonín Dvořák. A simply and warmly written account of the immigrants' cultural wealth, their skill and diligence, their struggles in the new land, and the depth of their love for each other and for the country of their adoption.

056. Lacko, Michael. Saints Cyril and Methodius. Rome: Pontifical Gregorian University, 1963. 235 p. Grades 6 and up.

Although popularly written, this is a well-documented biography of the two brothers, saints Cyril and Methodius, Christian missionaries and founders of the Slavic culture. They were born in Thessalonica, the second largest city in the Byzantine empire. Their father was a wealthy nobleman with a high political position. Cyril, the youngest of seven children, was born in 827 and was christened Constantine. He assumed the name Cyril much later. He studied philosophy and theology in Thessalonica. At the age of sixteen, Constantine was invited to attend the imperial school at Constantinople. There he studied mathematics, astronomy, rhetoric, philosophy, music, and other arts. He remained and excelled at the school for six years. Later he became a priest and served as a patriarchal secretary and librarian at the church of Hagia Sophia, as a missionary to the Arabs, and became a professor of philosophy at the imperial school. Not much is known about the youth and childhood of Constantine's older brother Methodius. He studied law and served as the governor of a province to the north of Thessalonica, which was inhabited by Slavs. He entered the monastery on Mt. Olympus where he was joined by Constantine around the year 855. When a delegation from the Moravian Prince Rastislav arrived, asking the emperor for missionaries to the Slavic people, both brothers willingly departed for the foreign land. Their knowledge of the Slavonic language was a great help to them. In addition to their missionary work Constantine devised, constructed, and organized the Slavonic alphabet and translated many liturgical books into the Slavonic language. The two brothers introduced and fought for the use of the Slavonic language in the liturgy, and they established schools for young people. They laid the foundations for the cultural life of all Slavs. Maps and photographic reproductions add clarity to many interesting historical details contained in the biography.

057. McSwigan, Marie. <u>All Aboard for Freedom!</u>. Illus. E. Harper Johnson. New York: Dutton, 1954. 249 p. Grades 4-10.
As explained by Dr. Jan Papanek in the introduction, this story is based on factual events which took place in September of 1951, when a group of daring, courageous Czechs escaped on a passenger train to an area of Germany occupied by U.S. troops. The story is centered around thirteen-year-old Franta Kristufels, who is, with the help of Anton Pavlik, the engineer of the train and a leader of the group of escapees. The young boy Franta personifies the yearning for liberty which is felt everywhere in Czechoslovakia, among both the young and the old. It is demonstrated in underground activities, in parents' refusal to send their children to Communist schools, in secret plans for escape, in feelings of hopelessness at not regaining freedom, and in the atmosphere of fear prevelant in Prague and throughout the rest of the country a few years after the war. The story is told with a deep compassion for Franta and his young friends, who are war orphans, and for the selfless woman, Millie Novak, who takes care of them and escapes with them. The fast-paced story is told in a simple style with much simple dialog and perceptive characterization. Black and white illustrations complement the adventurous spirit of the story.

058. Maiden, Cecil. <u>A Song for Young King Wenceslas</u>. Illus. Cary. Reading, Mass.: Addison-Wesley, 1969. 173 p. Grades 4-12.
Set in Bohemia at the beginning of the tenth century, this is an engaging story about King Wenceslas, his ascension to the throne, his struggle with the pagan

beliefs, and his courage, goodness, and piety. Upon the death of his father, Duke Ratislav of Bohemia, the upbringing and the education of the boy Wenceslas is entrusted to his grandmother, Ludmila, who is a devout Christian. Wenceslas' mother, Drahomira, still a pagan and a regent for the child, strongly resents Ludmila's influence on her son and begins instigating her death. Because of this and because of other intrigues caused by his mother and her supporters, Wenceslas decides at the age of fourteen to take the government into his own hands. Capable politically, struggling effectively for the unity of his country, and successfully curbing oppression of the serfs by the nobility, King Wenceslas, then 21 years old, becomes a victim of the jealousy of his own brother. The story is an authentic record of the historical period, of the clash between Christian and pagan cultures, and of the beautiful pageantry of the medieval times.

059. Mudra, Marie. <u>A Feather for His Cap</u>. Illus. Robert MacLean. New York: Dutton, 1959. 160 p. Grades 5-8.
This comprehensive portrayal of life in Czechoslovakia during the first years of the Republic after World War I is presented as the story of the Kral family whose members are impressive in their courage, patriotism, resourcefulness, and strong faith. The book is centered around the son, Jan Karl, who, after his father's tragic death, assumes most of the responsibilities for the family. The story places emphasis on Jan's selfless love for his mother, who is rendered mute and deaf by the shock of her husband's arrest, and on Jan's deep devotion to his country. In addition, Jan's relationships with his grandparents, friends, and schoolmates are presented with warmth and tenderness. The portrayal of the atmosphere of the historical period and of the Czech country seems to be authentic and convincing. The rich description of Czech customs, their homes, their food, and the celebration of their national and religious holidays form a framework for the simply written, fast paced story.

060. Pelzel, Helene. <u>Nanka of Old Bohemia</u>. Illus. Lucille Wallower. Chicago: Whitman, 1937. 254 p. Grades 4-8.
The story of eight-year-old Nanka, or little Anna, begins in 1865 in the small Bohemian village of Ratje. Nanka is a sympathetic child with a vivid imagination. She is fond of her father, the village tailor, and her hard working mother. Her younger sister Francisca, her Aunt Anna and Uncle Jan, and her friend, Hanka, a nine-year-old boy who tends his family's ducks and geese, are all very dear to her. Nanka also loves to climb the steep stairs to her grandmother's room to listen to her stories, such as the old tale that explains how the old country of Bohemia was founded. The simple way of life of these people, their struggle for existence, and their colorful social customs form

the background for this part of the the story. The
second part consists of the family's travel to America,
by wagon to Praha, by train to Bremen, by an old
freighter to New York, and again by train to Cincinnati.
During their fourteen weary weeks on the sea, lacking
food and water, they still manage to enjoy moments of
fun and laughter. There are even gifts from Kris
Kringle on Christmas: rag dolls for Nanka and
Francisca. The third part of the story portrays Nanka
and her family's adjustment to life in America. Many
amusing experiences arise from their lack of knowledge
of English. The proudest moment for Nanka comes when
she is selected to hold the American flag during the
school closing ceremonies. Warmly written, the story is
an excellent portrayal of life in the old world as well
as of immigrant experiences more than a hundred years
ago.

061.   Purdy, Claire Lee. Antonín Dvořák: Composer from
Bohemia. New York: Messner, 1950. 200 p. Grades 6-10.
A biography of the Czech composer written with
admiration for Dvořák's talents, his beliefs, his
accomplishments, and for Dvořák as a man. Antonin was
born in 1841 in the village of Nelahozenes. His father
was an innkeeper and a butcher, and his young son was
expected to follow in his footsteps in spite of the fact
that both parents and the village school master agreed
that Antonin possessed rare musical talent. After four
years of schooling at home, Antonín was sent to the
neighboring larger town of Zlonice to attend school
there. He was fortunate to get a teacher of unusual
musical ability. In addition to musical theory, his
teacher taught young Dvořák the organ, piano, violin,
and viola. Later, when Dvořák wrote the opera, "The
Jocobin," he immortalized his old schoolmaster in the
character of Beuda. At the age of sixteen, Antonín was
on his way to Prague. He was accepted by the famous
Organ School. There he practically supported himself by
playing in various orchestras. Dvořák's accomplishments
in musical composition, the acceptance and devotion he
received at home and abroad, and his travels to England
and to the United States are vividly and sympathetically
described. Although the biography is centered on Dvořák
himself, it also tells us much about the political
situation of the country, its cultural past, and the
richness of Bohemian folklore, an important source of
inspiration for Dvořák's music.

062.   Seckar, Alvena. Zuska of the Burning Hills. Illus.
Kathleen Voute. New York: Oxford U., 1952. 222 p. Grades
5-8.
Papa and Mama Stebina came from Slovakia sometime before
World War II. They settled in the East Camp in the
mining town of Pinet Hill, West Virginia. All of the
adults in the camp speak either Slovak, Polish,
Ukrainian, or one of the other Slavic languages. The

Stebina family lives in one of the thirty identical red framed houses. They are covered with gray dust and have no electricity and no running water. Papa and the other men of the settlement work in the Pinet Hill mines; Mama is busy with the family and the various household tasks. In addition, she cooks for and takes care of several borders who are rooming with the family. Ten-year-old Zuska and her older brother Walent go to school and do their share of the chores. Helping her mother, Zuska makes egg noodles and dumplings for the soup, and decorates Easter eggs with intricate Slovak designs. She nurses a baby chick to health and helps with the hoeing and the weeding of the garden. She scrubs the kitchen floor and helps Walent pick up coal to be used for heating and for Mama's cook-stove. When Papa's work becomes irregular and there is no money to pay for the groceries, Zuska is sent to the company story to bargain for a sack of flour. On another similar occasion, she offers for sale her collection of precious stones which Papa has brought to her from the mine. Most importantly, however, Zuska manages to befriend her classmate Olga and her naughty brother Arthur Junior, the grandchildren of the prosperous store owner. In addition to a wealth of information about the life of the Slavic people in the mining town, the story contains a number of adventurous twists and mystery-filled episodes, which, when brought to light, unexpectedly change the course of the family life for the better.

063.   Skurzynski, Gloria.   The Tempering.   New   York: Clarion/Houghton, Mifflin, 1983.   178 p.   Grades 6-10.
At the beginning of this century in Canaan, Pennsylvania, where the steel mills with their blast furnaces kept the night skyline orange-red and the days smoky gray, European immigrants struggled to make their living. For those young men life was just beginning to shape its course. Karl Kerner, the son of German parents and not yet sixteen, wanted to quit school and become a steel worker. His first love, a passionate distant love for his English teacher, Yulyona Petrov, who had come as a child from Russia, was a short-term incentive to finish high school. His three-year older friend Jamie Culley, Karl's ideal of manliness, who had his eyes on Karl's sister Kathleen, temporarily lost his job in the mill because of a practical joke he had played on a co-worker. Andy Stubak, however, a Slovak, had it the hardest. The Slavs, Hungarians, and other East-European immigrants living in the towns of the Monongahela valley were labled as "hunkies" and were considered second class citizens. Andy, an intelligent perceptive young man who felt fiercely about the labor injustices, finally decided to go to Gary with an exciting although dangerous task - to join the steelworkers in union work with the dream of returning to Canaan and organizing a union back home. This is a compelling story written with compassion and with a

great deal of understanding of the rich Slovak customs. The book appears on the American Library Association list of best books for 1983.

064.   Taylor, Sydney.   _A Papa Like Everyone Else_.   Illus. George Porter.   New York: Follet, 1966.   159 p.   Grades 4-6.

The story has a minimal plot, but is filled with interesting detail portraying the life of a Hungarian Jewish family in Czechoslovakia several years after World War I.   The Landesmans are typical immigrants. Papa has gone to America to earn a better living for his family.   He wants to get a job, work for a couple of years, find a place for his family to live, and when he has enough money, send for Mama and their two daughters, Szerena and Gisella.   Unfortunately Papa left in 1949, just before the war broke out.   This has delayed the family's reunion.   The last three chapters of the story deal with the departure of the mother and the two daughters from their relatives and their home and village of Helmecz, and with their trip to America, by buggy and wagon to the station, by train to Prague and Rotterdam, and finally by ship to New York City, where they meet Papa.   The girls finally realize that they are no longer orphans with only a Mama to love, but members of a real family.   Vivid and touching descriptions of life in a small village in Czechoslovakia and of several Jewish rituals such as going to school, preparing geese for the market, baking matzo bread, celebrating the Passover, raising silkworms, making "lechwar" from plums, and processing and spinning linen fibers, are all skillfully woven into the story.

065.   Winlow, Clara Vostrovsky.   _Barbora: Our Little Bohemian Cousin_.   Boston: Page, 1911.   95 p.   Grades 3-5.

In the spring, Barbora, the nine-year-old goose girl, and her friends Vlasta and Jirka, are out daily with their flocks.   For the most part it is a delightful life for them.   As their geese get bigger and the weather warmer, the children have time to wade in the ponds, sing to their geese, and play "froggies" and other games.   Sometimes, however, it happens that the geese run away or get mixed up, or go into the wrong grain or vegetable patch, which results in a scolding at home. There are, of course the other delights of spring time. Under a big linden tree, which is the national tree of Bohemia, wonderful stories are told, and wreaths and chains of flowers are made which are then used to decorate the image of the Virgin Mary at the crossroads. Then comes Easter and May Day, rich in festivities and in the blending of old pagan and Christian beliefs.   In the other three sections of the book, the author portrays in an easy, storytelling style, the world and the life of children in a Czech village before World War I.   Vivid descriptions of the children's special activities in the summer, autumn, and winter, including

their school life, the customs of the people, their
songs, their folktales, the historical monuments of the
city of Prague, and highlights of its history are deftly
interwoven into short episodes which are centered on
Barbora, her friends, her relatives, and her family.
Excellent reproductions of photographs add special
interest and appeal to the narrative.

066.   Young,   Percy   M.   <u>Dvořák</u>.   Illus.   Paul   Newland.
Masters of Music Series.   New York: White, 1970.   80 p.
Grades 6-12.
A short biography of the Czech composer containing an
abundance of detailed information about the historical,
political, and scholarly environment in which he lived.
Antonín Dvořák was born in the village of Nelahozeves on
the river Vltava about forty miles north of Prague.
Destined to become a butcher like his father, young
Antonin is sent to a village school where he receives
instruction not only in the languages, arts, and
mathematics, but also in music, including violin
playing. In order to sharpen his skill as a butcher and
to learn German, Antonín is sent to a trade school. The
love and talent that Antonín displays on numerous
occasions finally persuades his parents to send him to
Prague to study organ and composition. This marks the
beginning of Dvořák's impressive musical career. His
symphonies, overtures, chamber works, and operas soon
win him world-wide recognition. Dvořák's trips to
England, where he conducts, among other works his
"Stabat Mater" and his oratorio "Saint Ludmila", are
crowned with the honorary Doctor of Music degree awarded
in 1891 by the Cambridge University. His stay in the
United States between the years 1892 and 1895 proves to
be similarly fruitful. He is most impressed by the
negro spirituals and the Indian melodies. The
performance of his work in Carnegie Hall is greeted
rapturously. Upon his return to Prague Dvořák teaches
at its Conservatory until his death in 1904. The author
places a special emphasis on the fact that Dvořák's
music is an outgrowth of his national consciousness and
his love for the historic and folkloric treasures of his
native country.

067. Ziegler, Elsis Reif.   <u>The Blowing Wand: A Story of
Bohemian Glassmaking in Ohio</u>.   Illus. Jacob Landau.   (The
Land of the Free Series) Philadelphia: Winston, 1955.   212
p.   Grades 5-10.
Set in Wisconsin and Ohio in the middle of the
nineteenth century, this story is an absorbing account
of an adolescent boy, Jaroslav Piontek, a Bohemian
immigrant, and of his courageous search for family
treasure and its owner. Ever since his father told him
the story of his great-grandfather and of his expert
glass-making in Poland, Jaroslav has to live with the
compelling desire to become a glassmaker himself and to
find a ruby candlestick, a copy of the one his family

brought from Czechoslovakia several years ago. Because
of his revolutionary activities against the Austrian
Habsburg rulers, Yaroslav's great-grandfather was
condemned to die. Before he left for America, he
entrusted his motherless infant son to his brother,
showed him two ruby candlesticks, identical in every
way, both engraved with a deer and intricate scrollwork.
He took one of the candlesticks with him to America,
leaving the other with his brother, so that if his son
ever followed his journey across the ocean, he would
recognize him. With the precious candlestick, he also
left a notebook containing copies of his formulas for
making some of the finest Bohemian crystal and colored
glass. With the engrossing narrative of the young lad's
adventure in fulfilling his life ambition, the author
succeeds in telling a fascinating story of Bohemian
glassmaking craftsmen in America during a period when
the advent of the machine age and the struggle between
capital and labor threatened to strangle the glass
blowers' highly specialized art.

OTHER FICTION

068. Alger, LeClaire. The Golden Summer. Illus. Aldren
Watson. New York: Harper, 1942. 205 p. Grades 3-6.
The story about a kind country doctor and the children
who come to live with him takes place in the Slovakian
village of Poruba sometime before World War II.
Everyone in Poruba knows Pan Doktor Hrušik. According
to the schoolmaster, Pan Doktor is a learned man who has
traveled widely and has written several books. In the
heart of every man, woman, and child, Pan Doktor is the
most loved and the most respected person in Poruba.
What the people do not know, however, is the fact that
Pan Doktor is the loneliest person in town. He lives in
a large house with his cook Marta. She is a superb
housekeeper and her meals are like songs out of the
kitchen. When it comes to keeping him company, however,
Marta, in her simplicity, thinks she has nothing to
offer to a learned man. The situation changes
drastically when a poor orphan boy, Andrušik, supposedly
Pan Doktor's distant cousin, comes to live with him.
Not long after that, his only niece, Stefanya, comes
from Praha to recuperate from the measles and from the
unhappiness of living in a large town. Pan Doktor calls
the year of the children's coming to Poruba his Golden
Year. The year is filled with a whirlwind of children's
activities which he instigates. The Poruba children's
band is invited to play at the Song and Dance Festival
in a town forty miles away. Lacking money for the
train fare, the children reach their destination by
foot. Through some unfortunate coincidences, however,
Andrušik and Fanya do not participate in the festival
and do not share in the highest honors the group
receives. Other memorable events take place during the

year. Fanya's parents escape with important messages to America. Sensing trouble brewing in the country, Pan Doktor, with the children and Marta, soon follows them. Simply written, the narrative is a perceptive portrayal of the people, places, and times.

069. Alger, Leclaire. <u>Jan and the Wonderful Mouth Organ</u>. Illus. Charlotte Becker. New York: Hoyer, 1939. 177 p. Grades 4-8.
Gustik, Andrej, Bubenik, and Jan are four boys and friends from the little village of Poruba at the foot of the High Tatra Mountains in Slovakia at the beginning of the century. One day on their way home from school they spot a beautiful mouth organ in a shop window. It is not an ordinary mouth organ, the kind that are being sold in stalls on fair days; this one is long with a shiny horn along its silver sides and with a holder that can be fastened around the player's neck. The boys want to buy it, but none of them have any money. If they save everything they get, and earn what they can, they, perhaps, would be able to buy it in partnership. With a little bit of luck and with some help from their parents and relatives, the boys manage to save five kreutzers. In the end, however, they decide to send the mouth organ to a young crippled boy, a brother of Jan's favorite Hungarian soldier in the army exercises in Slovakia. After all, they can do so many other things: fly kites, run, play games, and march, while the little Pan Hussor's brother could play beautiful music if only he had an instrument. Their act of kindness eventually brings them a reward they never expected. Description of their stories, songs, their national costumes, their simple way of life and their festivities form a colorful background for this moving story of friendship. Illustrated with black and white drawings.

070. Bollinger, Max. <u>The Fireflies</u>. Trans. Roseanna Hoover. Illus. Jiří Trnka. New York: Atheneum, 1970. N. pag. Grades 2-4.
Written by an award winning Swiss author, this tender story seems to be based on themes found in the nineteenth century Czech classic authored by Jan Karafiát. Prosper, a young firefly, longs to become an adult. He wants to be like his father, with his own lantern to make the outside world beautiful. According to his father, the next Midsummer Eve, Prosper will fly out with him. But now it is only fall, and the fireflies have to get ready for their winter sleep. While the gentle, haunting sounds of the wind dwarfs' music warns the fireflies of the coming winter, Prosper spends the night with his father gathering tufts of moss and dried grass to fill the cracks in the walls and around the windows. In spring, when the cowslips are in full bloom, Prosper's real adventures begin. He visits his grandmother, who admires his strong wings and gives him his late grandfather's lantern to light up the

world. With Father, he makes the Midsummer's Eve
journey, learns to fly in the wind, has a sad adventure
with an owl, and finally meets Sally, the neighbor's
daughter, with whom, after another winter sleep, he
exchanges wedding vows. After that, Prosper becomes
busier and busier, for he and Sally suddenly have ten
small fireflies to think about. Delightfully gentle,
the story reflects the wonders of the cycle of life and
is imaginatively illustrated in rich colors by a Czech
artist. For the excellent illustrations, J. Trnka
received a prestigious international award - the Hans
Christian Anderson award in 1968.

071. Čtvrtek, Václav. The Little Chalk Man. Trans. Ivo
and Atya Havlů. Illus. Muriel Batherman. New York: Knopf,
1970. 81 p. Grades 4-8.
    This delightful fantasy was originally published in
Czechoslovakia in 1961. It received the Marie Majerova
Prize, awarded to the author of the best Czech book.
Translated in German, it received the Austrian State
Award in 1967. Told in first person by a young man who
is old enough to shave daily, a series of most original
episodes take place in a small space just outside the
boy's bedroom window. On the wall between the window
and the apricot tree, a little chalk man appears. He is
not happy with his forlorn environment. The wall is
empty and completely faded by the sun and rain. As soon
as the young man begins interacting with the little
chalk fellow, changes begin to take place. First the
young man draws a nail for him, and the chalk man hangs
up his hat. Then he gives him some lines: blue for
hope, the sky, and the flowers; green for the meadows
and trees; and brown for flower beds and skylarks. Now
the chalkman is able to create at least half of the
world according to his desires and ideas. This he
promptly does! Still, there is no end to his anxiety.
He needs someone who will listen to his troubles. But
who? Standa Novak, the neighbor, who just received a
terrible report card with the exception of a single A in
art, comes to the rescue. There is much humor in the
simple dialogues, and a full measure of child-like
imagination can be found in the lively written vignettes
that reveal how the chalk doll was created, how it got
lost in the jumble, how the chalkman's beautiful world
was nearly destroyed on account of the crooked blue
line, and how remaining close to the truth in the end
saves everyone.

072. Drdek, Richard. The Game. New York: Doubleday,
1968. 142 p. Grades 4-8.
    An absorbing story of a twelve year old Czech-American
boy, Sonny Novak, and the people around him: the man
who raises him and whom he knows as his uncle, the
people who question Unk's fitness to raise the boy, and
the parish priest who understands his people and is
close to them. Before every birthday or Christmas, or

whenever a present or any other special gift is given to Sonny, Unk invariably plays a game with the boy. There is always much teasing, curiosity, and suspense in the introduction of the gift. In the past it has always been the uncle who has given the gifts and, therefore, set the rules of the games. Then one day Sonny finds a shoebox filled with five- and ten-dollar bills while fishing by Lake Erie. Now the situation reverses itself. It is the boy's turn to set up a guessing game regarding what he has found. The uncle, however, is even wiser and more loving than Sonny could ever have imagined. He responds with a story that not only convinces him to give up his dreams about buying Unk a pair of glasses and a car, but has, in many other ways, a profound effect on the boy. There is mystery incorporated into the story, which is satisfactorily solved. Furthermore, many details concerning the life of Czech-Americans living in Cleveland's West Side between the two World Wars are deftly synthesized with the main events. The characters are sturdily and sympathetically drawn and are totally believable.

073. Hofman, Ota. Escape. Trans. Alice Backer. Illus. Alan E. Cober. New York: Knopf, 1970. 86 p. Grades 4-8.
His name is Alexander Tichy, but his friends call him Bronco. He is a fourth grader, and like many other boys his age, he forgets to take off his muddy boots when he enters the house, passes notes in class, sticks gum to his desk, and complains of a sore throat when he does not want to go to school. In spite of his effort to be careful and cautious, however, trouble usually catches up with him one way or another. Then he sincerely regrets his mischief and promises his father that he will never do anything foolish again. One day, however, after a fire burns down the shed on the hill, tragedy strikes. Law officials find a beer can buried in the shed with a piece of paper in it, on which Bronco and his two friends, nicknamed Geronimo and Speed, have written a secret oath in blood to protect each other at all costs. During their questioning it is revealed that while meeting in the shed the boys shared cigarettes among themselves. Word of the boys' involvement in the case spreads quickly. Returning home from school, Bronco catches a glimpse of a police car in front of his house. Although he knows he is innocent, Bronco, burdened by a heavy feeling of guilt, acts on impulse and runs away. In a masterful, vivid description of Bronco's escape, the author offers perceptive insight into the character of the young boy. Bronco emerges as an honest and sincere adolescent with unshakable loyalty to and a deep concern for his parents and friends. Brilliantly composed of short dramatic scenes which are accompanied by expressive line drawings, the book was listed among the best of the best in children's literature when first written in the original Czech language.

074.   Jacobs, Emma Atkins.   <u>A Chance to Belong</u>.   Illus.
Oscar Liebman. New York: Holt, 1953. 214 p. Grades 8-10.
A touching story of an immigrant Czech family working in
a plant nursery in Eastern Washington State.   Jan, a
high school senior, yearns to be accepted by his
friends, to make his own decisions, and to become a
full-fledged American.   It is especially difficult for
Jan to accept his father's stern authority, his constant
insistence on the ways of the old country, and his right
to make all of the important decisions for him just
because he lives under his roof.   Jan's resentment is
intensified when he is compelled not to participate in
special school activities and when he loses "a chance to
belong" because of his duties at home.   After an open
confrontation, Jan and his father attempt to understand
each other's thoughts and motivations and are willing to
compromise.   Jan's problems are gradually worked out,
and the family becomes part of the community when Jan is
invited to play in the school orchestra as a violinist.
The characterization is excellent, the relationships and
the situations are natural, and the solutions to the
problems are convincingly portrayed.

075.   Jarunková, Klára.   <u>Don't Cry for Me</u>.   Trans. George
Theiner. New York: Four Winds, 1968. 287 p. Grades 6-12.
Originally published in Slovak in Bratislava in 1963,
this is a lively story told in the first-person by a
fourteen year old girl, Olga.   In it she tells of her
family life, her relationship with her peers, her first
love, her heartaches, school, talents, and her deep
concern for the neighbor's neglected children.   As a
typical teenager, Olga believes her parents to be
"one-track-minded" people who invariably suspect the
worst.   Troubled by their strained relationship, Olga
begins to think about ending her life.   In her
imagination she composes a farewell note to them which
concludes with the words "Don't Cry for Me."
Fortunately, Olga can turn to Aunt Masha, who always
seems to understand and manage to put her finger on the
source of any trouble.   She does not scold, and does not
talk about morals or the wickedness of the world, but
listens, and in her strength identifies with Olga's
helplessness.   Above all she makes Olga think a lot.
The absorbing plot, the universality of the problems
portrayed, the problems of adolescence, as well as the
problems in marriage relationships, the insights into
and the understanding of a young life, and the
wonderfully real characters make this novel an
outstanding literary work.

076.   Kočí, Marta.   <u>Katie's Kitten</u>.   Illus. the author.
Salzburg, Austria: Neugebauer, 1982.   (Distributed by
Alphabet Press.) N. pag. Grades PreS-Gr. 1.
Written originally in German by a young Czech
author-illustrator who defected to Austria in 1964, the
story is about a little girl Katie who lives with a

kitten, a pig, a hen, and a family of mice in a cottage on a distant mountain. One day, after Katie leaves on her skis for school, the kitten follows her and gets lost in the deep snow. Before she is found again, she must escape from two dogs who growl fiercely at her, from a threatening owl, and seemingly from a huge bear with tiger's teeth. This is not much of a story, but the superb watercolor illustrations vividly convey Katie's love for her animal friends as well as the fright and relief the kitten experiences on her adventurous journey.

077.   Kožíšek, Josef. The Magic Flutes.   Illus.   Rudolf Mates. New York: Longmans, Green, 1929. N. pag. Grades 2-5.

All that Mother Mouse has left for her eight sons to eat are five lone grains, and each of them could eat all of those and still be hungry. While old Mother Mouse is desperate, Father Mouse goes to work. He makes the finest maplewood flutes. Every soul listening to their music finds that it makes sadness go away and worries disappear. With their flutes under their arms, eight hungry children bid their last adieus to their parents and march off, each in a different direction, to seek their fortune. As the first one plays his flute to a helpless frog who has been tormented by sickness, its sweet music makes his pain disappear. Joy and strength suddenly return, and the frog leaps to his feet in delight. The second son plays his flute beneath the courtroom window, where Liza, the Pussy-cat, is quarreling with the Dog, Lap, over a rabbit fur. The second son's music is as sweet as honey to them. They become completely still, they open their hearts to each other, and Liza gives Lap her paw as a sign of peace. Similar wonders occur to the other six children. The music of their flutes gives strength and wisdom to the weak and a spirit of cooperation and togetherness to the selfish. It finally brings all eight sons home with barrels of golden wheat and a storehouse full of bacon, butter, and gingerbread. The enchanting story is vividly illustrated with humorous colorful scenes, and richly designed borders.

078.   Macourek, Miloš. Curious Tales. Trans. Marie Burg. Illus. Alolf Born. New York: Oxford UP, 1980. 90 p. Grades 3-5.

The fourteen fantasy tales in this collection are the curious products of a rich imagination. There is a sink in one kitchen that sings so beautifully in its spare time that the clock stops ticking, and the pots and the glasses and the cupboard all think it should go to a music school. The little girl Ottilie is very talented; among other things she can play carols on her violin. She has dreadful handwriting however and has to be constantly refilling her fountain pen because of all those inkblots she makes in her exercise-books, on her desk, on her skirt, on her nose, and on the ribbons in her hair. When she makes one thousand, five hundred and eighty blots as she writes her dictation piece, the teacher soaks Ottilie in Fado. But as the inkblots fade away, Ottilie fades away too and becomes invisible, and this is the beginning of Ottilie's wonderful adventure. Other stories are about animals, such as the naughty frog who does not like her green plastic mac, and the small hedgehog who supplies a needle for the family gramophone. There is a home with six thousand alarm clocks that go on strike, and a box of Italian macaroni that is bored to the teeth and decides to go for a walk. Watercolor illustrations accentuate the comedy of the tales.

079.   Moric,   Rudo.   <u>Wild Duck</u>.   Illus.   Dagmar   Černá. Minneapolis, Minn.:   Learner, 1966. N. pag. Grades 2-4.
An adventure story about a brave mother duck, a wild duck that lives near the edge of a large stream. Following her motherly instinct, she lays her eggs in a nest under a tree and dreams of the time when her beautiful ducklings will be hatched and she will proudly swim with them, showing them off to the world. But while searching for food in a stream, a hedgehog comes along and devours the eggs. Heart broken, but never losing hope, the mother duck builds a new nest among the twisted roots of a huge tree right above the water. Here her ducklings would be safe and would live like duck princesses in their duck palace. Before the eggs hatch, however, a black weasel eats them leaving only pieces of shell floating in the water. The mother duck builds her soft nest in the knotted crown of an old willow tree a third time and lays her eggs again. These eggs do not hatch either. A martin, who is an even greedier egg-thief than the hedgehog and the weasel, discovers the nest and quickly empties it. Once again, terribly disappointed, the mother duck takes to her wings and finds a deserted eagle nest in a lovely fir tree. Repairing the nest and lining it with moss and feathers, she lays her eggs, and the hawks are afraid to touch her eggs and her ducklings. Finally, the mother duck's dreams come true. Told with gentleness and warmth and illustrated with expressive water colors.

080.   Říha, Bohumil. <u>Ryn, the Wild Horse</u>.   Trans.   Iris Urwin.   Illus. Mirko Hanák. New York: Doubleday, 1971. 104 p. Grades 5-8.
As the title suggests, this postwar adventure story is centered around Ryn, a lovable, tame horse, who frequently comes up with rather rambunctious ideas. During the war Ryn's parents arrived from the Caucasus. They were tough riding animals who looked more like ponies than horses. When they left the village on the Radim River, Ryn stayed on with the old man Antonin Jakub, who loved the animal with its tossed yellow mane, thick   brown   coat,   and   eyes   which   reflected   its

spiritedness. Jakub's wife was killed during the war in
an explosion of a German munition train nearby. Since
then the old man had lived in a cottage with a dog, a
cat, a few hens, and, of course, with Ryn - in a
timbered stable out in back. His animals, as well as
the local people, especially the children, are extremely
fond of Jakub. His granddaughter, Karolinka, worships
Jakub and is happiest when she is with him and his
animal friends. Ryn allows her to run with him as much
as she wishes. In addition to Ryn, the hero, and his
best friends, Jakub and Karolinka, there are several
other sturdy and distinct characters in the story:
Vaclav Turek, a revolutionary and his two rebellious
sons; Mr. Turnabout, the righteous chairman of the
village; Widow Spudilka, who grabs everything she can
lay her hands on, and her beautiful daughter, Daniela.
The story is written in eleven chapters, each introduced
by the author's opinion of what should or should not
happen at that particular time. Each chapter reads as
an independent short story with familiar characters,
colorful settings, and overtones of robust humor, warm
friendships, and a love for simple things in life.
Artful   watercolor   sketches   provide   enriching
accompaniments to the episodes of the story.

081. Seredy, Kate. Philomena. Illus. author. New York:
Viking, 1955. 93 p. Grades 4-6.
Philomena lives with her grandmother in a village near
Prague. She calls her grandmother Baboushka. This is
all the family she has. Her father and mother died when
she was small, and her aunt Liska lives in Prague.
Auntie went there when she was in her early teens to be
a servant girl; she married a rich man, and never
returned, in spite of Baboushka's pleading and Father
Matthias' letters. When Philomena turns eleven and the
old Baboushka knows that the time has come to leave her,
she advises Philomena to go to Prague after she is gone
in order to find her aunt and to follow the custom for
young girls from the village, to seek service in the
city - to learn to cook, sew, and clean. But when she
is sixteen she must come home. The homecoming is very
important, Baboushka emphasizes. At first Philomena
does not find her aunt, and no one seems to know where
her aunt lives. But Philomena never fails to ask
Baboushka in heaven to guide her. As a servant girl she
goes from one job to another, and in the end with the
special help from Baboushka she finds not only a loving
home, but also discovers her aunt Liska, not rich, but
poor and deserted. A gentle story with authentic
detailed drawings, giving a perceptive portrayal of the
life of the prewar Bohemia.

Hungary

082. Biro, Val. <u>Hungarian Folk-tales</u>. Illus. author. Oxford Myths and Legends Series. New York: Oxford UP, 1980. 192 p. Grades 4-8.

One of the best collections of Hungarian folktales in English intended for children, the volume contains twenty-one tales adapted from the original Hungarian collections of Emil Kolozsvári Grandpierre and Gyula Illyés. The tales reveal variants of ageless motifs as well as authentic Hungarian themes and elements. The youngest son, who is bolder, smarter, and kinder than his twenty-three brothers, receives the King's granddaughter in marriage as a reward for conquering a host of thieving goblins. At his wedding feast more good wine is served than there is water in the mighty Danube. A very poor man with ninety-nine children cleverly proves to a dragon that he is stronger in every way and cunningly swindles him out of three barrels of gold. A man called Peter Cheater hoaxes the town's mayor, not once, but five times; Sammy Lazybones, an only child spoiled by his elderly parents, becomes the hardest working young man in the village; Briar Peter, despised by his stepmother, is richly rewarded for his kind deeds and finds his good fortunes in some dangerous situations. The stories are told in a light, conversational manner, a style characteristic of the oral traditions of folklore. Expressive black and white drawings accentuate the rich wit and humor contained in these stories.

083. Curtin, Jeremiah. <u>Fairy Tales of Eastern Europe</u>. Illus. George Hood. New York: McBride, 1949. 259 p. Grades 4-8.

The author, a foremost scholar of languages and literature, personally gathered the eighteen stories presented in this collection in the course of his travels. As perhaps no American before him, J. Curtin

was not only a master of all Indo-European and even some
other languages, but was also most knowledgeable in the
nations' histories, in the achievements of these people
in their religious beliefs, their myths and folklore,
and in their overall literature. Being able to converse
with the common folk in their mothers' tongues, he
gathered their stories while mingling with them at their
festivals or chatting with them in their wayside inns.
The author presents these selections with a freshness
and a simplicity of style, bringing out the special
ethnic character of each nation and, at the same time,
preserving the universal themes that are common to all
East-European   nationalities.   Included   are   eight
Hungarian stories, seven Russian, three Czech, and one
Serbian. The Hungarian tale about the apples of youth
resembles a Russian story featuring an elusive firebird.
A kind-hearted youngest brother, aided by a horse which
speaks to him and advises him in a human voice, conquers
a host of deadly dangers, finds the three golden apples
with their power to restore youth, and delivers his two
older brothers from a dungeon, where they have been
thrown while unsuccessfully searching for the apples of
youth.   Other Hungarian selections are also highly
adventurous and are similar in their motifs and themes
to the stories of the <u>Arabian Nights</u>. Masterfully told
and enhanced by black-and-white drawings.

084. Dégh, Linda. <u>Folktales of Hungary</u>. Trans. Judit
Halász. Folktales of the World. Chicago: U Chicago P,
1965. 381 p. Grades 5 and up.
A distinguished collection of folktales selected and
translated mostly from the pioneer works of nineteenth
century collectors and authors Janos Erdelyi and Janos
Kriza. Seventy-two tales are presented under several
broad subject headings including: "Märchen," longer
folk tales with intricate plots which, in this
collection with one exception, are all hero-tales;
"jokes and anecdotes," shorter stories, containing
simple episodes and crisp dialogue and stemming from the
antagonism of the common people against their harsh,
often cruel feudal masters; "religious tales," centered
around Christ, Satan, the angels and Saint Peter;
"animal tales," a type of tale intended from the
beginning for children; "historical legends," dealing
mostly with the peasants' heroes, such as King Matyas,
Prince Rákóczi and Lajos Kossuth; and very popular
"local legends" which originated mostly in the northeast
region of the country and are additionally classified
under specific cycles and under such folktale characters
as   coachmen,   herdsmen,   persons   endowed   with
extraordinary knowledge, witches, and other supernatural
beings. The well-written forward, the introduction, the
glossary, the index, and especially the notes to the
tales give the adult reader a better understanding of
the folktales themselves as well as their relationship
to the folklore of other countries.

085. Domjan, Joseph. <u>Hungarian Heroes and Legends</u>. Illus.
author. Princeton, NJ: Nostrand, 1963. 120 p. Grades 6
and up.
A pictorial record of the history of Hungary, including
its art, folklore, and heroes. The collection begins
with a legend about two brothers, Hunary, and Magar,
who, in pursuit of a stag which lures them farther and
farther into the woods of unknown lands, begin the great
migration of Hungarian tribes from the western slopes of
the   Ural   Mountains   into   present   day   Hungary.
Interspersed   between   simply   written   historical
information are stories about King St. Istvan, Queen
Gisella, King Endre and his daughter, St. Erzsebet, King
Lajos the Great, János Hunyadi, Lajos Kossuth, and
several Hungarian heroes in America. Included are
legends about King Matyas who loved his people so dearly
that he frequently mingled with them in disguise. There
are stories about great musicians--Ferenc Liszt, Béla
Bartók, Zoltán Kodály--and short biographies of major
literary figures. An excellent collection, the book is
superbly illustrated with numerous black and white
pictures, some full page, all in the authentic spirit of
the rich folklore and history of Hungary.

086. Illyés,   Gyula.   <u>Once Upon a Time; Forty Hungarian</u>
<u>Folk-Tales</u>. Trans. Barna Balogh and Susan Kun. Budapest,
Hungary: Corvina, 1964. 268 p. Grades 4 and up.
Forty selected tales, translated and retold with a touch
of   humor   in   a   lively,   straightforward   style.
Transmitted orally from generation to generation before
they were written down, they still seem fresh and
original.   The   themes   of   the   tales   contain   the
unwritten, noble principles that must have governed the
early Hungarian society which created the stories. In
the preface of the collection the author writes that the
folktales contain more of the nation's experience and
more of the people's beliefs than it is possible to
express through poetry and other forms of writing. To
the Hungarians, the search for truth seemed to be the
most important concern in every aspects of life. In his
struggle for truth man is assisted by beings with
extraordinary powers, such as magic steeds and tree
fairies, or magical objects, like magic flutes, magic
dew drops, magic trees, and a powerful living water.
One is invariably compensated for his good deeds;
animals, such as foxes, fawns, rabbits, fish, and
serpents are especially grateful for acts of kindness
done to them. The collection's animal tales, the tales
about their heroes, such as King Matthias, and the
stories about poor peasants and kings and queens all
contain   bits   of   moral   justice: the   good   and
simple-hearted are rewarded, those who break the law or
the customs of the people are severely punished, and
those who are fake and deceitful come to an even worse
end. A rich collection of wise and amusing folktales.

087. Kovács, Freda B. Selected Hungarian Legends. Trans. Elizabeth M. Wass de Czege. Illus. Joseph Mór. Astor, Florida: Danubian, 1979. 95 p. Grades 6 and up.

Twenty-three legends, defined as the most ancient form of folktale, are presented in this collection in three parts. The first part contains the only existing Hungarian myth, the story of the creation by the God Ur and the story of the establishment of the Hungarian nation by Hunor and Magor, the two sons of King Nimrod, who follow an enchanted stag across the mountains, through swamps and marshes into a land of matchless beauty, where they each begin a new nation. Five legends are about the Huns, who are believed to be descendents of Hunor, and about their mighty king Atilla, who conquers the Goths and threatens Rome and Byzantium in the fifth century. The majority of the legends, however, deal with the Magyars, thought to be the descendents of Magor. Some are historic and give accounts of the nomadic life of the Magyars and of their encounters with the neighboring Slavs: the coronation of their great king Istvan in the year 1000; the bravery, kindness and piety of their eleventh century King Laszlo, and the marriage of King Istvan's granddaughter, Princess Margit, to the King of Scotland. The last four legends are geographical in nature. They explain the miraculous beginning of Saint Anna Lake, the great beauty of the Valley of the Vag, the raging waters of the Lake Balaton, and the peace of Balvanyos' castle. The captivating legends, compiled by Albert Wass from a collection of Freda B. Kovács, are accompanied by vigorous, full-page black and white drawings.

088. Manning-Sanders, Ruth. The Glass Man and the Golden Bird: Hungarian Folk and Fairy Tales. Illus. Victor G. Ambrus. New York: Roy, 1968. 194 p. Grades 4 and up.

The title story is one of twenty-one tales contained in this collection. It tells of the good King Andrew and how he finds a lovely bride with the aid of a sprig of rosemary, a grateful golden bird, and a talking white horse. First, however, he has to pull a magic glass arrow out of the shoulder of a white horse and save the Diamond King from a two-sworded spider witch. The other stories also contain magical beings, animals with extraordinary powers, and a myriad of magical objects. One tells of a wonderful tree that has branches reaching to heaven and of the king's beautiful daughter who is carried by a fierce whirlwind to its top. There she is held prisoner by a dragon with nine heads. She is saved from the furious dragon through the magic of the huge tree by the king's swineherd, Jack, a lad with the heart of gold, and by his helpers, a piglet, and a golden horse with wings. Earlier Jack had shown a special kindness to both. The piglet and the horse would have died without his help. Similarly, other tales in the collection prove that one good turn deserves another, that kindness to the poor and weak is especially well

rewarded, that a marriage between loving couples lasts
forever, and that the haughty and the envious eventually
receive their deserved punishment. Expressive black and
white drawings alternating with strong, full-color
paintings perfectly match the humor and grace of the
stories.

089. Pogány, Nándor. The Hungarian Fairy Book.   Illus.
Willy Pogány. New York: Stokes, 1913.   287 p.   Grades 5
and up.
   A collection of twenty-six tales, most based on some
type of historical background. As indicated in the
foreword, most of the stories are probably fragments of
the great Hungarian epic that once existed and has been
lost in the chaos of invasions occuring throughout
centuries. The collection contains such favorites as
the "Miraculous Stag," illustrating the beginning of
Hungary as a nation; "The Funeral of Attila," reflecting
the beliefs and the social conditions of the Huns after
the death of their King in the fifth century; and
"Botond and the Emperor of the Greeks," a kind of
tall-tale mirroring the strong, fighting spirit of the
Magyars. "The Chapel of Karcsa" explains the origin of
a strange chapel, built upside down, its tower buried in
the ground, the ruins of which can still be seen today.
The same story also explains why the fairies will never
again appear on earth and that what we call the drops of
dew are really the tears of Prince Hajnal, who weeps
afresh every night for the death of his Fairy Queen.
"The Cattle of Molvos" clearly portrays the long
historical period when most of Hungary's peasants worked
for the powerful nobles and did not possess even those
scraps of land on which their miserable cottages stood.
The miniature pen drawings, ornamented initial letters,
and full-page black and white illustrations add drama to
the tales.

090. Pogány, Nándor. Magyar Fairy Tales from Old Hungarian
Legends.   Illus. Willy Pogány.   New York: Dutton, 1930.
268 p.   Grades 5-8.
   Twenty-one folk tales told in a lively prose and
enriched with vigorous, decorative black and white
drawings and borders. None of these are simple stories.
All have subplots, a myriad of fascinating characters,
and magic galore. "Prince Argyilus" is a love story in
which the youngest son of a King falls in love with the
beautiful fairy Ilona, who descends in the form of a
raven upon an apple tree bearing fruit of pure gold.
Within the story is related the extraordinary journey of
the Young Prince in search of his beloved. Neither the
Sun, the Moon, Wind, or the one-eyed King of the Animals
can offer any good advice. A lame wolf is the only one
who knows anything about the whereabouts of the fairy
Ilona. There begins another adventure for the Prince,
in which he has to outwit three little devils and an old
witch. With the aid of four magic items - a cloak, a

pair of boots, a whip, and finally the witch's whistle - the fairy Ilona is freed from her spell and can finally marry the handsome Prince. Similarly, in other stories, unexpected events (as well as characters) appear and disappear and new parts begin. The characters include talking animals, royalty, deities, angels, evil spirits, fairy folk, and all kinds of human creatures, rich and poor, smart and foolish.

091. Schwimmer, Rosika. *Tisza Tales*. Illus. by Willy Pogány. Garden City, NY: Doubleday, Doran, 1928. 225 p. Grades 3-8.

There is no other place in the world which the Hungarian fishermen love more than the river Tisza and the valley through which it zig-zags. Tisza is one of the four rivers appearing in the Hungarian coat-of-arms and the only river with its source and mouth on Hungarian soil. Since Tisza never leaves the boundaries of Hungary, the fishermen consider it the most wonderful river of all. Encouraged by the old man Karad, a group of fishermen in a hut on the bank of the river take turns selecting and telling stories. Everyone knows that Uncle Karad tells stories better than anyone else, so he has to tell the first tale. He is asked to begin with a legend explaining the origin of their beloved Tisza. According to Uncle Karad, it was created in the beginning by the Father of Creation with the help of an archangel, who harnessed a donkey to a golden plow and made a long furrow across the land all the way to the Danube River, with Tisza, the lonely creature, following and filling the grooves. Other stories are told and exchanged by the fishermen. Several tales are about King Mathias the Righteous, others are legends about saints, like the legend of St. Elizabeth, and still others are about most unusual characters. They include Hary Janos, a peerless hero, whose deeds of bravery surpassed the heroic deeds of all the heroes of the world, and a poor tailor, who outwits no one but two devils and gets the sack of gold they drop right in front of his door. All thirty-two tales in the collection are told in a spirited, poetic style and are accompanied by distinctive black and white drawings and color plates.

092. Wass, Albert. *Selected Hungarian Folktales*. Trans. Elizabeth M. Wass de Czege. Illus. Béla Petri. Astor Park, FL: Danubian, 1972. 135 p. Grades 4 and up.

Twelve tales carefully chosen to represent the various types of rich Hungarian folklore. In their themes they emphasize victory for the morally strong, however physically poor they may be. They stress the existence of a rich reward for those who are willing to help the poor and needy. In the story lucky Pista, the youngest brother in a family with "more children than there are holes in a sieve," sets out into the world to search for a kingdom in need of a king. On his way, Pista rescues an eagle trapped in a briar bush and shares his meager

food with him; he offers an old woman help and carries a
bundle of heavy firewood to her hut; he greets a witch,
the Iron-Nosed Baba, with gentleness; and he keeps a
freezing snake warm under his shirt and shares his last
bite of food with him. For his good deeds, the young
lad   receives   invaluable   advice   and   tokens   of
appreciation   containing   extraordinary   powers   which
enable him to lift the curse of the evil warlock off the
Golden Kingdom.   He becomes a king and marries a
beautiful princess.   Other fascinating stories about
dragons, giants, golden castles, silver meadows, flowers
of precious stones, wheatfields of pure gold, good and
wise kings, ugly witches, arrogant warlocks, and witty
maidens,   all   contain   manifestations   of   goodness,
unselfish love, justice, integrity and hope. A rich
collection in a smooth translation and pleasing format,
with handsome illustrations and typography.

TRADITIONAL LITERATURE: SINGLE EDITIONS

093. Ambrus, Victor G.   Brave Soldier Janosh.   Illus.
author. New York: Oxford UP, 1967. N. pag. Grades K-3.
Since none of the villagers have ever traveled from
home, they believe and marvel at the old soldier's
stories. Janosh, a popular character in Hungarian folk
literature, is particularly fond of telling them about
his encounter with Napoleon.   According to Janosh, as
soon as he had a chance to draw his sword, Napoleon and
his grenadiers fled for their lives.   Neither their
heavy cannon nor their swift horses could save the
French army.   But out of the goodness of his heart,
Janosh spared their lives. In gratitude Napoleon filled
Janosh's pockets with gold. If Janosh had not had such
large holes in them, he would have been the richest man
among the villagers who listened to his tales.   The
short narrative is enhanced with large waterpaintings in
glowing colors, making the puffed-up character of Janosh
even bigger and taller than he ever actually could have
been.

094. Ambrus, Victor G.   The Little Cockerel.   Illus.
author. New York: Harcourt, Brace, and World, 1968. N.
pag. Grades K-3.
First published in England by Oxford University Press,
this story is based on an old Hungarian folktale. It is
centered around a little cockerel and his efforts to
make the Turkish Sultan return the golden coin which he
has taken away from him. The little cockerel believes
that the golden sovereign, which he found in a poor old
woman's pile of rubbish, belongs to the old woman and
that the Sultan has no right to take it from him.
Determined to retrieve the golden coin, the little
cockerel flies to the palace shouting his demands in the
middle of the night. Furious for being disturbed in his

sleep, the Sultan roars for his guards who try to get rid of the noisy villain. But the cockerel survives a deep well, a fiery oven, and a lively beehive. Pursuing the Sultan not only with his loud shouting to return the golden sovereign, but also with a swarm of bees which he swallowed when he was thrown into a beehive, the cockerel convinces the Sultan to give in. Needless to say, when the little hero brings back the golden coin, he gains a special place in the old woman's heart as well as in her house. Brilliant watercolors perfectly match the humor and the simple liveliness of the text.

095.   Ambrus, Victor G.   The Seven Skinny Goats.   Illus. author.   New York: Harcourt, Brace, and World, 1969.   N. pag.   Grades K-3.

About the only thing that the simple lad, Jano, could do was play his flute. When Jano takes the innkeeper's goats to the meadow, he plays such merry tunes that they begin to dance and do not eat a single blade of grass. They soon become a very sorry sight indeed. Trying to find out what was happening in the pasture, the innkeeper follows Jano secretly and hides behind a bush. He does not stay there long. As soon as Jano begins to play his flute, the goats start to dance. Before the master can get over his surprise, he too is kicking his heels and cannot stop dancing until Jano stops playing. When he is taken before the judge for making the goats the skinniest animals ever seen, Jano again makes everybody dance with his music. The townsfolk and the judge leap about until they reach the point of exhaustion. Driven from the town, Jano vows never to stay any place where good music is not appreciated. Large illustrations in brilliant colors add a note of humor to the imaginative text of the old folktale.

096.   Ambrus, Victor G.   The Sultan's Bath.   Illus. author. New York: Harcourt Brace Jovanovich, 1972.   N. pag.   Grades 1-3.

The Sultan, who rules over a dry country where water is scarce, loves his morning bath. Every day his servants search the wells and the houses of his kingdom to collect enough water for his royal dip. How surprised he is one morning when he discovers that the water, so carefully gathered, was stolen overnight. After searching the kingdom, the servants find the thief in the Sultan's courtyard. It is Gul-Baba, the gardener, who is using the bath water for the beautiful plants in his secretly walled garden. While Gul-Baba is waiting in a dungeon to be executed, the Sultan visits the garden and is amazed at its beauty. Sitting under sunflowers, surrounded by birds, peacocks, and hedgehogs, he feels happier than he has ever felt before. But without the gardener's care the flowers soon begin to fade, and the Sultan grown sadder and sadder. Finally, he sends for Gul-Baba. They work out a compromise to the satisfaction of each, and are both

happy for the rest of their lives. The brightly colored
illustrations augment the story's charm, humor, and
affection. In Great Britain the book was awarded the
Greenaway Medal for the excellence of its artwork.

097. Ambrus, Victor G. The Three Poor Tailors. Illus.
author. New York: Harcourt, Brace, and World, 1966. N.
pag. Grades K-3.
    A simple folktale about three busy tailors who decide to
go to a nearby town, which, for lack of time, they have
never visited before. They enjoy themselves immensely
by sightseeing and dancing and eating at the inn, but
get themselves into much trouble when they lack enough
money to cover the bill. In his anger the innkeeper
calls the police who chase the three tailors through
town; they catch and punish them by forcing them to mend
all the townspeople's old coats. Because the poor
tailors believe that their bad luck is due to the
slowness of the nanny-goat, on whose back they ride to
town (as well as use to attempt an escape from the
infuriated guards), they decide to work harder than ever
before. If they save enough money they can buy a
billy-goat which is much faster than their old
nanny-goat. The brevity of the text is supplemented
with richly colored large paintings which bring out the
details of the Hungarian folk design and the silliness
of the old folktale's scenes. The book received the
Kate Greenaway medal for most distinguished
illustrations in Great Britain where it was first
published a year earlier.

098. Cleaver, Elizabeth. The Miraculous Hind: A Hungarian
Legend. Illus. author. Toronto: Holt, Rinehart, and
Winston, 1973. 64 p. Grades 2-5.
    A retelling of an old Hungarian legend based on
historical events, the story describes the westward
migration of the old Hungarian tribes from Asia to the
steppes of Eastern Europe between the fifth and eighth
centuries, and tells of the establishment of the
Hungarian nation. It tells about two brothers, Hunor
and Magyar, and their one hundred horsemen, who, in
pursuit of a mysterious hind wander far away from their
kingdom into a new land, where the grass grows soft, the
water is fresh, the mighty river has a multitude of
fish, and where the forests are alive with wild game.
Moreover, they discover that at twilight beautiful fairy
maidens that live in the woods come out of their tents
to dance and sing. Enchanted by the goodness of the
land and by the loveliness of the maidens, the two
brothers and their companions decide to remain in the
newly discovered country and, with brides selected from
among the fairy maidens, establish their homes and found
a new nation. Transmitted orally from generation to
generation, the legend was first written down in the
late thirteenth century. Accompanied by distinguished
illustrations reflecting Hungarian folk art, it contains

valuable historical information and a variety of unusual, highly effective print, and received the Canadian Library Association Book of the Year Award.

099. Colos, Francois. The Student Who Became King in Spite of Himself: A Hungarian Folktale Retold. Illus. author. New York: Holt, Rinehart, and Winston, 1974. N. pag. Grades 2-5.
An intricate tale about a student who leaves his home and becomes a king. It is said that the story was written on the tooth of a fish living in the great sea beyond the Glass Mountain. The story tells about a poor student's desire to see the world. Since his father has taught him to keep his eyes open and to pick up everything that has any value, the student gathers some dry green peas when crossing a field and puts them into his pocket. The peas became instrumental in convincing a king and queen in a distant palace that the young man is a prince disguised as a student, although he has no intentions of proving himself to be of royal blood. In spite of his objections, they begin to call him "Your Highness" and give him their beautiful daughter in marriage. Before his kingly affairs are settled once and for all, however, he has to overcome a seven-headed dragon with the help of an old witch and with the help of a wise talking loaf of bread that has been baked seven times. The accompanying illustrations are most unusual. There are full-page paintings in rich colors and fascinating, complicated collages, incorporating many elements of modern art as well as old folktale motifs.

100.   Domjan, Joseph.   The Little Cock.   Illus. author. Retold by Jeanne B. Hardendorff. New York: Lippincott, 1969. N. pag. Grades 1-4.
In a small house at one end of the village, lives a poor woman with a pet cock, Kis Kakas. One day as the cock is searching and scratching for a worm in the yard, he finds a diamond halfpenny. While crowing the good news to the old woman, a Turkish Sultan comes by with his army and orders the soldiers to take the diamond halfpenny from Kis Kakas. The cock, however, is determined to retrieve the treasure. He follows the Sultan to his palace, annoying him with his constant crowing. The persistent cock outsmarts the cunning of the Sultan's three wives. He emerges unharmed from the deepest well in the palace yard, from the hot fire of the biggest stove in the palace kitchen, and from the largest beehive in the palace garden. He returns to the old woman not only with the diamond halfpenny but also with all the gold, silver, diamonds, and rubies of the Sultan's treasure room. The exuberant woodcuts, alternately in rich colors and in black and white, enhance the authentic setting of the simple folktale.

101. Galdone, Paul. The Amazing Pig; An Old Hungarian Tale. Illus. author. New York: Houghton Mifflin, 1981. N. pag. Grades K-3.
In a land across the sea lives a king who promises his beautiful daughter in marriage to any man who can tell him something he cannot believe. When a young peasant's son tells him about his father's amazing pig, who provides the family with milk and eggs, from whose side father cuts slices of bacon and which then instantly grow back again, the king smiles, saying he believes him. But when the poor man says that he hired the king's own grandfather to look after the pig, who is getting blind, the king yells in disbelief. In his pride he cannot allow anyone to call his grandfather a swineherd. The peasant's son, of course, marries the beautiful princess and proves to be the wisest ruler the kingdom ever had. Colorful, humorous illustrations could tell the story on their own.

102. Lederer, Charlotte. The Golden Flock. Illus. author. New York: Farrar and Rinehart, 1931. N. pag. Grades 1-3.
Traditional ornamental edging in bright primary colors and full page illustrations with folklore motifs accompany the text of this old legend. Because of their kindness and friendliness to the villagers of Szent Andras, Aunty Mari and Uncle Pista are very much loved by all. Even the birds sense their goodness. When the swallows return to Szent Andras, they first fly to their nest under Aunt Mari and Uncle Pista's roof whose red brick chimney is occupied by the stork couple and their long-necked babies. But, although she is grateful to the Lord for His many blessings, Aunty Mari cries frequently because she has no child running in and out of the house. To console her, Uncle Pista invariable comments: "The Lord will provide." In the end, the Lord does provide. The happy couple get a little boy, a shepherd to watch over their lambs, but not before Uncle Pista returns from his wanderings around the world when he searched for and found a golden flock. A precious story reflecting a simple joy and an authentic Hungarian atmosphere of times gone by.

103. Seredy, Kate. The White Stag. Illus. author. New York: Viking, 1937. 94 p. Grades 5-9.
An exceptional rendition of the best known Hungarian legend, the story tells of the role of the mysterious white stag in the early history of the Hun-Magyar tribes. Beginning in the fourth century, it traces the tribes wanderings from the headlands of wild Altain-Ula, the barren land in Asu (Asia), to the promised land, the land of beauty and riches in Ereb (Europe). It tells about their wise leader, old Numrod, and his brave sons, Hunor and Magyar. It traces the widening rift between the tribes led by the two brothers. Those who are more warlike and reckless follow Hunor; those who are gentler and serious look to Magyar for guidance. The white stag

points the way to the twin eagles, Hunor and Magyar, and also appears periodically to the younger leaders, Hunor's son, Bendeguz, and later to his son, Attila, the Conqueror. When the Huns are threatened by enemies, and their future seems to be dark and without hope, the luminous bright figure of the White Stag appears for the last time to young Attila, the Red Eagle, and leads his army to victory. The author's superbly drawn illustrations strongly support the poetic retelling of the beautiful epic. The story received the Newbery Medal for the most distinguished contribution to children's literature in 1938 and the Lewis Carroll Shelf Award in 1958.

104. Severo, Emöke de Papp. The Good-Hearted Youngest Brother. Illus. Diane Goode. Scarsdale, NY: Bradbury. 1981. N. pag. Grades K-3.
The youngest of three brothers renounces his right to his parents' inheritance and wishes only that the others remain good brothers to him. While setting out to seek their fortune, the three brothers come upon one unusual wonder after another. Out of each unexpected episode, they emerge without harm, and in the end each marries a beautiful princess because of the acts of kindness performed by the youngest brother. First he begs his oldest brother not to shoot wild doves in the forest, then he pleads with his middle brother not to kill the wild loons swimming on the green lake. While the other two feast at the table, magically laid for them with every kind of good food and drink, the youngest brother dreams of how he would thank the provider for all those blessings. Because he possesses such a good and gentle heart, he is able to undo the terrible bewitchment cast on the three princesses by finding three pearls hidden in three wild doves' eggs, by recovering three crowns from the bottom of the green lake, and by guessing which of the three princesses is the oldest and which is the youngest. Superb paintings in gentle colors underscore the charm of the story and bring to life the authentic Hungarian setting. This is the author's first translation and adaptation of an old Hungarian folktale.

HISTORICAL FICTION, BIOGRAPHY, AND AUTOBIOGRAPHY

105. Dickinson, Peter. The Dancing Bear. Illus. David Smee. Boston: Little, Brown, 1972. 244 p. Grades 6-12.
This rich piece of historical fiction is set in the middle of the sixth century, when Hunnish warriors under the Khan Zabergan plundered Byzantium and began weakening the Justinian Empire. The story is about a Greek slave, Silvester, who is in service to the prominent Lord Celsus, the Lord's only daughter, Lady Ariadne, and a she bear named Bubba, who saved Ariadne, at the age of two, from a male bear. Silvester, an intelligent boy, the same age to the day as the bear and

the young girl, takes care of Bubba, who was trained to dance to the rhythm of the drum and flutes. During the raid on Byzantium, when her Lady Ariadne is taken away by the Huns, the faithful, loving Silvester begins a long journey with Bubba in search of his dear friend. Silvester's adventures are presented with a deep understanding of human tendencies and aspirations and of animal capabilities and with much insight into the Byzantine civilization as well as into the lives and customs of the early Hunnish and Slav tribes. The author admits, however, that aside from well researched historical facts pertaining to sixth century Byzantium, which reached its greatest size under Emperor Justinian and to the plundering of the Empire by the Huns, the story is purely fictional. Especially day-to-day living customs of the savage tribes are the author's own innovation. The adventurous absorbing story is accompanied by stylistic black and white drawings and a map of Silvester's journey. In 1973 the book received a special commendation by the Greenaway Medal Committee of the British Library Association.

106. Eyerly, Jeannette. <u>Good-by to Budapest</u>. New York: Lippincott, 1974. 159 p. Grades 5-10.
   Megan Moore's father, an outstanding physicist in the field of cosmic radiation, is attending a conference in Budapest. As Megan waits at the crowded Frankfurt airport for her flight to the Hungarian capital to join him, she notices the same handsome young man standing nearby wearing a brown raincoat that she had seen that same morning in London's airport and a day before at the Hungarian consulate. He must speak English, Megan thinks, otherwise he would not be reading <u>The London Times</u> and <u>Newsweek</u>. But, once aboard the Hungarian airplane, Megan notices him talking to the Hungarian pilots and emerging nonchalantly from the cockpit. He must be a Hungarian. In her lively imagination Megan decides that the good looking young boy must be "somebody," perhaps a courier for his government carrying important documents. His role in the suspenseful drama, involving a blackmail plot to force Megan's father to reveal scientific secrets to the Russians, is soon revealed. From several adventurous episodes, Megan emerges as an intelligent, resourceful heroine. As expected, she is in love with Andras, the young man in the brown coat, who is now engaged in a desperate and daring attempt to get Megan and her father out of the country and out of danger. The story provides much information about life in postwar Hungary.

107. Finta, Alexander and Jeanette Eaton. <u>Herdboy of Hungary: The True Story of Mocskos</u>. Illus. Alexander Finta. New York: Harper, 1932. 166 p. Grades 5-10.
   A perceptive story told in the first person by Sandar, a young Hungarian boy who lives with his family in the

village of Puspoki toward the end of the nineteenth
century. When he is four years old, his father brings
him some penknives from the fair and immediately
proceeds to teach him how to carve the letters of the
alphabet out of wood. With the primitive tools, Sandar
learns not only manual skills, but also how to put
alphabet letters together in order to read. With this
accomplishment, new joys come into Sandar's life. To
the surprise of the old school master, Sandar is able to
read better than most of the older students. He learns
quickly, but cannot stand constant repetitions. When,
because of his age, he is placed with the younger
students, school becomes an agony for him. Completely
bored with school and not learning anything, Sandar
misbehaves and plays many a trick on the old
schoolmaster. He is expelled from school. Only nine
years old, Sandar is destined to become a cowboy. He is
taken by his father to his uncle's ranch on the
Hungarian plains located two days walking distance from
his home. There he learns the hard way to herd cattle
and horses and to ride his own horse, Mocskos. It is
his love for the brokendown horse that helps Sandar
survive the unusual hardships imposed on him by the
herdsmen on the range. He risks his own life to steal
clover in order to feed his emaciated friend. Sandar
fills his free time on the range by collecting specimens
of rare birds' nests, eggs, and feathers. His knowledge
of the birds that live in the swamps of the region
becomes known to Otto Herman, a famous ornithologist.
When Otto comes to the ranch to study birds, he promises
Sandar a scholarship in the Gymnasium of Nagyvarad.
Sandar's youthful courage, his endurance of hardships,
his love of animals, and his ingenuity and intelligence
are clearly reflected in a most absorbing story.

108. Finta, Alexander. My Brothers and I. Illus. author.
New York: Holiday House, 1940. 185 p. Grades 5-10.
    A sequel to the story Herdboy of Hungary (107). Sandar
arrives home just after his father receives a letter
from the Minister of Education of Hungary informing him
that a very attractive scholarship has been granted to
his oldest son to attend the classical high school.
Unfortunately, Sandar is not able to accept it. In his
strict Calvinist convictions, his father decides that
all of his five sons should have an equal chance in
getting an education, and the offered scholarship for
the prestigious Gymnasium of Nagyvarad is declined.
Sandar and his five brothers register at the public high
school. Their life in the ancient city of Nagyvarad is
quite adventurous. Deserving special mention is the
fact that the almost militant activities of the youth
gangs on Inferno Street, their aeronautical experiments,
their efforts to outdo each other in strength and
recognition, as well as the difficulties they experience
with adults, are convincingly described and are
timeless; they could happen today in any city. The

story contains captivating passages and narrow escapes.
There are clever mischievous pranks and tender moments
of sadness over injustices, and moments of love which
overcome greediness. The story abounds with various
superstitions and folkloric myths and beliefs. Overall
an appealing story, though it lacks the strength and
depth of the earlier Herdboy.

109. Gárdonyi, Geza. Slave of the Huns. Trans. Andrew
Feldmar. Illus. Victor C. Ambrus. New York: Bobbs-
Merrill, 1969. 358 p. Grades 7 and up.
This story is told in the first person by Theophil,
whose Thracian father sold him into slavery when the boy
was twelve years old. Father had no choice. The people
in the Eastern Empire were taxed to death because of the
demands of the Huns. Besides, the boy's mother died,
and there were six children to be fed. Under the first
master, Maximinus, the boy is treated with utmost
cruelty. Fortunately he is purchased by Priscus who is
the emperor's adviser and a teacher of history and
rhetoric. Priscus is a good, kind man. Because of the
boy's excellent memory and ability to learn Homer,
Plato, Aristotle, Herodotus, and other classical
authors, he is named Zeta, for the letter in the Greek
alphabet. After eight years Zeta is given his freedom
but decides to stay with the good, learned man. He
accompanies Priscus on his diplomatic mission to the
camp of Attila, the Hun. There he meets Emmo, a noble
lady, and falls in love with her. In order to declare
his love for her, Zeta sacrifices his freedom and joins
Attila's army. Distinguishing himself in the service of
the Huns, Zeta finally becomes Attila's scribe and thus
enters Emmo's world. A most colorful historical drama,
first published in Hungary in 1901, it has been
considered a classic ever since.

110. Hámori, László. Dangerous Journey. Trans. Annabelle
Macmillan. Illus. W.T. Mars. New York: Harcourt, Brace,
and World, 1962. 190 p. Grades 5-8
A spellbinding adventure story of two Hungarian boys
who, in search of freedom, escape from Russian occupied
Hungary to Austria. Twelve-year-old Latsi Kerek loses
his grandmother who has taken care of him ever since his
parents left Hungary and fled to Sweden in hope that the
boy would be allowed to follow them. Left alone after
the death of his grandmother, Latsi submits a request to
the government for the documents needed to travel to
Sweden. Again, permission to leave Budapest is denied
to him. Pishta Gati is in a similar situation. His
father was killed during the war; his mother must now
work long hours to earn their living, and Pishta rarely
sees her at home. When Pishta tries to sneak away from
the flag parade in school, he is expelled and taken away
from his mother. Both boys are now on a train to a home
for orphans, accompanied by the Comrade Youth Warden.
Courageous, bright, and determined, the boys fool the

Warden and, with the help of some good-hearted friends,
escape from the children's home and cross the border.
The fast moving story includes exciting accounts of
narrow escapes, of dramatic but fully believable
episodes, of catastrophic incidents, and of the boys'
deep concern for each other. The completely believable
and moving story contains interesting background
information regarding the life of Hungarians and the
political situation of the country in its post
revolutionary period.

111. Hersh, Gizelle and Peggy Mann. <u>Gizelle, Save the
Children</u>. New York: Everest House, 1980. 319 p. Grades
7-12.
    In 1940 when Hungary became an official ally of Hitler's
    Germany, one half of the Romanian province of
    Transylvania was ceded to it. The size of the Hungarian
    Jewish population increased tremendously with the influx
    of thousands of Transylvanian Jews and Jewish refugees
    from Poland and Czechoslovakia. Until 1944 nearly a
    million Hungarian Jews, although deprived of much of
    their livelihood, had been spared from the Eichmann's
    plan of the "Final Solution." When German troups
    invaded the country in the spring of 1944, the merciless
    program of extermination also began in Hungary. Against
    this background, the engrossing story of the family of
    Emmanuel and Miriam Hersh, their son Sander, and their
    four daughters Gizelle, Lenci, Mitzi, and Katya,
    develops. "Gizelle, Save the Children," called the
    mother to her oldest daughter, aged sixteen, when the
    parents were separated from their children at the death
    camp at Auschwitz. From that moment on it was up to
    Gizelle to watch over her younger sisters during their
    horrifying months in Auschwitz, in the forced labor camp
    at Geishingen, during their stay in Dachau, another
    living hell, and in their final horrible train ride in
    packed boxcars, until finally were freed by American
    soldiers. With Gizelle's courage, resourcefulness,
    intelligence, and loyalty, the four sisters managed to
    keep together and survive. A moving, unforgettable
    story of endurance and love in a sea of evil and hatred.
    It is masterfully written.

112. Jacobi, Elizabeth. <u>The Adventures of Andris</u>. Illus.
Kata Benedek. New York: Macmillan, 1929. 124 p. Grades
3-5.
    A story centered around two children, the boy Andris and
    his six-year-old sister, Kati, living after the First
    World War on the big Hungarian estate called Kelnek
    Puszta in the middle of the Great Hungarian Plain. The
    one-thousand acre farm belongs to Squire Kelneky. The
    children's father, Istvan Kerekes, is the Squire's
    coachman. The coachman's family, as well as the
    families of others in the service of the Squire, has a
    bit of land of their own, where they grow vegetables and

raise poultry and other animals. For the work they do
the families receive additional land, grain, firewood,
and money. The twelve-chapter narrative paints an
intricate picture of life on the estate and of the
social and political conditions in Hungary. It offers
glimpses into the history of the country and into the
people's struggle for freedom. The stories of their
heroes and the religious life of the people, from Easter
to   Christmas,   are   interwoven   with   the   quietly
adventurous life of the villagers.   Bright orange
borders and black and white folkloric ornaments and
illustrations heighten the appeal and warmth of the
book.

113. Kalnay,   Francis.   The Richest Boy in the World.
Illus. W.T. Mars. New York: Harcourt, Brace, 1959. 92 p.
Grades 4-6.
    This picturesque story takes place just before World War
I in the Royal Institute for Underprivileged Boys, a
boarding school in Hungary for sons of the railroad
workers.   Based on the author's childhood experiences,
the story is a vivid portrayal of the life in the
boarding school, of the educational concepts prevalent
at the beginning of this century, and of the level of
understanding of children as human beings. The director
of the Institute does not interact with the boys except
in cases when he inflicts harsh punishment upon them.
While the boys are kept just a notch above starvation
level, the director's favorite place in the building is
his own pantry which is filled with smoked sausages and
salami.   From the window of this pantry the director is
able to slightly observe the activities of the boys on
the playground. He watches them intently at their play
of shooting marbles, the only game they are allowed to
play, but only for exactly one hour each afternoon. For
the boys the marbles become a symbol of wealth, a means
for trading their meager portions of food and other
precious items.   When the boys catch the director spying
on them during one of their games, all of their precious
possessions are confiscated.   At the end of the school
year, however, the smallest boy in the school is given
all the marbles.   To him they are worth more than gold
and money. He learns soon, however, that sudden wealth
can cause big problems.   A perceptively written story,
strong in its characterization and development of
relationships.

114. Lasker, David. The Boy Who Loved Music. Illus. Joe
Lasker. New York: Viking, 1979. N. pag. Grades 2-4.
    Prince Nicolaus Esterhazy is the richest Hungarian
nobleman of the eighteenth century. He spends most of
his time in one of his luxurious summer castles,
Esterlaza.   With him reside his Viennese musicians,
singers, painters, and dancers. They are considered his
servants just like his cooks, butlers, maids and
stableboys.   They are forbidden to leave to visit their

families except during a short period when the Prince leaves the castle for his winter palace. Among the musicians is a young man Karl, a horn player in the orchestra. Although he has tried, he fails to persuade Prince Nicolaus to return to Vienna so that he can visit his family. When the annnouncement comes that the Empress Maria Theresa is planning to visit Esterhaza and that the musicians are to stay there even longer, Joseph Haydn, the famous composer and music director at the castle composes the symphony, "Farewell," with an unusual, effective ending, solving, for once, Karl's problems, as well as the problem of his colleagues. Based on historical fact, the story vividly portrays the customs of the eighteenth century Hungarian and Austrian nobility and shows how important music was in their lives. For its strikingly beautiful illustrations in rich colors, this pictorial narrative was recognized as an outstanding book of the year by the New York Times, School Library Journal, and by the American Library Association.

115. Lengyel, Emil. Lajos Kossuth: Hungary's Great Patriot. Illus. author. New York: Watts, 1969. 145 p. Grades 7-12.
The biographer presents Lajos Kossuth as an ardent patriot, able orator, and the first journalist to advocate reform in Hungary; Lajos is also portrayed as a man with warm feelings for his fellowmen, especially for the poor and powerless. He was born in 1802 in the villge of Monok in northern Hungary to a family of lesser nobility, known as gentry. At the age of twenty-one he became a lawyer. He entered parliament in 1825 and soon became the leader of the liberal minded patriots. Influenced by the readings of Jean Jacques Rousseau, by the American Constitution and Bill of Rights, and by the revolutionary movements in the western European countries, Lajos Kossuth became the most ardent spokesman for government reforms and for more independence and freedom from Metternick's absolutism under Habsburg rule. In 1848 Kossuth led an unsucessful anti-Habsburg revolution. In 1849, as a result of the defeat, he fled to Turkey. President Fillmore helped him to immigrate to the United States, where he was hailed as the Hungarian George Washington. A chronological list of events, a detailed index, a map of nineteenth century Hungary, and several photographs add to the authenticity of the biography and to the description of the historical period in which Lajos Kossuth lived and fought for the freedom and independence of his beloved Hungary.

116. Noble, Iris. Physician to the Children: Dr. Béla Schick. New York: Messner, 1963. 189 p. Grades 5-10.
In the later part of the nineteenth century, man's knowledge of medicine was increasing rapidly. Louis Pasteur proved that many illnesses were caused by

bacteria, and he introduced vaccinations as tools for fighting infectious diseases. More great scientists followed with medical discoveries. The bacteria for typhoid, tuberculosis, and cholera were isolated. Moreover, areas of specialization, such as pediatrics, were beginning to germinate. Bela Schick was born during this exciting time in science. In 1867, when Mrs. Schick was visiting her brother Dr. Telegdi, a dedicated physician, Bela was born prematurely in the Hungarian resort town of Boglar. Dr. Telegdi saved him and prayed that someday the child's life would be dedicated to saving other people's lives. This absorbing narrative tells about the development of Bela's vocation, his courageous struggle to reach and stand upon his convictions, his success in his studies, his dedication to pediatrics, his scientific discoveries, and the well deserved recognition he received in Europe and in the United States, where he worked during the last decades of his life. In his eyes, more important than all the medals and awards bestowed upon him during his ninety-year life span, was an honor that he received in 1933 in New York: he was presented with an enormous album signed by one million of America's children in gratitude for saving millions of children's lives from the threat of diphtheria by developing an immunity test, which became known as the Schick test. An intimate, well written biography of a great scientist and an even greater humanitarian.

117. Petersham, Maud and Miska Petersham. **Miki**. Illus. authors. New York: Doubleday, Doran, 1929. N. pag. Grades K-3.

This old story is about a boy, named Miki, the son of Hungarian parents living in the United States, of his visit to Hungary a half century ago, and of his many experiences there. It describes the Hungarian homes, with their white-washed clay stoves and their feather-filled beds topped with gayly embroidered pillows, and the deliciously prepared Hungarian specialties, like poppyseed strudel and filled paprikas. It portrays Budapest, the capital of the nation, and the festivities of Christmas and Saint Nicholas Day. Miki visits a kind old couple in their snug house, sleeps on a soft pillow bed, takes a goose to the mountain pasture, eats with the shepherds from a common bowl, listens to their stories, dances to gypsy music, visits cities, rides on a merry-go-round in the park of Worstly, the place where one buys Hungarian sausages, and meets a girl named Maruska and celebrates Christmas with her family. Miki returns to the United States with a lot of presents and is dressed in a new suit with a richly embroidered shirt and vest. Superbly illustrated in bright colors and authentic folklore designs.

118. Ritchie, Rita. <u>The Enemy at the Gate</u>.   New   York:
Dutton, 1959. 250 p. Grades 7-10.
In 1526 at the battle of Mohacs, Turkish Sultan
Suleiman's army conquered most of Hungary and threatened
central and western Europe.   While cities throughout
Europe continued to strengthen their walls, Vienna
appeared to be safe. It was encircled by a high stone
wall, which had been built three centuries before and
had kept the city free from attack since. The year 1529
was different.   Vienna was being transformed into a
military depot, and more earthen embankments were built
behind its walls.   It was during this year that the
Turkish cavalry, under their crescent banner, attacked
the city.   Against the background of this ravaging
siege, which proved to be the beginning of Ottoman
decline, develops the story of a Hungarian apprentice
gunsmith, Michael Laszlo, who, in fear for his family in
Hungary, leaves Vienna during the raging battle around
the city with the hope of returning to them to help
them. Caught and branded as a traitor, he has to run
from the Viennese army as well as from the Turks.
Michael's skill with wheellock guns, which he himself
forges, along with his great courage, play an important
role in saving Vienna from destruction.   An exciting
story with some fascinating historical details vividly
portraying the dangers, adventure, and complicity of the
period and the tragedy of the historical conflict.

119. Sawyer, Ruth. <u>The Christmas Anna Angel</u>. Illus. Kate
Seredy. New York: Viking, 1944. 48 p. Grades 3-5.
The First World War is raging. The Christmas season is
approaching, but the shops seem empty.   The baker's
window has only a few loaves of rye bread and no buns
and no cakes. Anna cannot imagine what the Christmas
tree will look like without Christmas cakes.   Every
night until the coming of Bethlehem, Anna watches the
splendor of the western sky, believing that the angels
will bake cakes for the children of the world. Among
them must be one of her own, named Anna Angel, who will
bake her Christmas cakes for their family tree. Does
she actually exist?   Anna thinks she does, as she
admires her clock-cake with a pink frosting face, which
she finds hanging just below the star, with its hands
pointed to midnight, the time at which the Christ Child
had been born.   The Hungarian celebration of the
Christmas season with the feast of St. Nicholas, St.
Lucy's Day, and Christmas Eve are vividly presented in
this story.   In the background of the colorful
festivities, however, one spots the chilling effects of
the war: the strict control of the people's food
supplies by the government and the lack of everyday
provisions. Warmly and cheerfully illustrated in pencil
drawings, as well as in rich color, the book appears on
the Caldecott Honor List for 1945.

120. Seredy, Kate. <u>The Chestry Oak</u>. Illus. author. New
York: Viking, 1948. 236 p. Grades 5-10.
    Chestry Oak is a giant of a tree, older than any other
tree in the valley, and even older than nearby Chestry
castle itself. It was planted during the reign of the
first Hungarian King, Stephan, around the year 1000.
Since then, countless giant oaks have grown from its
acorns, all planted by the men of Count Chester, who has
been in charge of Chestry Valley for centuries. In the
twentieth century, six-year-old Prince Michael is
determined that he too will plant an acorn from the
Chestry Oak with the oath which has been repeated by the
Chestry men in the past. The time comes when
ten-year-old Michael fulfills his promise and his dream.
He plants the acorn with the same love for the good
earth and with the same courage in his heart as that of
his ancestors, but not in the same soil. Rather, he
plants it in America, his adopted homeland, where he is
brought as an orphan of the World War I. Masterfully
integrated into this gentle story are beautiful
Hungarian legends, episodes from history, especially
those which describe the error of the World War II, and
descriptions of the brave, proud spirit of the Hungarian
people. This absorbing, moving story is written in a
flowing, poetic style and illustrated with most
appropriate, sensitive pencil drawings.

121. Seredy, Kate. <u>The Good Master</u>. Illus. author. New
York: Viking, 1935. 210 p. Grades 4-8.
    A warm story about ten-year-old Jancsi Nagy, who lives
at the turn of the century with his parents on a large
ranch, and about his cousin, Kate, who comes from the
city of Budapest to live with his family. Kate is not
the delicate city cousin Jancsi had pictured her to be.
When she arrives she is a spoiled, stubborn, screaming
little girl. But living and working on the farm along
with Jancsi, Jancsi's loving mother, and wise father and
with her understanding Uncle Marton, the "Good Master,"
Kate changes into a happy, husky little farmer. With
the help of Jancsi, Kate drives the geese and ducks to
the brook, feeds the chickens, learns all about horses,
takes care of her garden, and listens attentively to
stories about fairies and witches, and to legends about
the constellations, like the Milky Way, called the
Skyway of the Warriors. She especially enjoys animal
tales and stories of Hungarian heroes, like King Matyas
and his servant, Matyi. With Jancsi, she participates
in the round-up of horses, in the celebration of Easter
and Christmas, and in the country fair. With his help
she emerges without a scratch from a dangerous encounter
with the river and from a gypsy camp. A touching story,
it gives a colorful picture of life on the big Hungarian
plains several decades ago. The illustrations add
vitality and strength to the text and an atmosphere of
charm and gayety to the Hungarian festivities. In 1936
the book appeared on the Newbery honor's list.

122. Seredy, Kate. <u>The Singing Tree</u>. Illus. author. New York: Viking, 1939. 247 p. Grades 5-9.
In this sequel to <u>The Good Master</u> the Nagy's homestead in the Hungarian plains is described as rich and spacious. Marton Nagy and his family are the second generation to live in peace on their beloved ranch. They think of people in other countries as their brothers. They live in contentment with their neighbors and love the good earth that provides so generously for their needs. Through their loving hearts they open their door to Kate and her father, Sandor Nagy, Marton's brother, to a young mother and her baby, to a city girl, Lily, who is in need of a good healthy home, and even to a litter of homeless kittens. A year or so later, when the World War I disturbs and changes their peaceful, unhurried ways, they often offer Russian prisoners, as well as homeless German children, warm shelter with them. Their caring home is like a singing, giving tree, alive with fruit and birds, all from different nests, the birds chirping and singing side by side. The affectionate Hungarian family life, the beautiful Hungarian customs, especially a traditional wedding, as well as the absurdity of the war are deftly portrayed. An absorbing story supported by engaging full-page illustrations, ornaments, and folk motifs. The book was selected by the American Library Association for the Newbery honor award.

123. Seroff, Victor. <u>Franz Liszt</u>. New York: Macmillan, 1966. 152 p. Grades 6-10.
A biography of the Hungarian composer and great piano virtuoso of the nineteenth century. Franz Liszt was born in 1811, in Raiding, a small village in Hungary. As a young boy Franz showed remarkable musical aptitude. According to the author, before his feet could touch the floor from his piano bench, he was able to repeat on the piano what he heard his father play. At the age of nine Franz made his piano debut. With his own improvisations of well-known melodies, Franz scored such a tremendous success that a group of the Hungarian aristocracy, who were to patronize his later concerts, offered to finance his musical education. At the age of ten Franz began a two-year study in Vienna under Karl Czerny, a pianist and composer. He continued his studies in Paris, where he became famous for the brilliance of style found in his piano music. The biographer gives a rapid account of Liszt's further successes, his concerts throughout Europe, his appointment as a musical director at the court of Weimar, Germany, of the women he loved, his loneliness, his famous contemporaries, his life in Rome, and of his unsurpassed compositions. Reproductions of old photographs and paintings add much to the biography. A selected Liszt's discography and index are appended.

124. Seymour, Alta Halverson. <u>Toward Morning: A Story of the Hungarian Freedom Fighters</u>. Chicago: Follett, 1961.

144 p. Grades 6-9.
   The setting of the story is the tragic Hungarian
Revolution of 1956. The revolution began with a
peaceful demonstration by groups of Hungarian workers,
students, soldiers, both young and old, even including
children, who gathered at Radio Building in Budapest in
an effort to broadcast their demands for more freedom.
The revolution ended a month later with Russian tanks
rolling into the streets of the capital and with the
terror-filled retaliations they brought. The absorbing
story is centered around the involvement of the Nagy
family and their friends in the heroic struggle. Janos,
a student, joins a group of young patriots in their
teens and becomes their leader. The group is determined
to fight the Russian tanks, but soon realizes that they
have no chance for victory. When the Russians begin to
persecute them they decide to escape across the border
to Austria. Fourteen-year-old Teresa plays a decisive
role in their dangerous flight to safety. The integral
theme of this well-plotted story, in which tense
episodes follow quickly one after another, is the
intenseness of the Hungarian's national pride and the
Hungarian's intense courage in defending their freedom.

125. Siegal, Aranka. Upon the Head of the Goat: A Childhood in Hungary, 1939-1944. New York: Farrar, Strauss
Giroux, 1981. 214 p. Grades 7 and up.
   From the time Piri is five years old, she spends her
summers with her grandmother in the Ukrainian village of
Komyaty. There she enjoys the open countryside, the
sounds of the Rika River, and the mystery of the nearby
forest. In 1939 when Piri is nine, she is unable to
return to her family home in Beregszasz, Hungary.
Travel between the two countries is not possible because
of the battle the Ukrainian Resistance Fighters are
waging against the Hungarians over disputed borders.
During the year she stays with Babi, Piri learns much
about her Jewish religion and becomes aware of the
hatred directed against the Jews, a hatred which gets
increasingly more intense as the European nations become
entangled in World War II. Upon her return to Hungary
this hatred drastically changes the life of her family
and of her friends. Her father is forced to serve in
the Nazi army. Piri is no longer allowed to attend
school, the food supply to all Jews is rationed, and
their freedom of movement is restricted due to the
imposed curfew. Forced to wear the Star of David on
their clothes, they are in constant danger of being
robbed or beaten. The worst comes when Piri's oldest
sister Lili is taken away and is not heard from, while
the family is herded into a ghetto and, from there, to
Auschwitz. An impressive, dramatic story, based on the
author's own childhood experience, it provides many
important insights into the devastating years of war in
Hungary. The book was selected as the Newbery Honor
Book in 1982 and appears on several notable books lists.

126. Smith, S.S. (pseud.)   The Falcon Mystery: A Boy's
Story of the Hungarian Plain. Illus. James Reid. New York:
Harcourt Brace, 1936. 326 p. Grades 7-10.
     The setting of the story is the Great Hungarian Plain or
puszta, as it is called by the Magyars, the people of
Hungary. When the Magyar herdsmen conquered the puszta
in the ninth century, they were so attracted by its rich
grassy expanses that they decided to stay.   There they
gradually built the nucleus of the Hungarian nation.
Like their forefathers, the two Pogany boys, Stefan and
Bela, love the puszta.   They have no use for the
hopelessly dull town of Ugricum, where they were born.
They prefer to camp in the puszta tending their herds of
wild horses, providing them with water and fresh grass
and keeping them from harm.   Moreover, they totally
enjoy falconry, the ancient sport brought from Asia to
Europe by the Magyars. The younger brother Bela never
leaves his falcon, Nol, out of his sight, except when he
releases it to pursue wild ducks and other game birds.
To catch a bird, the falcon plunges upon it from above,
passes over it, and slashes it with a hind claw.   The
victim dies instantly and falls into the hands of the
falconer.   The hawk, of course, gets the skin, head,
feet and the entrails.   This spring, however, the
herdsmen have been noticing disturbing, threatening
signs.   The chief nobleman of their district, His
Excellency Sigismund Rakoczy, wants to purchase Bela's
falcon for any price.   Shortly after that, a strange
man, also a falconer, appears in the puszta and hides
his game hastily before the two brothers.   Then Nol is
shot, and fear spreads among the puszta's horseherders
and swineherders that falconry would be outlawed and the
puszta pasturage destroyed.   With intelligence, courage,
and determination, Stefan and Bela finally expose
Rakoczy's pearl-smuggling operations which involve
falcons and carrier pigeons and thus save the age-old
puszta for the Poganys and the other horse-herding
Magyars.

127. Zalan, Magda.   In a Big Ugly House Far From Here ....
Illus. Julius Varga. Toronto, Canada: Porcepic, 1982.   87
p. Grades 5-8.
     A compilation consisting of ten autobiographical
vignettes containing themes from the author's childhood
in Hungary. Magda Zalan was six years old when Hungary
became involved in World War II.   She lived with her
family in the hilly part of the capital, called Buda,
which was destroyed by bombs in the fall of 1942.   The
family was evacuated and moved into a two-room flat in a
gray house in Pest.   In six of the short stories, the
author reminisces about the events which took place in
and around this house as well as in the air-raid shelter
in the basement of the house during the war; the
remaining four episodes describe events immediately
after the war. Among the war narratives, three accounts
are especially memorable.   In one the author describes

how a blast from an ear-splitting bomb explosion
returned hearing and speech to an old man, who had lost
both of these facilities during World War I. The story
of two Christmas candies is a moving account of a little
girl, who shared a small gift brought to her by a
Christmas angel, or so she believed, with her friend,
who was killed by a bomb and buried under a flat mound
at the end of their courtyard. The most absorbing
event, so well remembered and retold, took place at the
beginning of 1945, when the city became the battleground
for two opposing armies. Magda's father, who deserted
the Nazis, was hiding in a hole behind a brick wall and
was almost betrayed by Aunt Lola's chicken, which was
shot by a soldier and fell through a pipe at his feet.
Accompanied by a glossary, pronunciation guide, and
detailed pencil sketches.

OTHER FICTION

128. Anderson, Mary. <u>That's Not My Style</u>. New York:
Atheneum, 1983. 162 p. Grades 6-12.
   On his birth certificate his name appears as John, but
to his Hungarian-born parents he is Janos, or, more
endearingly, Janci. His father, Joszef, and his mother,
Anna, fled Hungary with their families during the
uprising in 1956. Although they came to Manhattan as
children, they frequently revert to the use of the
Hungarian language and maintain the old Hungarian ways.
They believe in strong family ties, which, to their
sixteen-year-old son means interfering with a guy's
business. Whenever they sit around the dining room
table they are most likely to talk about the virtues of
togetherness. Mom works in Dad's butcher shop on
Broadway, which they purchased six years before and
which has been their pride and joy ever since. Dad
comes from a long line of butchers and intensely enjoys
his work. Perhaps their son Janos will continue with
the family business. But there is no doubt in John's
mind that he will be a writer someday, a second
Hemmingway. The story is an absorbing account of John's
simple-minded ways and of his growth to maturity. In
the end he discovers not only where and how ideas for
novels are born, but also the character of true manhood
and the values of friendship. A psychologically
perceptive and entertainingly written story.

129. Brown, Margaret Wise. <u>Wheel on the Chimney</u>. Illus.
Tibor Gergely. New York: Lippincott, 1953. N. pag.
Grades 1-3.
   It is considered a great honor and a promise of good
luck for Hungarian countrymen to have storks build their
nests on the roofs of their houses. In order to attract
storks to land in spring, some farmers tie cart wheels

to the top of their chimneys or prepare piles of twigs
and straw for them. All during the spring and summer
one can hear the rustle of white birds above the roofs,
first as they build their nests, then as they feed their
hungry babies, and finally as the young storks grow up
and try to use their longer legs and bills. While the
other animals in the barnyard are noisy all summer, the
storks, with the exception of an occasional gentle
clapping of their beaks, remain silent. Then on a
certain chilly day in autumn, black storks from the wild
forest in the North arrive and invite their white
cousins to join them in their flight to the South. This
simple, poetical text explains the flight of the storks
over the countries of Europe to their destination in
Africa. It is enveloped by brightly colored
illustrations, some of which are double spreads. They
certainly add strength, beauty, and drama to the story.
The book was selected for the Caldecott Medal Honor in
1955.

130. Donászy, Magda. **Fun and Hullabaloo**. Trans. Alexandra
Ribiánszky.   Illus.   Károly   Reich.   Budapest,   Hungary:
Corvina, 1978. N. pag. Grades 3-5.
Thirteen humorous poems, each illustrated in full-page
colorful crayon drawings.   Eight poems are about
animals: a fox cunningly outmaneuvers a gullible crow
and wrestles a piece of cheese from him; a squirrel
tells a story of his feasting on pumpkin seeds and
acorns; a lamb expresses her sorrow over losing her
wool; a cock strikes the morning hour with the clock in
the tower; busy bees in the hollow of a tree collect and
make honey; a dog and a cat lose their way and encounter
a fox with evil intentions. The themes of other poems
include merriment at a fair, the joy of summer rain, the
fun of blowing bubbles and playing hide-and-seek, and
the cleverness of a young maid.

131. Ginsburg, Mirra.   **Two Greedy Bears**.   Illus.   José
Aruego and Ariane Dewey. New York: Macmillan, 1976. N.
pag. Grades K-2.
This lighthearted story tells of two greedy bears and
how they learn their lesson. As they set out to see the
world they become thirsty, and trying to outdo each
other, they drink water from a brook until they are
ready to burst, feeling an agonizing discomfort. They
continue their foolish rivalry until a clever fox brings
them to their senses. Continuing on their journey, they
become hungry and find a large piece of cheese by the
roadside. Immediately they begin to argue as they try
to break it into two equal parts, each afraid the other
will get a larger part. The fox solves the problem for
them by eating some of the cheese from the piece which,
to the cubs, seems to be the larger piece. The box
keeps dividing the cheese until she is fully satisfied,
leaving only two tiny, but equal, crumbs for the foolish
bears who, in their fight for absolutely equal justice,

are unable to comprehend the joy of sharing. Brightly
colored, joyful illustrations add a comical note to this
short, simply written narrative.

132. Hirsh, Marilyn. <u>Deborah the Dybbuk: A Ghost Story</u>.
Illus. author. New York: Holiday House, 1978. N. pag.
Grades 2-4.
    Originally written in Swedish, this amusing story of the
    mischievious girl, Deborah, takes place in a nineteenth
    century Shtetl in the Hungarian village of Voolatz,
    where the author's father was born. Without exception
    the villagers agree that Deborah is the naughtiest child
    ever to live. She runs into other people's houses
    without knocking, picking up not only household objects,
    musical instruments, food, and other things, but also
    babies from their cradles. She eventually returns each
    thing to its owner, but her behavior causes constant
    confusion and upheaval. She stops running only to feed
    the birds or to relax by hanging upside down from a
    nearby tree. In addition, Deborah makes it known to
    everybody that she is not happy as a little girl. She
    wants to be something with wings - an angel or a
    chicken - or a fast flying bird. Her wishes are only
    partly fulfilled when she becomes a dybbuk, a ghost who
    enters the body of a quiet girl, Hannah, and changes her
    into an immensely restless child. Finally, with the
    help of the great Rabbi Isaac, all ends well for
    Deborah, as well as for the villagers. The
    illustrations in gray and orange halftones perfectly
    complement this light-hearted, well-told story with an
    unusual theme.

133. Illyés, Gyula. <u>Matt the Gooseherd</u>. Illus. Károly
Reich. New York: Penguin, 1979. N. pag. Grades 2-5.
    The only work that Matt, the son of a poor widow, is
    willing to do is to look after his mother's geese. As
    soon as the sixteen goslings become plump and lively,
    Matt takes them to the market in the nearby town. When
    he requests no less than two gold crowns for a pair from
    the rich landowner and mayor of the town, Dobrogi, the
    goslings are taken away from him. Matt is whipped and
    thrown into the road. As he staggers away, Matt vows in
    his anger that the cruel master will pay three-fold for
    the gross injustices done to him. Matt's first
    opportunity to retaliate comes when Dobrogi decides to
    build a new mansion for himself. Disguised as a
    reputable foreign carpenter, Matt is hired as a lumber
    consultant. At the first opportunity, however, he
    reveals his identity, takes money from Dobrogi's
    pockets, and belabors the landowner with a supple branch
    from a nearby tree. Twice more he returns, under
    disguises of a physician and a horseman, and he bestows
    on Dobrogi twice the strokes Matt received and helps
    himself to his money, twice the price of the geese. An
    amusing tale with a strong plot, accompanied by colorful
    expressive illustrations.

134. Konigsburg,   E.L.   <u>Throwing Shadows</u>.   New   York:
Atheneum, 1979. 151 p. Grades 7-12.
Five stories featuring young men discovering the meaning
of true humanity in other people, and who, by finding it
in others, discover it in themselves. In the story, "At
the Home," Philip first meets Mr. Molin (short for
Molinkowsky) an immigrant from Ukraine, who in his youth
had been a singing troubadour and who longs for the
young man's friendship. Another character in the old
folks' home is Miss Ilona Szabo, a Hungarian from
Budapest, who tells Philip her life story bit by bit, a
part every day, in order to insure his return the next
day. She insists on telling him how her ugliness saved
her life. After she was born it was suggested that she
be educated, as she would never be able to catch a man.
She was sent to Paris and learned how to speak French
fluently, without an accent, which saved her from being
sent to Auschwitz. More than one other subject enters
her narrative. The facts that Hungarians are most proud
of two things, their cooking and their language, figures
prominently in her story. Philip's handling of Mrs.
Silverman, who has a number tatooed on her forearm, and
his success in persuading fiery Miss Ilona and Mr. Molin
into taping the stories of the other old folks reflect
Philip's sensitivity and his mature attitude toward his
fellowman. It is a perceptive, short story, written
with freshness and a touching sense of humor, and it
should leave a powerful impression on any reader's mind
and heart.

135. Kormos, István.   <u>It All Started with the Big Green</u>
<u>Fish</u>. Trans. Alexander Ribiánszky. Illus. Károly Reich.
Budapest, Hungary: Corvina Kiado, 1979. N. pag. Grades
2-4.
One day old Bob Brandt, a highly esteemed fisherman of
Pebblebury on the Danube, catches a green fish three
times larger than his boat. The moment old Bob reaches
the bank with it, an enormous seven-headed dragon swoops
down upon the fish and tries to snatch it away. In his
fight with the dragon, old Bob hits the dragon's feet,
causing it much anguish and pain. The ferocious dragon
retaliates   and   devours   a   beautiful   maiden,   the
golden-haired Susie, who is betrothed to old Bob's
grandson, little Bobby. With the help of his friends,
the   red-horned   owl,   the   splendid   peacock,   the
dapple-green pony and his brother, and the magic steed,
little Bobby reaches the dragon's citadel over the seas.
With their support and with the sweet music of his
flute, which he uses to enchant the dragon, Bobby
rescues the golden-haired maiden and brings her home to
a joyous jubilation. They celebrate their wedding to
the music of three gypsy bands and to the tune of the
old fox violin. Distinctive illustrations, rich in
color and folkloric decorations, make up for some
weaknesses in translation. The story was originally
published in 1977.

136. Kormos, István. <u>The Painted Kitten</u>. Trans. by Judith Elliot. Illus. Éva Gaál. Budapest, Hungary: Corvina, 1977. N. pag. Grades 2-4.
In the land of Tintonia the sky is always blue, the grass is deeply green, and everything else, the walls, the rooftops and even the dust-carts, dazzle with the brightest colors of the rainbow. A long string is stretched over the beautiful land, with the Sun tied to one end and the Moon to the other. The man who pulls the string with the appropriate machinery to make the Sun and the Moon rise sometimes makes a mistake and causes both to appear in the sky at the same time. Sometimes just the opposite happens, and the Land of Tintonia is enveloped in darkness. There are numerous other wonders in Tintonia. It has a marvelous zoo, a fairy park, musical clowns, and many famous painters. The love between young couples is so intense that the Sun closes his enormous eyes when it sees a young man meeting his maiden. The land, however, also has its troubles. Its greatest enemies are Cloud Sentinels. When they attack the country, the rain comes and washes away all the glittering colors. This is exactly what threatens the land of Tintonia one day. Fortunately along comes a little Puppet, a kitten "cut out of magic paper and painted with fairy paint," who is the hero of the story and saves Tintonia from losing its colors. The brilliantly alive illustrations perfectly complement the charm of the fantasy.

137. Lesznai, Anna. <u>The Wanderings of the Little Blue Butterfly in Fairyland</u>. Trans. Caroline Bodoczky. Illus. author. Budapest, Hungary: Corvina Kiado, 1978. 23 p. Grades 2-4.
Originally published in Hungary in 1912, this is the delightful fantasy of the birth of a little blue butterfly and her journey to Fairyland. She is born in the autumn in a red-petaled morning glory in Aunt Anna's room. Yearning for freedom, she makes for the windows, and listens to the chat of white lilies, daisies, mignonettes, flowering pots, robins, and apple trees and to the village church bells that bid her Godspeed on her way to Fairyland, which lies beyond the blue mountains. The brave little blue butterfly has to fly a long, long way before she reaches her destination. In the end, there is not one, but three Fairylands, each one a thousand times more beautiful and brighter than the one before. In the third Fairyland she finds people and flowers, and dreams and stories that have never been born, sumptuous fruits and cakes, birds singing unceasingly and kisses that have never been kissed. But after an entire fairy-year in the enchanting Fairyland, the little blue butterfly feels a need to fly back home to the beautiful Leszna garden, where the flowers grow and bloom at peace with the world. Delectable illustrations, borders, and end papers greatly expand the charm of the story.

138. Molnar, Ferenc. <u>The Paul Street Boys</u>. Trans. Louis
Rittenberg. New York: Macy-Masins, 1927. 292 p. Grades
7-12.
     To the children of Budapest, even at the beginning of
the twentieth century, a vacant lot was the only open
grassland to the children in rural areas. The "grund,"
as the Paul Street lot was called, was fenced in on one
side and bordered by tall buildings on the other; to the
rear, however, it was adjoined by another spacious site
which was filled with piles of lumber and stacks of
firewood in symmetrical blocks. The vacant lot and the
short alleys among the huge blocks of lumber were an
ideal playground for the city boys. In this environment
a story of two rival gangs of high school boys develops.
The long standing controversy between the two groups is
intensified when the Pasztor boys disrupt the Paul
Street boys' marble game, declare "einstand," in which
the physically stronger boys take possession of the
marbles belonging to the winner of the game and are
prepared to use their fists against any kind of
resistance. The victim this time is the youngest and
the smallest of the Paul Street boys. He is Nemecsek,
the only private in the military group. All of the
other boys enjoy issuing orders and are, therefore,
officers, captains, and lieutenants. Nemecsek remains
in the center of the action during the Paul Street boys'
fierce defense of their playground. Sadly, he also
becomes a victim in the final struggle. His loss,
however, is the beginning of a genuine reconciliation.
Although written more than half a century ago, this
compelling novel proves that, in some aspects, life in
the larger cities has not changed much over the decades.

139. Surany, Aanico. <u>Kati and Kormos</u>. Illus. Leonard
Everett Fisher. New York: Holiday House, 1966. N. pag.
Grades 1-4.
     This is the story of a prize hunting dog named Kati
Vizsla who belongs to a rich Hungarian Count. She is
well provided for. Living in a grand kennel on a large
estate, she eats the best food, and her sleeping box is
always filled with fresh cedar shavings. The Count,
however, is rarely home and Kati is lonely. When she
notices a rip at the bottom of the wire fence, she
wiggles through and streaks over the fields. She does
not stop until she skids into a troup of bawling sheep
grazing in a pasture. Meeting their sheep dog, Karmas,
and the old shepherd, Imre, proves to be the beginning
of a new life for Kati, a life of companionship and warm
friendship. The text, with interpretive full-page
illustrations, provides some interesting details about
the Hungarian countryside.

140. Varga, Judy. <u>Janko's Wish</u>. Illus. author. New York:
Morrow, 1969. N. pag. Grades K-3.
     Instead of working out in the fields, a lazy peasant
named Janko just slouches on the wobbly bench outside

his house and stares at his farm. The vegetable garden
is neglected, rain trickles through the hole in his
roof, and the chickens and cows are unhappy in the
littered barn. When there are no clean cooking pots
left in the kitchen and Janko does not feel like
scouring the dirty ones, he decides to go into the woods
and gather berries for his supper. There he meets an
old Gypsy who persuades Janko to push her caravan out of
the mud. Trying to think of a place where he can hide
the pot of gold he is expecting to receive from the
Gypsy in return for his good deed, he begins to put his
house and fields in order. One day, as Janko is
admiring his crop of harvested gold wheat, he meets a
pretty young girl who likes the hard-working farmer.
Janko finally realizes that everything he has wished for
has already come his way. A lively tale with colorful,
engaging illustrations.

Poland

TRADITIONAL LITERATURE: COLLECTIONS

141. Bernhard, Josephine Butkowska. <u>The Master Wizard and</u>
<u>Other Polish Tales</u>. Rev. E. Frances Le Valley. Illus.
Marya Werten. New York: Knopf, 1934. 181 p. Grades 4-10.
   The title story, "The Master Wizard, Pan Twardowsky and
   his Spider" is about a Polish nobleman who lives and
   studies in Krakow. People love him, for Pan Twardowsky
   is not only very knowledgeable, but also very kind.
   Never has anyone in distress appealed to him in vain.
   He is also very pious. He composes hymns honoring the
   Holy Lady and the Lord Jesus. The time comes when all
   his knowledge and his secrets of wizardry are not enough
   for him. He wants power. In search for it, he signs
   his soul to the Devil. With his help Pan Twardowsky
   enjoys the promised prosperity and on several occasions
   outsmarts the Devil out of the contract. At last, in
   order to get Twardowsky into his power, the Devil, too,
   resorts to trickery. When everything seems to be lost
   it is Twardowsky's sad remembrance of the words of the
   hymn he had composed to the Holy Lady and her Son that
   somewhat saves him. At the sound of the hymn, the Devil
   drops him, but falling out of his clutches, Twardowksy
   gets caught on the horn of the moon, where he has to
   hang until the final Day of Judgment. The other ten
   stories in this collection also contain highly magical
   and unusual adventures. Genuine folkloric illustrations
   add appropriate spice to the tales.

142. Borski, Lucia Merecka.   <u>Good Sense and Good Fortune</u>
<u>and Other Polish Folk Tales</u>. Illus. Erica Gorecka-Egan.
New York: McKay, 1970. 96 p. Grades 4-8.
   A collection of twenty-three tales, translated and
   retold from some of the most representative sources of
   Polish folklore, these reflect an admiration for some of
   the most prominent characteristics of the Polish people,
   their resourcefulness, cleverness, humor, determination,
   their straight-forwardness, and their strong faith that

hard work eventually pays off and that good luck
frequently comes to those who know how to use their
wits. The stories contain a variety of fascinating
characters: poor and clever peasants, pretty and lazy
maidens, haughty kings and beautiful princesses, fair
mermaids and enchanted animals. There are stories about
a wandering cobbler, a sly gypsy, a silent fisherman, a
smart astrologer and a not so smart physician, and of
course about Good Fortune, who proves to be more
powerful than Good Sense. Included is the author's note
regarding the origins of the tales and a list of
sources. A pleasant format and spirited black and white
drawings add to the richness of the collection.

143. Borski, Lucia Merecka and Kate B. Miller. The Gypsy
and the Bear and Other Fairy Tales. Illus. James Reid. New
York: Longmans, Green, 1933. 129 p. Grades 3-8.
Faithfully and smoothly translated from noted Polish
folklorists, this is a collection of thirteen stories,
all containing animal characters endowed with human
traits with unmistakenly Polish elements. The last line
or lines in each story bear a cleverly expressed gentle
lesson or a conclusion that involves the teller in the
action of the tale. In the title story, a crafty gypsy,
a servant to the bear, decides to get the better of him.
He never does a stitch of work, but pretends that he is
the stronger and harder worker of the two. Even in the
end the bear does not catch on, in spite of the fact
that his friend, the fox, tries to convince him that the
gypsy is really a cheat. A wolf helps out a mother
lark, distressed over the safety of her brood, but plays
a trick on a fox, and the fox repays his provocation on
manifold occasions. Some stories are written in the
"pourquoi" tradition. One explains why animals lost
their freedom, one tells why goats have short tails, and
another why the flounder has a crooked mouth. Told in
simple, but expressive language, the stories are
accompanied by vigorous pen-and-ink sketches. Notes on
the origins of the stories and a well-written commentary
are appended.

144. Borski, Lucia Merecka and Kate B. Miller. The Jolly
Tailor and Other Fairy Tales. Illus. Kazimir Klepacki. New
York: McKay, 1967. 158 p. Grades 3-8.
Originally published in 1928, these ten tales contain a
great deal of humor, wit, magic, and a strong feeling
for what is just, good, beautiful, and brave. To stop
the rains the jolly old tailor, Mr. Nitechka, sews a
torn piece of the sky, through which the water has been
pouring down, and promptly is made king. The funny
cobbler, who can shoot a slingshot farther than anyone
else, hits the ascending moon in the face and knocks out
his front teeth, so that the next day the poor moon
appears all red and with a bandaged face. A wicked
youth is rewarded beyond his dreams when he comforts the
sad with his merrymaking. A king's beautiful daughter

is allowed to rule her country when she proves to be
patient, courageous, and above all, loving. With her
gentle heart Princess Marysia melts an immense iceberg
and marries a Black Swan, who changes into a Prince at a
wedding lasting seven years. A little boy with a great
heart breaks a spell and rescues his mother from the
powers of the mighty witch of the waters. A glossary of
names and a list of sources are appended. Black and
white illustrations appropriately highlight the spirit
of the stories.

145. Byrde, Elsie. The Polish Fairy Book. Illus. Livia
Kádár. New York: Stokes, 1925. 231 p. Grades 4-10.
   As "Aunt Elsie" explains in her introductory letter,
Poland once belonged to fairies. When people from the
eastern lands came to live there, they frightened the
beautiful creatures, so the fairies hid in all kinds of
dark places, in old abandoned houses and in the crevices
of mysterious forests. At times, when the good and the
innocent need special help, the fairies emerge and
deliver them from their difficulties. Sometimes they
transform themselves into lovely flowers or animals,
thus, it is never known if a fish, a bird or a daisy is
exactly what is seen: they could be hidden fairies at
any time. It is best, therefore, to be kind to them and
to be their friend. In the story "Bogdynek," a handsome
young man is warned by the splendid horse he is riding
not to pick beautiful lilies because they would bring
misfortune. When Bogdynek helps three dogs, a griffin
and a whale out of their troubles, they return the favor
and come to his rescue when he is required to perform a
series of enormous tasks imposed on him by the King.
This and the other twenty-seven stories in the
collection are some of the loveliest fairy tales ever
translated and adapted from the rich and extensive
treasure of Polish folklore. Seven color plates are a
graceful complement to the fresh, simply written tales.

146. Crown, A.W. Kunegunda: Tales from Poland. Illus.
Jacqueline Grippando. New York: Pergamon, 1971. 47 p.
Grades 4-8.
   The book contains four Polish folk tales, originally
published in Great Britain. The title story,
"Kunegunda," is about a beautiful girl who lives with
her parents in the Opole castle on top of a rocky-crag
in the south-western section of Poland. Even as a
little girl she was unhappy because she had no children
to play with. She is destined to marry a famous knight
someday, but she falls in love with Franek, a commoner,
who brings food and supplies to the castle. Completely
devoted to him, but forbidden to see or marry her
beloved, Kunegunda despairs and dies. It is said that
even now a beautiful lady frequently is seen walking
sadly over the cragy hills at the foot of the old
castle, searching for Franek. The theme of the loving,

hard working youngest brother who is rewarded beyond his
dreams, and the lazy older brothers who is punished is
beautifully interwoven into "The Legend of the Glass
Mountain." In the "Popiel and the Mice" a wicked duke,
who lives in a tower on Lake Goplo, is justly punished
for his evil deeds. It is believed that Slavic tribes
lived in today's Poland as early as 2000 B.C. These
tribes were involved in great migrations between 400 and
800 A.D. "The Legend of Lech, Czech, and Rus"
beautifully explains how three brothers founded the
Russian, Czechoslovakian, and Polish nations. Under the
sign of an eagle, the sign of watchfulness and
greatness, Lech established the first Polish capital,
Gniezno, meaning "a nest," on the hill where he first
spotted the white eagle. Each story ends in a verse
with a suitable theme. A delightful collection of the
most typical Polish stories and legends.

147. Ficowski, Jerzy. _Sister of the Birds and Other Gypsy_
Tales. Trans. Lucia M. Borski. Illus. Charles Mikolaycak.
Nashville: Abingdon, 1976. 74 p. Grades 3-7.
    It is believed that gypsies originated in India and
began to wander westward around the tenth century,
eventually arriving in Eastern Europe during the early
fifteenth century. Although they can be found in all
parts of the world today, the largest number of gypsies
still lives in Eastern Europe. Jerzy Ficowski, a Polish
poet, writer and world-known scholar of Gypsy lore lived
among the gypsies of Poland for two years, studying
their way of life, learning their language, and
collecting their stories and songs. Six of these
folktales appear in this collection in an excellent
translation. The title story tells about a young maiden
who has power over the singing of the birds. It tells
of her rescue form the castle tower in which she has
been imprisoned by the evil witch Urma and of the
celebration which follows her deliverance. One of the
stories tells of the origin of blond people, and one
tells how a violin came into the world. Another story
relates how a Gypsy violinist saves a beautiful princess
from her enchantment, and the last tale is about a poor
Gypsy boy, Andrusz, who decides to be faithful to his
Gypsy tradition and remain poor, rather than betray his
loyalty and keep the riches offered to him. The
illustrations and decorative borders perfectly
complement the stories.

148. Haviland, Virginia. _Favorite Fairy Tales Told in_
Poland. Illus. Felix Hoffman. Boston: Little, Brown,
1963. 90 p. Grades 2-5.
    A collection of six stories retold in an easy, joyful
and flowing style. They tell of a hedgehog becoming a
prince, of grateful animals rewarding a poor couple for
taking them along on their journey, of the wolf and fox
helping the lark take care of her young, of the old
jester fooling the king, and of the good hearted

youngest brother catching the flamebird and winning the
Princess Wonderface in marriage. Included is also one
of the favorite folktales about the wise tailor, Mr.
Joseph Nitechka, who sews up a torn piece of the sky
above the town of Pacanow and stops the rain.
Illustrations in soft colors and in black and white add
just enough detail to convey the spirit of the stories.
A list of sources of the stories is appended.

149. Kimmel, Erica A. **Mishka, Pishka and Fishka and Other
Galician Tales.** Illus. Christopher J. Spollen. New York:
Coward, McCann, and Geoghegan, 1976. 64 p. Grades 3-6.
    Five humorous traditional tales from Galicia, the
country which is today part of both Poland and Russia.
An independent kingdom during the Middle Ages, Galicia
was intermittently part of Poland for several centuries,
including the period just prior to World War II. Most
of eastern Galicia is currently in the Soviet Union
while the western part is in Poland. The stories are
told by Lazer-Yancov, a great-grandfather and a very
clever man too, who sits on his porch with his two dogs
at his feet; he plays a special role in the episodes as
well. He tells of Ropenose, a frightful brigand, and of
the clever photographer, Anton Antonovich, who is able
to prevent the animals, the Gypsies, the German imperial
army with its dignitaries, and even Kaiser Franz Joseph
himself from passing along the road. The old wise man
also tells about the Cossack and the Tartar, two best
friends who become bitter enemies, and about Baba Tsygan
(which means Gypsy woman), who lives in a little green
cabin on the mountain and is able to foretell the future
shuffling her cards. Finally, Lazer-Yancov tells about
three soldiers, Mishka, Pishka, and Fishka, who exhibit
the most beautiful moustaches in the emperor's army. It
is Fishka's moustache, the longest one, that wins him
the love of a beautiful maiden. Black-and-white
spirited illustrations are quality reproductions of the
artist's original etchings.

150. Nolan, Paul T. **Folk Tale Plays Round the World.**
Boston: Plays, 1982. 248 p. Grades 4-8.
    A collection of sixteen, one-act, royalty-free plays,
containing some of the most popular folk tale themes,
mostly from European countries. "Stanislaw and the
Wolf" is a play based on a folk legend, set in the
Golden Age of Poland, when men, like St. Stanislaw,
coexisted with animals endowed with human
characteristics. It contains nine characters: St.
Stanislaw, the patron saint of Poland, an old woman, a
school boy, a blacksmith, and five animals. Observing
the animals in their pursuit of delicacies, St.
Stanislaw does not seem to understand how things can be
so right with the world and at the same time how all his
animal friends constantly hunger after the bad. They
cannot learn to like only those things that belong to
them. Ivan the wolf cannot keep his nose out of the

beehive; Sam the squirrel and Masha the rabbit feast on the neighbor's carrots and lettuce; Audrey the fox thinks of eating the rabbit, and Adolph, the wolf, wants meat, tender human meat when he could have the plentiful fruits of the forest. Even good Saint Stanislaw has to almost tell a lie and use all his wits to save his friends, including some forest creatures, from the greediness of the more powerful combatants.

151. Singer, Isaac Bashevis. When Shlemiel Went to Warsaw and Other Stories. Trans. author and Elizabeth Shub. Illus. Margot Zemach. New York: Farrar, Straus and Giroux, 1968. 116 p. Grades 5 and up.
Eight Jewish stories, five of which are folktales with their origins in Eastern Europe. The story of Shlemiel, who always dreamed about taking a trip, is the funniest of all. When one of the recent visitors to Chelm tells him about the numerous marvels of the city of Warsaw, Shlemiel decides that he must start for the famous city immediately. Following Warsaw Street in Chelm he is convinced that it will lead him directly to his destination. When he decides to take a nap on the long journey, Shlemiel places his worn-out boots by his side with the toes facing toward Warsaw, so that he will know which direction points to Warsaw and which back to Chelm. When he is found asleep, however, a prankster comes along and turns the boots around. Consequently, Shlemiel arrives back home, but refuses to believe that he has returned to his town. He is convinced that he has arrived at Chelm Two, where the houses and the people look just like those in Chelm One, the place where his real family lives. This and other imaginative and highly amusing stories in the collection are accompanied by spirited pencil drawings. In 1969 the book appeared on the Newbery Honor List.

152. Uminski, Sigmund H. Tales of Early Poland. Detroit, Mich.: Endurance, 1968. 100 p. Grades 4-10.
Twelve legends explaining the establishment of Poland and its early history. In "The Legend of Lech, Czech and Rus," three brothers in search of land follow the directions of three eagles which appear in the air above them. Lech selects a white eagle and goes north, Rus follows the black eagle to the northeast, and Czech the third eagle to the northwest. Each brother establishes his own nation. Lech settles on an immense plain, called "Pola" and calls his descendents "Po-Lachs." "The Story of Lech and Gniezno" relates how a brave white eagle becomes the symbol of Poland and how the city of Gniezno (meaning "nest") is founded. "The Legend of Wanda" is a story of freedom, always considered by Poles the most precious gift of individuals and nations. Other legends contain characters representing real historical personages, living from the tenth to the thirteenth century, that are described in the oldest documents recording Polish

history. One legend is of the good, wise King Krakus
who saves the city of Krakow from terrible danger;
another is of the blind Prince Mieszko, who miraculously
regains his sight and christianizes the entire Poland.
There is also King Boleslaw the Brave, Saint Albert,
Otto the Third and, of course, the trumpeter of Krakow.
A good collection of stories embodying the ideas of
freedom. heroism, Polish national pride and Christian
ideals.

153. Zajdler, Zöe. <u>Polish Fairy Tales</u>. World Fairy Tale
Collections. Illus. Hazel Cook. New York: Follett, 1959.
190 p. Grades 4 and up.
A collection of seventeen tales which were once told by
potato pickers, timbermen, charcoal burners, shepherds,
travellers, and other storytellers. The stories were
told in the foothills of the Carpathian and Tatra
Mountains, in villages of the Pripet marshes and the
Mazovian plains, in dwellings in the coastal lowlands,
and in the great blue belt of the Polish lakes. The
more popular characters in the stories are animals who
interact with humans. A dog, a cat, and a fish help
Jan, the only son of a poor widow, to find the powerful
crown of the King of Snakes. When he finds it, the King
of Snakes teaches Jan that happiness does not come in
having material possessions, nor by being envied or
admired, but through love. In another story, a crafty
fox pressures a wolf, the most credulous of all the
animals, to make him a pair of charming boots, and in a
way he keeps his word. The wolf, of course, pays dearly
for his vainness. The forces of nature - the power of
water, wind, thunder and lightning - have important
parts in the stories, as do legendary creatures such as
dragons, earth spirits, and enchanted princesses. As in
many other folktales of the world, the most winsome
human characters include the youngest of three brothers,
a poor peasant, and a neglected stepchild. The
environment in which these beings live and the manner in
which they act and respond to each other, however, are
characteristically Polish. Most of the stories are
illustrated with appropriate black and white drawings.

154. Zand, Helen S. <u>Polish Proverbs</u>. Scranton, PA:
Polish American Journal, 1961. 54 pp. Grades 4 and up.
A collection of proverbs in Polish and English arranged
under sixty-six subject headings. Included are those
proverbs which are of purely Polish origin and express
the people's struggle with the soil, the weather, and
poverty. Also included are proverbs which express the
historic events of the Polish nation, and the patience,
courage, and endurance of the Polish people.

TRADITIONAL LITERATURE: SINGLE EDITIONS

155. Bernhard, Josephine B. <u>9 Cry-Baby Dolls</u>. Illus. Irena

Lorentowicz. New York: Roy, 1945. N. pag. Grades 1-4.
    Based on the version originally written by Janina
    Porazinska, this folktale is centered on a one-year-old
    boy, Tolus Bartosh, and on the nine crying dolls his
    mother has made. In spite of the boundless love with
    which his mother takes care of him, and in spite of the
    lovely world of sunshine in which he and his mother
    live, Baby Tolus is a dreadful cry-baby. He howls and
    wails day and night for no apparent reason. At the end
    of her wits and wondering what to do, his mother asks a
    wrinkled old Granny who comes knocking with her cane to
    the Bartosh cottage, for advice. Granny has traveled
    across the world and has an answer for everything.
    Granny suggests to the mother to cut the sleeve from an
    old shirt and with fine stitches sew nine crying dolls.
    Then, she is to take these to the market square and toss
    them on the farmers' wagons that pass by. According to
    Granny's promise, whoever drives off with a cry-baby
    doll will also carry away Tolus' crying. Mother Bartosh
    does exactly what she is told, and immediately Baby
    Tolus stops his yowling. This, however, is only the
    beginning, as all the other children in the village
    begin to scream. Unhappy because she has hurt others,
    Mother Bartosh, with Granny's help, finds a better and
    final solution to the problem. Bouncy, brightly colored
    illustrations greatly enliven this version of the old
    humorous tale.

156. Domanska, Janina. <u>The Best of the Bargain</u>. Illus.
author. New York: Greenwillow, 1977. N. pag. Grades K-3.
    A superb recreation of a Polish folktale about Olek, an
    untypically foolish fox, and Hugo, a shrewd hedgehog.
    Olek owns the apple orchard which lies next to the field
    belonging to Hugo. Olek suggests that as neighbors they
    should help each other in their work. In return for
    half of Hugo's crops Olek is prepared to work with him
    in his field. In addition, he offers him half of the
    fruit from his own orchard. When Olek chooses as his
    half that which grows above the ground, Hugo suggests
    planting potatoes. When Olek selects the half which
    grows below the ground, Hugo suggests wheat. Hugo ends
    up getting all the potatoes and all the wheat and half
    of Olek's apples. Feeling tricked, Olek takes Hugo to
    court where Olek is outsmarted again. In the end, Olek
    the fox learns his lesson and refuses to be Hugo's
    partner. Bright watercolor illustrations most
    effectively complete the simply-written humorous
    narrative.

157. Domanska, Janina. <u>Din Dan Don It's Christmas</u>. Illus.
author. New York: Greenwillow, 1975. N. pag. Grades K-3.
    While on their pilgrimage to the manger, the speckled
    ducks play the bagpipes, the gander and the turkey beat
    the drums, the rooster plays the trumpet, the
    nightingale sings, the goldfinch twitters and the
    sparrow joins in with the chorus. The procession of

birds and people, young and old, is joyously and
reverently portrayed in rich, colorful illustrations
embellished with authentic Polish motifs and geometric
designs. A splendid rendition of an anonymous Christmas
carol as remembered by the author from her childhood in
Poland.

158. Domanska, Janina. <u>King Krakus and the Dragon</u>. Illus.
author. New York: Greenwillow, 1979. N. pag. Grades K-3.
A retelling of the tale of King Krakus, who founded the
old city of Krakow. At first it was a very small and
simple town. When the roosters crowed in the morning,
the king gave orders to wake the town, and at twilight
the night watchman announced that it was time to sleep.
There was no better place in the world until a
voracious, thousand meter long dragon appeared and
threatened to devour every living creature in sight. It
was clever Dratevka, the shoemaker's apprentice, who
finally saved the city from the flame and smoke-spouting
beast. Domanska's dramatic illustrations in rich color
and lavish design complement and bring to life this
enchanting old tale. The title was selected by the <u>New
York Times</u> as one of the best illustrated books of the
year.

159. Domanska, Janina. <u>Look, There Is a Turtle Flying</u>.
Illus. author. New York: Macmillan, 1968. N. pag. Grades
1-3.
King Powoj of Poland enjoys talking to his people, but
most of all, he enjoys talking with his hundred-year-old
turtle, Solon. During one of his conversations with
him, Solon accuses the King of talking too much. In his
hurt and disappointment the King seeks comfort with his
two favorite herons, Heba and Helen. The herons, too,
become indignant and decide to teach Solon a lesson.
Their opportunity to do this comes when the turtle
expresses a desire to learn to fly. Solon suggests to
his winged friends that each take one end of a stick in
their beaks and that he hang on to the middle with his
teeth. Warning him that while in flight he would not be
able to talk is in vain. The wise old turtle is not
like the King, who talks all the time. Solon speaks
only when he is spoken to. He knows when to talk and
when not to talk. He takes immense pride in being the
first flying turtle in the world and, more than anything
else, wants the King to notice him. When the two herons
refuse to fly lower over the shores of the lake where
the King sits playing his flute, Solon cries to them in
anger and, of course, plunges into the water. After his
climb ashore, he has no choice but to admit to the King
that it is he, the wise old turtle, who talks too much.
The wisdom and humor of the story is enhanced by the
amusing pen drawings in washes of orange, blue, and
brown.

160. Domanska, Janina. <u>Marek, the Little Fool</u>.   Illus.
author. New York: Greenwillow, 1982. N. pag. Grades 1-3.
   Marek, the youngest of three brothers, is a simpleton.
   When he is asked to take porridge to his older brothers
   in the field, he throws it at his shadow, thinking it a
   hungry man. When he is told to tend the sheep, he
   gathers them together and binds their legs. In this
   way, he is able to keep them from scattering all over
   the field. When he buys a table at the market, he
   places it on the road thinking that its four legs would
   bring it home. He covers bare tree trunks with newly
   purchased pots and pans to keep them dry in case it
   rains. He pours a sack of salt into the river thinking
   his horse would drink if the water were salty. Whenever
   he is asked to perform a task or run an errand, the
   result is always different than the one expected. The
   superbly composed illustrations could tell the story on
   their own. They are often made up of geometric designs
   in rich colors. Full page illustrations contain
   enlarged details on the opposite pages, with an
   admirable effect. Although no source is given, the
   story seems to be of Polish origin.

161. Konopnicka, Maria. <u>The Golden Seed</u>.   Adapted by
Catherine Fournier. Illus. Janina Domanska. New York:
Scribner, 1962. N. pag. Grades K-3.
   A translation and adaptation of the famous story of a
   king who wishes and wishes for gold in order to help his
   impoverished country. A sack of greenish-brown seeds
   given to him by an old wise merchant with a promise that
   they would grow into gold brings flax to his people. In
   the king's judgment, as well as in the opinion of his
   subjects, flax is richer than gold. Obtaining flax
   becomes a cause for joyous celebration throughout the
   kingdom. Four-color gentle drawings add to the reader's
   appreciation of medieval times.

162. Pellowski, Anne. <u>The Nine Crying Dolls: A Story from
Poland</u>. Illus. Charles Mikolaycak. A Storycraft Book. New
York: Philomel, 1980. N. pag. Grades K-3.
   The author translated and adapted this story from the
   original Polish version of a fable which was first
   published in 1930 in Lwow. When their baby Anatolek
   cannot be stopped from crying, and Tatus Bartosz and
   Mama Bartosz do not know what to do, along comes an old
   babka, who has seen much of the world and has a wise
   word for any query. She tells Mama Bartosz to make nine
   rag dolls from old blouses and shirts and throw them one
   by one into the wagons of people who come to the market.
   As Mama follows babka's instructions, the crying
   disappears from her house. However, it appears in nine
   other households, and it returns to her, as nine other
   mothers take the same advice from babka. Eventually,
   the crying of Anatolek is carried away by the current of
   the swiftly flowing river. Masterfully illustrated with
   colorful, expressive collages in traditional Polish

papercutting technique, this is a delightful story from
the award-winning author and illustrator.

163. Reid, Barbara and Ewa Reid. <u>The Cobbler's Reward</u>.
Illus. Charles Mikolaycak. New York: Macmillan, 1978. 28
p. Grades K-3.
   A young cobbler, Janek Dobry (whose name means John the
Kind One), lives in a Polish village outside great Piska
Forest and must go out into the world to seek work.
Singing on his path through the forest, he comes upon a
trampled ant hill with a multitude of ants scurrying
about trying to rebuild their home. The kind-hearted
cobbler immediately takes off his cap and with it
gathers scattered sand and pine needles into a pile.
Grateful for his help, the queen ant promises Janek her
help should he ever be in need. On his way through a
meadow, Janek helps a band of swarming bees to rebuild
their hive, which had been broken by a bear. Again, the
queen bee pledges her help in times of trouble. After
he feeds wild ducks nesting on the bank of a lake, the
oldest drake offers Janek his aid if bad luck should
befall him. When Janek approaches the town of Kolno and
finds out about the beautiful maiden who is imprisoned
in a great stone tower by the old witch, he decides to
rescue her. As he solves a riddle and performs two
humanly impossible tasks imposed on him by the evil
witch, Janek is helped by the ants, the bees, and the
wild ducks who come back to rescue him. They not only
save him from death in his dangerous undertakings, but
also win him a beautiful, loving maiden for a wife.
Numerous black and white illustrations edged with gentle
pink hues add a wealth of authentic detail to this
charming folktale.

164. Singer, Isaac Bashevis. <u>The Fearsome Inn</u>. Trans.
author and Elizabeth Shub. Illus. Nonny Hogrogian. New
York: Scribner, 1967. N. pag. Grades 3-6.
   Doboshova, the witch, lives with her husband Lapitut,
who is half man, half devil, in an inn on a hill
overgrown with thistles. Together they inflict torture
and cast spells on travelers who get lost or become
stranded. Serving them are three beautiful captive
girls. They have tried to escape many times, but each
time they fail and have to return to the inn because the
roads are under a spell and lead nowhere but back to the
inn. Then one stormy winter day, three young men arrive
seeking shelter at the inn, and everything changes for
the better. One of them, a clever cabala student with a
knowledge of the mysteries of heaven and earth, outwits
the evil pair with the help of a magic piece of chalk
given to him by his master. After Doboshova and Lapitut
are forced to sign their oath in blood and to leave the
inn forever, they vanish into the darkness of the
netherworld. The three girls marry the travelers, and
the fearsome inn becomes a warm shelter for people to
stop and rest. With time it becomes a famous school for

the study of cabala, an inexhaustible source of wisdom.
Expressive illustrations in gentle watercolors add
immeasurably to the beauty of the book.

165. Swiderska, Barbara. <u>The Fisherman's Bride</u>. Illus.
author. New York: Scroll, 1971. N. pag. Grades 1-4.
A content young fisherman thinks his life lacks nothing.
He owns a boat for sailing and nets for catching fish.
He fishes early in the morning, sells his catch in the
afternoon and rests by his fire in the evening.
Consistently he goes to bed early and rises early the
following morning. Then one day the King's messengers
arrive at his village searching for a husband for the
King's daughter. As soon as the fisherman sees the
picture the messengers have brought with them, he knows
at once that she must be his bride. With his goodness,
cleverness and determination the young fisherman
eventually wins the hand of the princess in marriage.
First, however, he has to prove to the King that he is
worthy of the beautiful maiden. With some special help
from a small ant and a whistle given to him by an old
woman for his acts of kindness to her, the fisherman
presents the King with the ten most beautiful pearls in
the world, separates the individual grains in three
sacks of wheat, oats and barley, and keeps a hundred
wild rabbits together on a pasture. After performing
the seemingly impossible tasks, he and the princess
begin their happy life together. Richly colored scenes
from the story bring out its beauty, its fun, and its
wisdom.

166. Turska, Krystyna. <u>The Magician of Cracow</u>. Illus.
author. New York: Greenwillow, 1975. N. pag. Grades K-3.
The story is a variation of the legend about Pan
Twardowski, a famous astronomer and alchemist of the
sixteenth century. He is known throughout Poland for
his enormous knowledge of the secrets of the world. Yet
he never stops studying. In his immense desire to
become the most learned and the most powerful man in the
world, he continues with his investigations and
experimentations. Above all else he wants to discover
how to get to the moon. With the help of the devil he
reaches the moon, where he sits even to this day. His
only companion is a little spider which gets caught in
his cloak when they fly from earth. Every so often, the
magician sends the spider to earth to bring him news of
the places in Poland which are still dear to his heart.
The author's own colorful illustrations and border
designs make this simply written story one of the most
authentic and most distinguished folktale picture books.

167. Turska, Krystyna. <u>The Woodcutter's Duck</u>. Illus.
author. New York: Macmillan, 1973. 32 p. Grades K-3.
A vividly written version of the familiar folktale about
a poor woodcutter boy named Bartek who lives alone with
his pet duck in a small hut on the edge of a forest.

Day after day Bartek ventures into the woods searching
for the duck's favorite food. On one of his trips he
encounters a frog in danger and saves his life. The
little creature, who happens to be the Frog King,
rewards Bartek for his kindness by giving him a magic
whistle. When he uses it correctly to whistle a magic
tune, the whistle has the power to create or quell
violent storms. Its power proves especially useful to
Bartek when an army commander passes by his hut and
demands Bartek's pet duck for dinner. The howling wind,
the terrible thunder, and the sudden rains created by
the magic whistle save Bartek's beloved duck from being
eaten by the Hetman and aid the army in getting rid of
their greedy chief and in making Bartek their leader.
Stylized colorful illustrations add warmth, authenticity
and humor to the story. In Great Britain, where the
book was first published a year earlier, it was awarded
the Kate Greenaway Medal, which is given annually to the
author-illustrator of the most distinguished picture
book.

HISTORICAL FICTION: BIOGRAPHY AND AUTOBIOGRAPHY

168. Aaron, Chester. <u>Gideon</u>. New York: Lippincott, 1982.
181 p. Grades 6-10.
This gripping, harrowing novel of Poland and Polish Jews
during the Second World War is based upon conversations
the author, who was with the American troops in April
1945 when they liberated Dachau, had with the survivors
of German concentration camps. In addition, the author
used diaries, histories, and reflections of the
survivors, as well as many well researched secondary
sources. Told in first person by Gideon, a teenage
Jewish boy, the novel succeeds in giving a graphic and
powerful portrayal of the horrors of World War II, of
the undescribable suffering of the Poles, especially
Jews in the Warsaw Ghetto and in the Treblinka
concentration camp, and of the strength of the young
boy's spirit to survive. Gideon lives in the Warsaw
ghetto with his family. His father considers him a
scholar. Before the war he was a good student; he
learned languages quickly and studied Hebrew and the
Torah seriously. Now, however, Gideon becomes a man of
action. He first escapes from the ghetto when he is
thirteen. Stealthily he slips through the walls to the
Aryan side of Warsaw in the morning and returns in the
evening with food for the family. A conflict arises
between him and his proud Jewish parents: his father,
who is in the process of organizing a resistance against
the Nazis, and his mother, who is devoted to the care of
the ghetto orphans. Gideon does whatever guarantees his
survival. He buries his religion and joins a gang of
thieves. His views change after his father's death,
when he witnesses his mother and a group of ghetto
orphans bravely marching to death. Now Gideon fights

not only for his own existence, but more so for the
survival of his fellow men.

169. Abodaher, David J. <u>Freedom Fighter: Casimir Pulaski</u>.
New York: Messner, 1969. 190 p. Grades 6 and up.
   In the middle of the eighteenth century Poland was
   dominated by the Russians. After Empress Catherine the
   Second succeeded in having Stanislaus Poniatowsky
   elected king of Poland in 1764, the legislative body,
   the Diet, became completely ineffective. The reform
   measures which King Stanislaus advocated weakened the
   position of Poland and strengthened Russia's
   interference in Poland's affairs. There were reactions
   to the sad political situation, but the majority of the
   Polish nobility were concerned with their own welfare
   and their own safety, and did not dare provoke the
   Russians. One of the few who wanted to change the
   situation was Josef Pulaski, a wealthy nobleman from the
   province of Mozavia, southwest of Warsaw. With the help
   of his three sons, Francis, Casimir, and Antoni, he
   approached selected trusted nobles, asking them to
   participate in an armed confederation against the
   Russians. Casimir himself was distinguished in military
   leadership. He trained the soldiers, led them to
   victories against Russian forces, and suffered defeats,
   but was able to reorganize and strike again. His
   enthusiasm inspired the Polish patriots. After four
   years of futile fighting for a free Poland, Casimir had
   to flee his own country. While in France, he learned
   about the American Revolutionary War through Benjamin
   Franklin and decided to offer his services. In 1777 he
   arrived in America and joined the forces of George
   Washington, becoming distinguished as a most able
   leader. He was named brigadier general and the
   commander of the cavalry. At the age of thirty-two
   Pulaski was mortally wounded in the siege of Savannah.
   The Congress and the country eulogized him as a
   courageous leader and a man of honor. A well written
   biography reflecting the fervor and the tragedy of the
   conflicts in Poland, as well as of those in the United
   States.

170. Adams, Dorothy. <u>Cavalry Hero: Casimir Pulaski</u>.
Illus. Irena Lorentowicz. American Background Books. New
York: Kenedy, 1957. 192 p. Grades 4-8.
   A biography written for younger readers about the Polish
   freedom hero and military leader, Count Casimir Pulaski.
   The author ably portrays Casimir's childhood where he
   lived on a large estate which belonged to his
   aristocratic family. Adams stresses Casimir's training
   as a horseman and a soldier, and his upbringing in the
   spirit of patriotism, which instilled in him pride for
   his Polish background and a strong desire for his
   country's independence. The biography gives a
   comprehensive account of Pulaski's courageous, although
   unsuccessful, fight against the Russian domination of

Poland, his escape to Paris and his meeting with Benjamin Franklin, who persuades him to go to America in order to join the colonies in their struggle for independence. Pulaski's distinguished contributions to the cause of the American Revolution, his superior knowlege of war tactics, his establishment of the first American cavalry unit, the Pulaski Legion, his valor and leadership in the battles of Brandywine and Savannah, where he is mortally wounded, and the honors and awards he receives are clearly brought to life. The book is a well-written, effectively illustrated biography, and it offers an informative view of Polish and American eighteenth century history.

171. Adams, Dorothy. We Stood Alone. New York: Longmans, 1944. 284 p. Grades 6 and up.
After the Allied victory in 1918, an independent Polish republic once again became a reality. In 1919, under the treaty of Versailles, Germany returned the territory along the Baltic coast to Poland. Disputes between Poland and the Soviet Union over the Polish eastern region led to war in 1920. The treaty signed in Riga in 1921 between the two nations represented a compromise. Poland gained some of its territory from Russia, only to be once again devastated at the beginning of World War II when Germany and Russia secretly agreed to partition the country. This is the historical substance that forms the basis for a very personal and intimate narrative mirroring the political, social, and familial life in Poland during the period between the two world wars. The author's romantic story begins when, in 1926, as a student at the London School of Economics, she and Jan Kostanecki, the son of the rector of Cracow University, meet, fall in love, and decide to marry. Moving to Poland, she becomes a strong supporter of her husband's work as an economist and diplomat and begins to share his family's love of Poland. Despite the loss of her husband in a tragic airplane accident, she wants to remain in the country. In 1939, following the insistence of her relatives, she finally decides to return to the United States with her young son. She concludes her narrative with a touching farewell and a moving tribute to the country of her adoption and to the enduring courage of the Polish people as shown in their willingness to fight for justice and freedom.

172. Arnold, Madison. Polish Greats. New York: McKay, 1980. 114 p. Grades 6-12.
Presented are biographies of twelve famous Polish men and women, who distinguished themselves in the areas of religion and extraordinary personal virtue, in science, government, arts, or in the military. Arranged chronologically, the biographies begin with Jadwiga, a beloved fourteenth century Polish ruler, a fervent promoter of Christianity and a benefactor of the University of Cracow. The other Polish greats include:

Nicholaus Copernicus, an outstanding mathematician, linguist, Greek scholar, and the founder of the sun-centered theory in astronomy; Tadeusz Kosciuszko, who fought bravely in the American Continental Army as well as in the Polish Army; Count Casimir Pulaski, another general who battled the Russians to free Poland and fought the British during the American Revolution. Biographies of men who excelled in the area of literature include biographies of Adam Mickiewicz, Poland's greatest poet, and novelists Joseph Conrad and Wladyslaw Reymont, a Nobel Prize winner. Included are biographies of pianists and composers: Frédéric Chopin, Ignace Paderewski, and Arthur Rubinstein; moreover, there are stories of two women: the famous Shakespearean actress, Helena Modjeska, and the scientist, Marie Curie Sklodowska. The last biography is of Karl Wojtyla, Pope John Paul II. The biographies seem to be factual, but sources of information are not acknowledged.

173. Boucourechliev, André. Chopin: A Pictorial Biography. New York: Viking, 1963. 144 p. Grades 6 and up.
Prints of authentic portraits, drawings, paintings, engravings and photographs accompany this story of Frédéric Chopin, a Polish-born composer. He was born on March 1, 1810 to his French father Nicolas Chopin and his Polish mother, Justyna Krzyzanovska. According to the Polish legend, musicians from the neighboring villages played that night beneath the windows in their house. Music was an important part of life in the Chopin family. Chopin's father played the flute, his mother the piano. She also had a beautiful voice. Even as an infant, Frédéric showed a very keen aptitude for music. At the age of six he began taking piano lessons from a reputable musician, Adalbert Zywny. Frédéric composed his first work, Polonaise in G minor, at the age of seven. When he was eight years old, Frédéric gave his first concert, which was enthusiastically received. The great families of Warsaw began competing for the young musician. Frederic played in palaces of renown Polish nobles and enjoyed private studies under Joseph Elsuer, the director of the Warsaw Conservatory. At the age of nineteen his studies at the Conservatory were completed. His concerts and compositions won him the title of musical genius. The following year, Chopin went to Paris, and, with the exception of some travel to neighboring countries, remained there until his death in 1849. Chopin's personal life, his enormous creative power and the poetic style of his music, are portrayed against numerous revolutionary events in Poland as well as in France. A chronology of events, a set of notes on the pictures, and an index of names add clarity and authenticity to the text.

174. Brandt, Keith. Marie Curie: Brave Scientist. Illus. Karen Milone. Mahwah, NJ 1983. 48 p. Grades 2-4.

Written in a simple, lively style and printed in large clear type, this biography of Marie Curie will appeal to young readers. Major portions of the slender volume deal with Manya Sklodowska's childhood. It portrays her father, a professor of mathematics and physics, and her mother, a principal at a girl's school, who contracts tuberculosis and, after a long struggle, dies, leaving five children of whom Manya is the youngest. The author highlights Manya's amazing memory, her ability to read at the age of four, her extraordinary skill at completely blotting out the noise around her when reading, her fascination with her father's physics apparatus, her ability to speak perfect Russian, the language used in school, her overall success in her studies, and her love for Poland and Polish history. Only a few pages are dedicated to the scientist's later life. Manya's hard work and willingness to help her family and her constant desire to study science at the University of Sorbonne are emphasized. Finally, the author tells how Manya Sklodowska becomes Marie, a student and chemist in Paris, how she marries the physicist, Pierre Curie, and becomes the world-known discoverer of radium and a two-time Nobel Prize winner. Delightful pen drawings illustrate the biography.

175. Crew, Helen Coale. Under Two Eagles. Illus. Henry C. Pitz. Boston: Little, Brown, 1929. 298 p. Grades 5-9.
In 1913, when Vasily Milneff was born in a one-room cabin on the flat shores of the Vistula River near Warsaw, Poland was still an enslaved nation occupied by Austria, Russia, and Prussia. By the time the story of Vasily takes place, the country is once more a united Poland. Now the soldiers in the barracks no longer wear Russian uniforms, and long-desired change is felt everywhere, on the streets and in school. After World War I, which Vasily hardly remembers, Poles who have lived apart for over a hundred years, are beginning to feel and act as one nation, under the leadership of the Premier Ignace Paderewski and General Jozef Pilsudski. Ever since the twelve-year-old Vasily met General Pilsudski by chance, he was moved by the spirit of patriotism in his decisions and his actions. A red lapel button with white outspread wings of an eagle, emblem of Poland, given to Vasily by the famous General, inspires the youth as he assumes manly responsibilities toward his impoverished family, as he uses every opportunity for learning, and as he fills his heart with dreams of building new bridges, new churches, and new and better lives. When Uncle Vidar comes from America to visit the family and decides that the boy should go with him to New York to earn a better living for himself and to help the family, Vasily does not hesitate. Living in a new land, under the wings of another eagle, he is even more determined to work hard and to learn everything he can. This absorbing story, unlike most literature written in the 1920's, which was

characterized by presenting a child's world without
conflicts, is sensitive to the problems of real life by
portraying Vasily's world (e.g. the irresponsibility of
his father, the lightheartedness of his older brother,
the feebleness of the government, etc.) in a most
realistic and appealing way.

176. Curie, Eve. <u>Madame Curie</u>.   Trans. Vincent Sheean.
New York: Doubleday, 1938. 412 p. Grades 7 and up.
The most complete, most true to life, and most artfully
written biography of the life, the personality, and the
achievements of one of the greatest woman scientists,
the discoverer of radium, Marie Curie. Written by her
daughter, Eve, the biography is based upon her own
recollections, on the accounts of her sister, Irene, on
the narratives and letters of her closest French and
Polish relatives and friends, on Marie Curie's personal
papers and autobiographical notes, as well as on
innumerable official documents. According to the author
all the phrases used in dialogue were actually said, and
all the anecdotes related really took place. Not even
the slightest ornament was added. With warmth,
remarkable storytelling technique, clarity, and power,
Eve Curie narrates the childhood of Manya Sklodowska in
Warsaw, Poland and the dark days of Manya's first
encounter with death, the death of her sister Zosya and
of her dear mother. She chronicles Manya's adolescence,
her life in high school under the strict supervision of
Russian inspectors, her successes, and her sensitivity
and gayety. The author recounts Manya's friendship and
love for her older sister Bronya and for her father and
the measure of responsibility she feels toward both.
She documents Marie's studies in Paris, her scientific
achievements, her distinguished career, and her
internationally recognized honors. Without resorting to
an adulatory tone, Eve Curie is especially forceful in
portraying her mother's marriage, her family life and,
best of all, her personality and the corruptionless
simplicity of her soul. Filled with first-rate
photographs and accompanied by a list of Marie Curie's
prizes, medals, decorations, numerous honorary titles,
and a detailed index.

177. DiFranco, Anthony M. <u>Pope John Paul II; Bringing Love
to a Troubled World</u>.   Taking Part Books. Minneapolis:
Dillon, 1983. 71 p. Grades 3-6.
A simple, direct and warmly written biography of Carolus
Joseph Wojtyla who was chosen as Pope John Paul II in
1978. The book explains the difficult political
situation of the country in the period of Karol's
childhood and youth. In 1920, the year of his birth,
Russia invades Poland. As a young man, Karol witnesses
the invasion of the Nazi's, the almost simultaneous
attack of Poland by the Soviet Union, the tragic Warsaw
revolt, and finally, the imposition of Communism upon
Poland. Forced labor, school closings, concentration

camps, and gas chambers all become part of his everyday experiences, as does the underground university, the underground theater group, and the underground seminary. Father Wojtyla's study in Rome and his first years as a priest, his love of literature and sports, and his work with young people are all touched upon by the author. The major events of his life, his election to the papacy, his world-wide travels, including his first jubilant return to his native country, and his reaching out to the world with a message of hope, peace, goodness, and joy, are grippingly described. Enriched with excellent photographs.

178. Donaldson, Margaret. <u>Journey Into War</u>. Illus. Joanna Stubbs. London: Deutsch, 1979. 152 p. Grades 4-9.
The ten-year-old twins, Tadek and Stefek Pulaski have come a long way from Poland to St. Quentin in northern France. Their father, an officer in the Polish cavalry, died in battle against German tanks in September of 1939. Their mother, who was English, was taken by the Gestapo and the boys do not know whether she is still alive. The twins manage to hide and, with the help of their father's friend, get out of Poland. On their way to their grandmother's in England, they walk many miles through Hungary into Yugoslavia and, as stowaways, enter France in May of 1940. A few miles away from town, hiding in a deserted cottage they meet an English girl, Janey, who is approximately their age and has also become accidently stranded on the way to England. Caught between the advance of the German army across northern France, the three children decide to wage their own war against the enemy. They cut telephone wires and smash a radio transmitter. Unfortunately, on their next sabotage endeavour, Janey falls into the hands of the Gestapo. With some help from a sympathetic German officer, and through their own daring ingenuity, the twins rescue Janey from the prison. Moreover, they aid a French prisoner, Gaston, in his escape. Gaston later becomes instrumental in guiding the children to Janey's father, now a member of the French underground forces, and eventually they reach England. An action-filled story.

179. Donaldson, Margaret. <u>The Moon's on Fire</u>. Illus. Joanna Stubbs. London: Deutsch, 1980. 138 p. Grades 4-8.
A detailed narrative, the story takes place in London from Wednesday, September 4th to Sunday, September 15, 1940. The Germans are beginning their heavy bombing of the city in preparation for their invasion of England. Two boys and a girl in their early teens are determined to fight the Nazis in their own way. The Polish twins, Tadek and Stefek, and their English friend Jarrey are staying with the girls' aunt and uncle. Convinced that the uncle is a German spy, the boys decide to trail him. This episode ends in a temporary disaster. Stefek and Tadek are forced to run away the very day the harrowing

bombing of London begins. They narrowly escape death, taking shelter in an underground tube station. When they emerge two hours later, the whole world seems to be ablaze. Even the pale moon seems to be on fire. The story vividly recreates the terror of war with its constant air raids and other deadly dangers. The children's undaunted spirit, the boys' attempts to join the Polish squadron in the Royal Air Force, the friendship they develop with the old bootman, and their enhancement by the crook, Wattie the wolf, are described with deep insight and perception. Black and white drawings nicely complement the powerful narrative.

180. Doorly, Eleonor. <u>The Radium Woman: A Life of Marie Curie</u>.   Illus.   Robert   Gibbings.   London,   England: Heinemann, 1939. 184 p. Grades 5-10.

A lively written biography of Marie Curie Sklodowska, the discoverer of two highly radioactive chemical elements, radium and polonium. The biography is based on the <u>Life of Madam Curie</u>, written by Marie's daughter Eve. Marie was born as Marya Sklodowska in Warsaw in 1867 as the youngest of five children. At the age of five, Manya, as she was called, showed great devotion to her family and to her country, which was then under Russian occupation. All classes in school were taught entirely in Russian, and the use of the Polish language was forbidden. Brighter than most children, Manya learns how to distract Russian inspectors and how to cleverly resist their demands. And she loves her school. At sixteen she graduates from high school with highest honors and with a gold medal of excellence. Since the University of Warsaw was closed to women, Manya goes to work as a governess, studying on her own and saving money to go to Paris to study at the best European University, the Sorbonne. Her dream comes true when, after two years in Paris, Marie passes her master's examination in physics and chemistry with the highest score. Marie's complete dedication to the study of science, her love and marriage to the French physicist Pierre Curie, her devotion to her family, her single-mindedness in her experimentation, her extraordinary patience with scientific research, and her deep humility with respect to her great successes and scientific discoveries are vividly and movingly portrayed. The book is illustrated with numerous beautiful woodcuts. In 1940 it was awarded the Carnegie Medal, which is given annually to an outstanding children's book published in Great Britain.

181. Eringer, Robert. <u>Strike for Freedom! The Story of Lech Walesa and Polish Solidarity</u>. New York: Dodd, 1982. 177 p. Grades 7 and up.

The story of Walesa begins with the events of December 1981, when the ten-million member Solidarity union is suspended, the rights it has won are lost, the military "Council of National Salvation" is established to be in

command of Poland, and when martial law is implemented.
The succeeding chapters give a quick review of Poland's
history, the development of the then sixteen-month-old
Solidarity, and the impact Lech Walesa has on his
country and the world. He was born in 1943 as the son
of a carpenter in the village of Popowo during a period
when Poland suffered under German occupation. Lech, the
youngest of four children, is only three years old when
his father dies after his return from the forced labor
camp. As a young lad, Lech partially earns his living
by carrying raw bricks to the furnace at the brickyard.
His formal education consists of attendance at an
elementary school in the village of Chalin and a trade
school in Lipno. He is remembered by his teachers more
for his daring and bravery than his academic
achievements. The report of his two-year military
record also points out Lech's decisiveness and
leadership abilities. In 1967 Walesa accepts a job as
an electrician in the Lenin Shipyard in Gdansk. Here,
after studying on his own, Walesa rises as the leader of
the Polish labor movement which threatens not only the
Polish government, but also the Soviet Union and the
very foundations of Communism throughout Eastern Europe.
Written in a light, storytelling style by a young
American correspondent with the help of an unnamed
Polish journalist and illustrated with excellent
photographs, the book is a rare testimony of the
dedication to freedom and courage of Lech Walesa as well
as of the entire Polish people. The book appears in the
School Library Journal's best book's list for young
adults.

182. Forman, James.   My Enemy, My Brother.   New   York:
Meredith, 1969. 250 p. Grades 7 and up.
For Dan Baratz and his Jewish family in Warsaw, the life
they have been accustomed to is over on the first of
September 1939. Dan remembers the first German planes
over the city and his father playing the "Grande
Polonaise" for the last time. When a few weeks later
the German army occupies Warsaw, Dan's father, a Pole, a
Jew, and a lawyer, is in special danger, so he changes
his law office into a watch repair shop. Soon
afterwards all Warsaw Jews are herded into the ghetto.
"Resettlement" follows. Refusing to submit, his mother
and father perish as underground fighters. It is his
father's wish that Dan leave the small doomed band of
resisters so that someday he would be a witness of the
tragic events. He and his grandfather escape, are
captured by the Gestapo, and, having convinced the
guards that they are skillful watchmakers, are sent to a
small concentration camp near Zambrov, a factory for
ammunition. Here, by the Russian army in the spring of
1945, they are found with a hundred or so other
prisoners, emaciated, weak, and ill. The remaining
story deals with their search for their old home and
with Dan's decision to leave with three other people for

Israel. At the age of sixteen, Dan and his companions journey mostly on foot to Krakow, into Czechoslovakia, through Austria, Yugoslavia, Italy, and finally into Kibbutz, called "Promise of the Future." This gripping story of the evil of war, of human love and endurance, and of the discovery of the difficult road to real peace and understanding received the Spring Book Festival Award for the year 1969.

183. Golden, Grace. Seven Dancing Dolls. Illus. David Stone. New York: Bobbs-Merrill, 1961. 96 p. Grades 3-6. This story takes place in the 1830's in a Polish castle near Warsaw, which was under Austrian rule. At that time Poland was divided among Prussia, Russia, and Austria. Prince Lenki travels frequently to Warsaw and Krakow to meet secretly with other nobles and to discuss the possibility of Polish freedom. Returning from one of such trips, Papa brings presents for Mama, for their older daughters, as well as for the youngest in the family, eight-year-old Wanda. This time there are two presents for Wanda. One is a young guest, a famous musician, Frédéric Chopin, who comes with Papa for a short stay with the family before he continues on his way to Vienna. The second present is a group of little figurines, seven dolls, held up by almost invisible bristles from a wild boar. When put on the piano, the dolls move about as though they are dancing. As the stories of some of the famous Polish heroes are told to Wanda, she names the dolls after Thaddeus Kosciuszko, Jadwiga, and the Trumpeter of Krakow. One is named Frédéric in honor of their beloved guest and the rest in honor of the most loved family servants and friends. When Chopin bids farewell to the family, one of the dolls, Thad, is missing. In the end it is Frederic Chopin who solves the mystery and at the same time presents Wanda with the famous composition "The Waltz of the Seven Dancing Dolls." A fast-paced story with sympathetic characters, authentic settings and much insight into the life of a Polish aristocratic family of the nineteenth century.

184. Greene, Carol. Marie Curie: Pioneer Physicist. Chicago: Children's, 1984. 112 p. Grades 4-8. In a pleasing, vivid style, the author presents the life of Marie Sklodowska Curie, the brilliant scientist and discoverer of radium. The biography traces little Marya's childhood in Poland, her growth to adulthood after the death of her mother, her constant desire for knowledge, her studies of physics and chemistry at the Sorbonne University in Paris, her marriage to Pierre Curie, her discovery of radium, the honors and awards which she received for her great scientific achievements, includng the Nobel Prize for physics in 1903 and again for chemistry in 1911, and the last years of her life. The historical period during which Marie Sklodowska lived as a young girl is simply and

objectively described. Living in the Russian occupied
section of divided Poland, Marya attends school, where
the study of Polish literature and history is forbidden.
Teachers and young students, however, break this rule
whenever the Russian inspector is not present and study
about their beloved homeland with great love and
determination. This devotion to Poland remains in
Marie's heart all her life. Her final journeys from
Paris to Poland take place after World War I when, with
her help, the Institute of Radium is established in
Warsaw and inaugurated in 1932. With the help of
President Hoover, Marie obtains a gram of radium from
the United States, which she donates to the Polish
Institute. In 1934, during her simple burial, her
sister and brother cover her casket with a few handfuls
of Polish earth. Much of the candid information
contained in the biography is related through quotations
and through selected incidents which are taken from a
biography of Marie Curie written by her daughter Eve.
Numerous reproductions of photographs obtained from
various archival collections, a table of major events
during Marie Curie's life, and an index accompany the
biography.

185. Haaren, John H. and A.B. Poland. <u>Famous Men of Modern
<u>Times</u>. New York: American Book, 1909. 352 p. Grades 3-6.
Of the thirty-three biographies of world famous men, two
are written about Polish patriots, one of John Sobieski
and the other of Thaddeus Kosciuszko. Both biographies
are written in a clear, simple style and seem to
describe the men's achievements realistically and
accurately. In addition to stories about the two men,
enough historical background is given to assist the
reader in fully understanding and appreciating each
man's strengths and his contributions to mankind. Since
each biography is only several pages in length, full
personalities including their more human side and their
personal life are not represented. Clearly, it was the
intent of the authors of the book to elicit in their
young readers a deeper interest in the study of history
by centering major historical events around the living
men who made history happen. The story about John
Sobieski emphasizes the fact that he was elected the
King of Poland in 1674 by the Polish Diet, who wanted a
Pole to govern Poland. Although his reign is described
as the most brilliant in Polish history, the biography
deals mostly with Sobieski's establishment of an
alliance against the Turks, who threatened all of
Christendom, and with his famous defeat of the Moslem
army at the gates of Vienna in 1683. The biography of
Kosciuszko brings to life the man's fight for the
freedom of Poland toward the end of the eighteenth
century, as well as his enthusiastic and brave
participation in the American struggle for independence.
The biographies are further enhanced by numerous, high
quality drawings and portraits.

186. Hautzig, Esther. <u>The Endless Steppe: Growing Up in Siberia</u>. New York: Crowell, 1968. 243 p. Grades 4 and up.

The city of Vilna in the northeastern corner of Poland with its university, parks, white churches, and old houses, was a spirited city, the best city in which a child could be raised. But in 1939 the German armies occupied Poland, and in 1940 the Russians, who were then allied with Hitler's Germany, occupied Vilna. One early morning in June of 1941 ten-year-old Esther waters the lilac bush in her garden for the last time. Her family and thousands of other Poles are transported on that beautiful summer day in crowded cattle cars to Siberia. Told in the first person by Esther and based on the author's own experiences of deportation and of her five-year stay in Siberia, the novel offers a moving portrayal of the harsh life on the endless steppe, the scorching heat of the summers, the howling winds of autumn and the bitter cold of winter, the crowded dung huts, the vermin, the scarcity of food, and the hard manual labor. The author's account of life in a Siberian village after amnesty is granted to the Polish prisoners, of going to school and learning Russian, of prejudices, ambitions, and first love, is told with vitality, individuality of style, affection, optimism, and much humor, without any trace of bitterness or hatred. This remarkable narrative about inexhaustible human endurance received numerous literary awards.

187. Hume, Ruth and Paul Hume. <u>The Lion of Poland: The Story of Paderewski</u>.   Illus. Lili Réthi.   New York: Hawthorn, 1962. 187 p. Grades 4-6.

A biography of the pianist, composer and statesman, Ignace Yan Paderewski, covering his entire career from his birth in 1860 to his death in 1941. The book relates how, even as a small child, Ignace showed an unusually great interest in music. He began taking piano lessons when he was six years old. At the age of twelve he left his home village in Podolia and went to Warsaw to study music at the conservatory. Later, he continued his studies in other European countries, Austria and Germany included. Paderewski gave hundreds of recitals in countries throughout the world. His many compositions, rooted in Polish folklore include operas, concertos, and minuets. As a statesman he served as the premier of Poland in 1919 and as the president of the exiled government in 1939. Paderewski's talent for music and his brilliant musical career as a concert pianist in the United States and Europe is especially vividly described. His devotion to Poland's freedom and his success as a statesman are related in straightforward yet sympathetic style. The book offers a minimally fictionalized biography of a great man as well as an honest account of the spirit and people of his time. A bibliography of sources and a pronunciation guide are appended.

188. Keller, Mollie. <u>Marie Curie</u>. An Impact Biography.
New York: Watts, 1982. 119 p. Grades 6-12.
   A biography of one of the most remarkable women
scientists, Marie Curie, which begins with her birth in
1867 in "Vistula Land," a Polish area under Russian
control and ends at her death in 1934 in France. The
book concludes with a paragraph appraising the
importance of her scientific discoveries. One of five
children, her father was a professor of physics and
mathematics and her mother a gifted pianist and singer,
as well as a housekeeper and a cobbler making who
repaired her own children's shoes. Marie learned early
that, in order to follow her dreams and ambitions, in
order to succeed and excel, she would have to work hard,
be patient and determined, and always do with less to
make more. Marie graduates from the gymnasium, the high
school as it is known in Poland, with a gold medal, the
top academic award, two years younger than her
classmates. After this, however, all roads to further
study seem to be closed. Because of her mother's death
and her father's uncertain job situation during the
Russianization of Poland, Marie has to go to work as a
private tutor and governess in order to send her sister
Bronya first, and then herself to France to study.
Through hard work and study, the two girls survive a
myriad of disappointments, make it to Paris, and
graduate from Sorbonne University. With her degree, her
reputation as a researcher, and her iron will, Marie is
given enough support to stay in Paris and to continue
with her scientific investigations. Stressing her
contribution to science, especially her work on the
isolation of radium and polonium, the biographer
presents a sensitive and authoritative look at Marie's
personal life, her vigor, perseverance, loyalty to her
home country, her devotion to her husband and family,
her dedicaton to the scientific community of the world,
and especially her deep humanity. A list of other
biographical works on Marie Curie and an index are
appended.

189. Kellog, Charlotte. <u>Paderewski</u>. New York: Viking,
1956. 224 p. Grades 6-12.
   Ignace Paderewski was twelve years old when he and his
father travelled all the way from Sudylkow, a village in
Russian ruled Poland, to Warsaw. It was hard for Ignace
to leave his sister Antonia, who had been a mother, as
well as a sister, to him. Their mother died soon after
his birth. Once in Warsaw, his father and he had to
arrange for his admittance to the conservatory, and find
a piano and a place for Ignace to stay while studying.
They brought with them a large scrapbook filled with
Ignace's compositions. The boy had no difficulty
getting accepted. That was in 1872. The formal musical
education of one of the best Polish pianists and
composers began. After the completion of the
conservatory in Warsaw, he studied in Berlin and finally

in Vienna. With debuts in Vienna, Paris, London, and
New York City, Paderewski became internationally known
and respected. His compositions, symphonies, minuets,
and sonatas reflected not only his musical genius, but
also his deep devotion to his native homeland.
Paderewski's career as a statesman, especially his role
at the Versailles peace conference and his
representation of Poland at the League of Nations, his
participation in the relief program for Poland, his year
as a Polish premier, and his mission as the head of the
Polish government-in-exile during World War II is
accurately presented within a historical context.
Incidents portraying Paderewski as a great humanist, and
those revealing his personal life, make this biography
especially appealing.

190. Kelly, Eric Philbrook.   The Blacksmith of Vilno: A
Tale of Poland in the Year 1832.   Illus. Angela Pruszynska.
New York: Macmillan, 1930. 184 p. Grades 5-10.
    At the end of the eighteenth century, Poland was
partitioned for the third time among Russia, Prussia,
and Austria. For several decades the country ceased to
exist as an independent nation. After a short interval
of independence under Napoleon I, the Congress of Vienna
in 1815 gave the largest part of the country to Russia,
which organized it as a kingdom of Poland under the rule
of the czar. Provoked by constant Russian interference,
the Poles revolted in 1830. They forced the Russians
out of Warsaw, only to lose their constitutional rights
the following year when the Russians came back into
power. Against this background of continuous relentless
attempts by the Russians to smother Polish nationalism,
a captivating novel centered around the ancient crown of
Polish kings develops. As a precious symbol of their
historic greatness and of their will for independence,
the crown is kept in hiding by the patriots in the hope
that someday it would be worn again by a Pole who would
be worthy of his ancestors and would govern a free
country. As the Russians try desperately to capture the
priceless crown, a group of daring nationalists meet
frequently in Peter's blacksmith shop at the edge of a
thick forest outside of Vilno. Pursued by spies and
enemy soldiers, they do not hesitate to risk their own
lives in their effort to hide the crown. A suspenseful
story illuminating the events of 1832, illustrated by
pen drawings as well as richly colored paintings.

191. Kelly, Eric Philbrook. From Star to Star: A Story of
Krakow in 1493.   Illus. Manning de V. Lee.   New York:
Lippincott, 1944. 239 p. Grades 6-12.
    The year 1493 was one of the years of upheaval that
marked the late Middle Ages. Constantinople had been
taken by the Turks. Their advances westward threatened
all of eastern and central Europe. Christopher Columbus
sailed to America, printing presses appeared in many
towns, and with these many books became available. A

new outlook, called humanism, was gaining ground among
students and scholars.   At that time, Poland was ruled
by Jagiellonian kings.   The empire was well advanced
politically, economically, and especially culturally.
The center of knowledge in Poland was the University of
Krakow, which had been in existence for more than 100
years.   There, Nicolas Copernicus, under the guidance of
his teacher Adalbert of Brudzevo, began to refute the
theory that the earth was the center of the planetary
system.   Against this historical setting the story of
Roman, the seventeen-year old son of a Polish nobleman
uncoils.   As the eldest, he is determined to serve in
the army, to uphold the honor of his country.   Roman,
however, has a yearning for knowledge and wants to study
at the University of Krakow before he assumes his duties
as a soldier.   With his mother's blessing, he leaves his
family   estate   though   much   against   the   will   of   his
father.   During the year of 1493, his first year in
Krakow, Roman experiences many hardships but manages to
establish friendships with many students, an extremely
special one with Nicolas Copernicus.   He plays an
important role in the changing of a custom that required
students   to   give   gifts   to   their   examiners.   Most
importantly, Roman is instrumental in helping to find a
secret treasure which had been entrusted to a Dominican
monk   during   the   fall   of   Constantinople   which   was
overtaken   by   the   Turks.   Written   with   accuracy   in
relation   to   historical   detail,   the   story   of   Roman
reveals the colorful student life at the University of
Krakow as well as the state of knowledge at that time.

192.   Kelly, Eric Philbrook.   Golden Star of Halich: A Tale
of the Red Land in 1382.   Illus. Angela Pruszynska.   New
York: Macmillan, 1931. 215 p. Grades 7-12.
A suspenseful historical novel, the story takes place in
fourteenth century Poland during the reign of Kasimir,
King of the Peasants, whom history knows as Kasimir the
Great.   When the King arrives from Krakow to Lvov in the
simple garb of a country gentleman to find out what is
going on along the eastern border of Poland, fifteen
year old Michael Korzets saves him from an assassin's
dagger.   For this brave action Michael is allowed to
accompany a group of noblemen to Halich, the ancient
city in the Red Lands to find out about the conspiracy
against their King and to probe into the mystery of the
Golden Star of Halich.   Separated from the company of
men, Michael falls into the hands of the Tartars, but
escapes.   Through his imprisonment and flight he learns
that the Golden Star is not a jewel or a precious
ornament, but a fourteen year old girl Katerina, of the
House of Lion, whom he meets on his dangerous journey.
On the night when she was born, a star never seen before
appeared in the sky; and, according to the legend, the
Golden Star was to rule the lands of the Tartars, as
well as the lands of the Slavs and Lithuanians in
prosperity and peace.   Connected with this mystery are

unbelievable intrigues, conspiracies, hatred, and bloody
wars. On his way to manhood Michael is able to put
someone else's need before his own, as he endures fires,
shipwreck, and enemy attack. Rich in theme and accurate
in historical detail, the novel gives sharp insights
into the dangers, romance, and adventure of the life in
medieval Poland.

193. Kelly, Eric Philbrook. The Trumpeter of Krakow: A
Tale of the Fifteenth Century. Illus. Janina Domanska. New
York: Macmillan, 1966. 208 p. Grades 6-10.
    This absorbing story, which won the Newbery Medal in
1929 when the book was first published, is set in late
fifteenth century Poland. The narrative gives a
fascinating view of the early Renaissance, its world of
learning and culture, the generosity of the people,
their search for truth and their unbelievable
superstitions. It describes the dangers of city life,
the greediness of the villains, the Tartar invasions and
armored knights, and the splendor of the courts.
Portrayed against this historically authentic background
is the dramatic adventure of the novel's hero, fifteen
year old Joseph Charnetski. After the Tartars destroy
his family's home in the Ukraine, he and his parents
escape with the great Tarnov crystal, a gem of great
value and symbolic significance. The crystal has been
in the family for more than two hundred years. The
ancestors of the Charnetski family have sworn to
surrender it to no other person than the King of Poland.
The promise is fulfilled after the morning song of the
young trumpeter, who sounds the ancient Heynal, a hymn
to Mary, from the tower of the Church of Our Lady and
after other dangers are bravely conquered by Joseph and
his father. The illustrations, resembling medieval
woodcuts, are a perfect accompaniment for this totally
engaging narrative. In addition to the Newbery Medal,
the book received special citation from the Boys' Club
in 1966.

194. Kelly, Eric Philbrook and Clara Hoffmanova. A Girl
Who Would be Queen: The Story and the Diary of the Young
Countess Krasinska. Illus. Vera Bock. Chicago: McClurg,
1939. 201 p. Grades 5-10.
    At the end of the eighteenth century the old Polish
Commonwealth fell to the politics and conspiracies of
the neighboring countries and its own self-seeking
gentry. During this time, however, there emerged
several strong personalities and patriots who in various
ways contributed much to the Polish patriotic
atmosphere. Tadeusz Kosciuszko was a forerunner of the
popular movement for independence, and General Pulaski
eventually came to the United States and fought for
American independence. One of the notable women of the
period was the Countess Francoise Krasinska, the subject
of the story. Her famous ancestral line went back to
the eleventh century, and her descendents founded the

male line of the Kings of Italy. Originally, the
Journal of Countess Krasinska was written on the basis
of her writings and her correspondence, which have been
kept in the Krasinski Library in Warsaw by the Polish
novelist Clara Hoffmanova. The Journal appeared in
several translations and editions. The present book is
based on the original novel. It also contains a few
additions concerning the life of the Countess and the
Polish political situation during the period. The story
reveals Krasinski's youthful years, her ambitions to
become a queen, her patriotism, the pride of her family,
her remarkable mind, her free spirit, and her devotion
to the man she married. In 1939 the book was the Junior
Literary Guild selection, and it received the American
Institute of Graphic Arts Award for the excellence of
its drawings.

195. Knight, David C. Copernicus: Titan of Modern
Astronomy. Immortals of Science Series. New York: Watts,
1965. 232 p. Grades 6-10.
Nicolaus was born in 1473 in Torun, a city in northern
Poland. Because he lost his parents in his early
boyhood, his uncle Lucas adopts him and raises him. He
sends Nicolaus to the Jagiellonian University in Krakow
to study, among other subjects, astronomy. Here
Copernicus begins questioning the theories of Aristotle
and Ptolemy, the Greek scientists, regarding the earth's
place in the universe. While in Italy studying church
law and medicine he continues with his astronomical
observations. When he settles as a church canon and a
physician in Frombork, Poland, he carries on his
astronomical studies. Using only basic equipment he
becomes convinced, with the help of his knowledge of
logic and mathematics, that the sun is the center of the
planetary system. The biographer emphasizes the
importance of Copernicus's scientific writings and
explains why the book containing Copernicus'
controversial theory could not be published for so many
years. Its first copy was not seen by the astronomer
until the very day of his death in 1543. A well-written
and carefully researched biography of one of the best
educated men of the sixteenth century, the book also
contains a brief history of astronomy prior to
Copernicus, an explanation of his heliocentric notion of
the universe, and the original introduction to his
writings as well as reproductions of all his known
portraits.

196. Korschunow, Irena. A Night in Distant Motion. Trans.
Leigh Hafrey. Boston: Godine, 1983. 151 p. Grades 7-10.
Until September 1944, Regine Martens blindly adhers to
the Nazi doctrine. Her father, who has been reported
missing in action in Russia, belonged to the Nazi party
since 1933; her mother is unquestioningly loyal to the
Fuhrer. During the night of September 12, after the
first enemy bombing of their town Steinbergen, Regine

meets Jan, a Polish prisoner, one of those subhumans who lives in the workers' barracks. He is twenty-two years old with the letter P, the symbol of all Polish workers sewn on his blue overalls. Regine does not really want to speak to a Pole because it is forbidden. If she was to be caught, she would get her hair sheared right to the scalp, and she would be put into prison; in addition, Poles who have relationships with German girls are either sent into concentration camps or are hanged without trial. But Jan's words of the unnecessary hatred, his mellow voice, and the goodness seen through his clear blue eyes draw Regine to him and open a new world to her. In the evenings they meet secretly in the garden shed, and Regine realizes that it is the war that is all wrong, not the fact that they are meeting together. Jan talks to her about his pre-war home in Cracow, the famous University, the market place Tynek Glowny, and about the Church of St. Mary. For the first time Regine realizes the horror of war and the evil of Nazism. As somewhat expected, they are soon seized by the Gestapo and separated. The story is told in the first person in a series of short episodes as recalled in parts by Regine, while she was in hiding on a farm after her escape from a prison. This powerful narrative, originally published in Germany in 1979, received the International Honor Award from the Jane Addams Peace Association, New York and from the Women's International League for Peace and Freedom, Geneva.

197. Kotowska, Monika. The Bridge to the Other Side. Trans. Maia Wojciechowska. New York: Doubleday, 1970. 164 p. Grades 5 and up.

In this collection of nineteen episodes, the Polish born author brings the experiences of children during World War II vividly to life. Written in first person as though told by the children themselves, the short stories reflect the inhumanity of the world of war around them and the despair that they experienced during the postwar period. Endowed with the power of imagination, the war orphans, who are constantly hungry and cold, who belong to no one and share only in the cruelty of the adult world, think of a better and different life; they think of the other side, the side that a chimney sweep must reach when he comes to the end of the thin ladder, or the side one reaches when crossing a long bridge. They think of warmth and of rivers flowing with milk, of having an uncle somewhere who would occasionally provide them with food and shelter. They wish to own something like a doll or a teddy bear or better still a kitten or a puppy, whom they could talk to so they would never be alone again. When the war ends, however, and the bombing stops, they are sadder than ever. With the world of war gone, the only world they have known disappears; there is nothing left for the children, nothing and no one. Only emptiness remains. A superbly written book, it displays an impressive understanding of the times and offers deep psychological insight into the feelings and brave struggles of the children on their horrid journey through the war.

198. Krasinska,   Francoise.   The Journal of Countess Francoise Krasinska. Trans. Kasimir Dziekonska. Chicago: McClurg, 1923. 182 p. Grades 6-10.
On New Year's Day in 1759 a sixteen year old girl, Francoise, daughter of the Count and the Countess Krasinski, possessors of an old, noble ancestry, began writing her diary. By then Francoise knew well how to write in Polish and French, and the idea of recording interesting facts and circumstances appealed to her. She decided to note in a special copy book, which she made for herself, as accurately as possible her own experiences, family events, and public affairs as they happened. Proud of her family, Francoise could recite her genealogy from the first Krasinski, Warcislaus Korwin from the old Roman family of Corvinus, who in the eleventh century came from Hungary to Poland to serve as General-in-Chief of the army under King Boleslaus II. More than anything else Francoise wished never to tarnish the respected name of the family. In her desire to add to the Krasinski's fame, she even felt sorry that she was not a man, as she would then have more opportunities to do so. Several years later, just the opposite happened. Francoise offended her family beyond all expectations when she married secretly without the blessing of her parents. Eloquently written and translated from Polish, the memories offer a profound account of the life of a young girl, her growth to maturity with its many joys, dreams, and expectations, as well as with its deep disappointments and sufferings. A superb portrait of life in the courts of Poland more than two hundred years ago.

199. Kresh, Paul. Isaac Bashevis Singer: The Story of a Storyteller. Illus. Penrod Scofield. Jewish Biography Series. New York: Lodestar, 1984. 149 p. Grades 6-10.
Based on the author's scholarly biography, Isaac Bashevis Singer: The Magician of West 86 Street, which was published in 1979, this book offers a colorful portrait of the world's foremost Yiddish writer, whose works are known and admired internationally. Isaac was born in 1904 in the small Polish town of Leoncin on the banks of the Vistula River. His father was a rabbi who spent most of his time studying sacred books, translating holy books into Yiddish, giving sermons, and handling local lawsuits. His mother, a daughter of a rabbi, was an independent, self-taught woman.   She learned Hebrew and read the Torah so faithfully that she knew almost the entire work by heart.   In this biography, young Isaac's relationship with his parents, as well as with his brothers and his older sister, is discerningly drawn.   The harsh life of the Jews in

Poland is vividly described and the customs and celebrations of various holidays amusingly and realistically explained. The author is especially successful, however, in portraying Singer's engaging personality, his early fondness for stories, and his fascination with books, reading, and writing. Mr. Kresh evokes Isaac's childhood, his short period of study in the Rabbinical Seminary, his years of poverty, his struggles as a writer, his decision to follow his older brother Joshua to the United States, his two marriages, his frequently uncertain path to literary acceptance, and finally, in 1978 his being awarded the Noble Prize for Literature at the age of 74.

200.   Landau, Rom.   Ignace Paderewski, Musician and States-man.   New York: Crowell, 1934. 314 p. Grades 8 and up.
A most inspirational biography of the great Polish pianist and politician. The book traces Paderewski's life from his early years of piano study to his acceptance by audiences around the world as a great pianist; then it describes his years of dedication to the founding of Poland as an independent nation and concludes with his expulsion from politics and return to the piano. Althouth the treatment of Paderewski's musical career is somewhat technical, and the French phrases interspersed throughout the book might not be appreciated by most American students, the author captures the spirit and genius of Paderewski throughout. The book is divided into three sections, each of which is broken into divisions, two or three pages in length. This allows the author to switch his viewpoint frequently without losing his reader. He illustrates personality traits using a short story or an event in the character's life, making the book very entertaining, which contrasts with the strictly chronological approach used by other biographers. In this manner Landau is able to bring his characters to life, for he effects a real life situation, giving the reader the feeling that he is almost there. This talent is no where better displayed than in the final chapter of the book, in which he relates the results of a series of visits with the great Polish patriot. The emotional bond one comes to feel for the pianist could hardly be greater than the one between the biographer and the subject himself. All in all, a most interesting and moving treatment of a most interesting and moving man. First class black and white prints are included.

201.   Malinski, Mieczyslaw.   Pope John Paul II: The Life of Karol Wojtyla.   Trans. P. S. Falla. New York: Seabury, 1979. 283 p. Grades 6 and up.
Written by his lifelong friend and chaplain at the University of Krakow, the biography portrays Karol Wojtyla from his youth until his election to the papacy. Tragedies filled his early life. His mother died when Karol was nine in 1929. His sister died as a child, and

his only brother, a physician, died of scarlet fever in
1938. He suddenly lost his father to a heart attack a
few years later.   At the beginning of the Nazi
occupation of Poland, Karol worked in a factory. During
his free time, however, he was a member of the
"rhapsodic theatre," whose youthful members were
determined to carry on the artistic Polish traditions.
They met in secret in private homes and listened to each
other's recitation of Polish poetry and poetic prose.
During the war, as the country was in a state of
constant terror and reprisals, Karol decided to become a
priest. He had to enter an underground seminary run by
Cardinal Sapieha. For a while he went on living the
life of a factory worker in Krakow, though he studied
hard whenever time permitted him to do so.   The
theological and philosophical studies were hard and
demanding. Wojtyla's work as a priest, bishop, cardinal, and especially his election as pope reflect his
enigmatic personality, his intelligence, extraordinary
courage, perseverance, wisdom, deep spirituality, and
warm humanity.   The biography richly manifests the
undaunted spirit of the Polish people at a sad period in
their history and their enthusiasm, their jubilation,
and their indescribable joy when Karol Wojtyla was
inaugurated as Pope John Paul the Second.

202. Maurois, André.   Frédéric Chopin.   Trans. Ruth Green
Harris. Illus. Everett Shinn. New York: Harper, 1942. 91
p.   Grades 3-5.
This brief account of one of the greatest musical
composers begins with the story of his parents, Nicolas
Chopin, a Frenchman, and Justine Krzyanowska, a typical
Polish girl, who, while in the service of the Countess
Skarbek, meet in the Countess' chateau near Warsaw.
They are married in 1806, when Poland was under
Napoleon's occupation. The young couple start their
independent life when Nicolas is appointed professor at
the newly established French high school. Like most of
Chopin's other biographers, Maurois points out that when
their third child, the boy Frederic was born in 1809, a
group of fidlers under the window seranaded the family
with popular Polish songs. Thus, these Polish melodies
were the first sounds the baby heard coming into the
world. In a warm and vivid style, and through short,
fascinating episodes, the author recreates the life of
Chopin, first as a boy, when, as an infant prodigy, he
enchanted audiences with his piano recitals, and then as
an adult, by depicting the outstanding events of his
productive latter life.   The account also contains
skillfully drawn sketches revealing Chopin's sensitive
personality, his tender love for Marie Wodzinska, his
association with the novelist George Sand, and above
all, his love for his motherland. Tailored to the young
reader, the biography also contains numerous sidelights
on the sad political situation in nineteenth century
Poland.

203. Mills, Lois. <u>So Young a Queen</u>. New York: Lathrop,
Lee, and Shepard, 1960. 172 p. Grades 5-9.
    A sympathetically written biography of the Polish Queen
Jadwiga, who ruled the country in the later part of the
fourteenth century. When she married the Grand Duke of
Lithuania, Wladislav Jagiello, they ruled both countries
together. The monarchs of the Jagiello dynasty then
ruled Poland nearly two hundred years. The biography
begins with Jadwiga's childhood in Buda, the Hungarian
court of her parents, King Louis the Great and Queen
Elizabeth. At the tender age of five, Jadwiga was
solemnly betrothed to the young Prince William, son of
Archduke Leopold, ruler of Austria. It was in their
parents' plan to unite the two countries some day in
order to strengthen their defenses against the
Lithuanian, Turkish, and Tartar invasions. From that
day on, the time of their engagement the royal pair
stayed alternatively in Buda, enjoying the warm family
life and excellent education provided by Jadwiga's
parents, and in Vienna, where their education continued.
Unfortunately, Jadwiga's father, King Louis I, who, in
addition to ruling Hungary also ruled Poland during his
last twelve years in power, died prematurely. Jadiwga's
older sister Mary became the ruler of Hungary, and the
teenage Jadwiga was sent to Poland to be crowned Queen
of the country. In spite of her youth, Jadwiga was
determined to incorporate into her rule her father's
outstanding virtues: intelligence, energy, and
self-control. Her personal sacrifice of leaving Prince
William of Austria in order to marry the pagan Jagiello,
who promised to convert to Christianity, is described
with sensitivity, compassion, and understanding. A
highly readable narrative, rich in compassion and true
historical details, but not lost in them.

204. Orlev, Uri. <u>The Island on Bird Street</u>. Trans. Hillel
Halkin. Boston: Houghton Mifflin, 1984. 162 p. Grades
4-8.
    An intensely moving story which takes place in Warsaw,
Poland during World War II. The book was originally
written in Hebrew in 1981 by the Polish-born author, who
spent six of his childhood and early teenage years both
in hiding and in a concentration camp. The story is
told in first person by eleven-year-old Alex, whose
mother has disappeared while visiting her Jewish friends
in another part of the walled ghetto and whose father
soon after is selected for transport. It is the third
year of the war. Alex is saved fom deportation by his
father's friend Boruch, who in all probability is shot
seconds after he pushes Alex through the window of a
moving train. Leaving him with a knapsack containing a
pistol, a bit of food, some water, and a flashlight,
Boruch instructs Alex to run to the bombed out building
on 78 Bird Street and wait there for his father, even if
it takes a month or a whole year. The boy first hides
in one of the storage rooms of the dark cellar, but soon

recognizes that it would be safer in the upper floor kitchen which seems to be hanging onto the broken-off part of the fourth floor. Courageously and intelligently, Alex makes a rope-ladder and moves to the upper quarters, carefully concealing it when he is home or when he leaves his cell at night to forage for food, clothing, and fuel. After five months of hiding and concealing his identity, he ventures out of the ruined building, accompanied by his pet mouse, to find that his father has really returned. Before they venture into the forest to join the Jewish partisans, however, Alex has to tell his father his stories about his narrow escapes, about his brave actions, and about the people who both helped and cheated him along the way. In 1981, when this well-written, fast paced story was first published in Israel, it received the Mordechai Bernstein Children's Literature Award, and in 1982 the book appeared on the IBBY honor list for Israel. In the United States it received the Mildred L. Batchelder Award for 1984. In the same year the book appeared on the American Library Associate's Notable Books list, on the Booklist Editor's list, and on the Hornbook Fanfare list. Finally, the Association of Jewish Libraries named it the best book for older children.

205. Pellowski, Anne. <u>Betsy's Up and Down Year</u>. Illus. Wendy Watson. New York: Philomel, 1983. 160 p. Grades 3-6.

Betsy is in the fourth grade. Many unpleasant things are happening to her this year. She becomes aware of the sibling rivalry in the family. The baby bottle explodes when snow and water freeze in it and her mother refuses to buy her a pair of clogs although all the girls in her class have them. While visiting their cousin Vic's buffalo farm with her grandparents, Betsy falls off the fence and with one foot caught in the fence is threatened by a buffalo. Borrowing her sister's pair of clogs for a school play, Betsy not only loses one of them while going off the stage, but the other one flies off her foot into the crowd and lands on her friend, Joey's head. One of the most difficult things for Betsy, however, is her new consciousness of the wide spaces between her front teeth. After being teased about it by her schoolmate Jimmy, Betsy decides to smile with her mouth closed, or not smile at all. She is convinced that it is because of her awful looking teeth that she is not selected to wear the costume for the Beauty and the Beast show in the Steamboat Day Parade. When Mama finally decides to send her to an orthodontist, she looses her retainer twice through almost unbelievable incidents. Another big tragedy is the death of Grandpa, who dies of a heart attack. There are, of course more than enough "ups" to outweigh the "downs". There is much good will, cooperation, and contentment offered in an extended family. Best of all, Betsy realizes that living with a dozen different

personalities at home is preparing her for the adult
life and that some sibling rivalry can actually
strengthen her family ties. Chronologically the last in
the series of five books by Anne Pellowski, the story
portrays admirably and affectionately, the fullness of
life in a large Polish-American family from the time
they first settled in the United States in the 19th
century to the present.

206. Pellowski, Anne. First Farm in the Valley: Anna's
Story. Illus. Wendy Watson. New York: Philomel, 1982.
189 p. Grades 4-9.
     Written in a lively, easy flowing style, this title is
chronologically the first in a series of several books
tracing four generations of a Polish-American family.
The story deals with the childhood experiences of Anna,
the author's great aunt. Because their birthplace in
Poland was then under the strict control of the Prussian
government, which forced their schools and their
churches to use the German language, Anna's parents left
the country and immigrated to the United States. They
were the first people to settle in Latsch Valley,
Wisconsin. By 1870, when Anna was six years old, there
were thirteen other Polish families in the valley.
Since they all spoke Polish at home, the children did
not learn English until they started going to school.
Anna loved farm life and accepted the chores naturally.
They were as much a part of her daily family life as
eating and sleeping. The family's celebration of such
events as the Fourth of July, mother's name day, and
Christmas and Easter reflect the warmth, togetherness,
and pride in the values and traditions which this family
shared. The family also undergoes difficult times. The
school burns down, diphtheria strikes and kills many
young children, two tramps appear at the house wanting
food and money when Anna and her sister Mary are home
babysitting, and Anna and her brother narrowly escape
death when an incoming train nearly hits the bobsled
loaded with logs on which they are riding. Expressive
pen drawings, a pronunciation guide, and a family tree
accompany the perceptively told story.

207. Pellowski, Anne. Stairstep Farm: Anna Rose's Story.
Illus. Wendy Watson. New York: Philomel, 1981. 176 p.
Grades 4-8.
     Anna Rose belongs to a family of third generation Polish
immigrants. She is not quite six years old yet. More
than anything else she wants to go to school. She can
already read the entire second grade book. She
practices by reading aloud with her older sister Angie.
Sister Pelagia, the principal, is impressed, but decides
that she cannot make exceptions for Anna Rose; she will
have to abide by the rules. So Anna Rose stays at home
and helps Mama with the work or plays with her younger
sisters. Although the chores are hard work, there are
also occasions to have fun. Everyone pitches in when

the new baby sister arrives in January. Daddy plays
lively polkas on his harmonica and dances with the girls
until they are quite dizzy. In February all the
relatives gather as Grandma and Grandpa celebrate their
fifty-fourth wedding anniversary. When her parents are
away, Anna Rose's older brother Lawrence makes a panful
of delicious oatmeal cookies. They spice up their
feather stripping work with a feather monster game. The
closeness of the family is again felt when the Grandpa
and Grandma die. Troubles seem suddenly to abound.
Little Janie is bitten by a gander and falls from a
swinging vine into a deep ravine. Tornado winds blow
the cupola off the barn and flatten the ripening oats
and corn. Lawrence, the oldest leaves home for Tacoma,
Washington, where he has found a job. When the day for
Anna Rose to get ready for school finally comes, the
buggy on which they were riding overturns and the horses
gallop away in fright. Based on the author's own
childhood and written with effortless fluency, the story
is a well drawn portrayal of the hard but good and rich
life on the farm a generation ago.

208. Pellowski, Anne.   <u>Willow Wind Farm: Betsy's Story</u>.
Illus. Wendy Watson. New York: Philomel, 1981. 176 p.
Grades 3-7.
In 1967 Betsy Korb was seven years old. She was the
seventh of ten children. Her family lives in a big old
house on a farm in Wisconsin which her daddy's
grandfather had bought when he came from Germany. In
order to tell their place apart from other Korb farms
nearby, Kathy, Betsy's older sister, named it "Willow
Wind." They had willows growing along the edge of the
road, and it had always been windy on the ridge of the
hill. Kathy even registers the new name in the county
courthouse. In addition to German, Betsy's mother uses
Polish words every once in a while. She learned Polish
from her parents and her grandparents. Although Dad now
owns a tractor with various implements which he uses for
planting, weeding, and harvesting, Betsy, her only
brother Danny, and her eight sisters still have many
chores to do. Betsy helps milk the cows, goes out with
the others to pick berries, helps to feed the pigs,
assists in the haymaking, and cleans the house.
Belonging to a large caring family has some very special
advantages. There are grandpa and grandma, and uncles
and aunts who come and help with the major work. There
are games and unforgetable gatherings, reunions and
family celebrations. Games in the moonlight, stories of
the missing pills, Christmas play at grandma's, dad's
story about grandpa's shaking hands with a bear, the
children's funeral for a calf, and Aunt Anne's unique
Christmas gift, all are vividly and sensitively
described. The story is written with humor, tenderness,
and appreciation and accompanied by expressive black and
white drawings and a pronunciation guide.

209. Pellowski, Anne. <u>Winding Valley Farm: Annie's Story</u>.
Illus. Wendy Watson. New York: Philomel, 1982. 192 p.
Grades 4-8.
   The story of Annie Pelagia, the fourth of seven children
   of a Polish American family. The Pelagias were second
   generation Polish immigrants. The adults still spoke
   Polish among themselves; however, the children used
   English also. In 1908, when the story begins, Annie is
   six years old. Many important events take place between
   the spring when the reader first meets Annie and the
   summer of the following year. There are delightful
   ethnic and religious holidays and ceremonies, such as
   the blessing of the fields, a birthday celebration for
   the eighty year-old patriarch of the family, Christmas
   festivities, the family's observance of Lent, a church
   picnic, and the young men's wooing in front of a tavern
   on Sunday afternoon. There are times on the farm filled
   with fun and mischief. Annie gets involved in the boys'
   buggy race, she wins the newspaper puzzle contest, and
   she witnesses the bumblebee school pranks. There are of
   course difficult times and times of sorrow. Mama is
   ill, the new baby Matthew dies, and Annie constantly
   worries that her parents will sell the farm and move to
   town. She even loses the tip of her finger while her
   older brother prepares to butcher the chickens. Annie
   also learns lessons on how to be honest and responsible.
   She enjoys planting the garden, preparing the cabbage to
   make sauerkraut, and tending the lambs while the ewes
   are being shorn. Details concerning work on the farm,
   the implements used, as well as Polish family customs
   are accurate, both as to place and to time. Black and
   white drawings enliven the impressive picture of a warm,
   close-knit family in which the author's own mother plays
   the main role.

210. Rubin, Elizabeth. <u>The Curies and Radium</u>. Illus. Alan
Moyler. New York: Watts, 1961. 112 p. Grades 3-6.
   The story of the lives and achievements of this
   remarkable husband-and-wife team is told in a simple and
   sympathetic style. Highlighting Marie's childhood in
   Warsaw, the author emphasizes the fact that Manya
   Skladowska, as she was called in Polish, grew up in a
   difficult climate, politically. Parts of Poland were
   under control of foreign powers, Warsaw was under
   Russian rule, and Tsar Alexander was determined to crush
   the people's spirit of independence. General education
   suffered the most, but Manya's parents taught their
   children to value knowledge above everything else.
   Moreover, the Russian authorities forbade women to enter
   a university; therefore, Manya and her sister Bronya
   soon realized that they had to leave Poland in order to
   get a university education. Manya accepts a job as a
   governess in a distant province to help her sister with
   her expenses while she works toward a medical degree at
   Sorbonne in Paris. Finally, her own chance to study at
   Sorbonne comes in 1891, after Bronya marries a young

doctor and Manya has saved enough money for her own trip to Paris and for her tuition. Manya Sklodowska, now called Marie, does not have an easy life in Paris. The author very ably portrays her ascetic living, her complete devotion to study, her meeting with Pierre Curie, a professor of physics and chemistry, their marriage, and their most successful research work together. Their scientific discoveries, as well as the highest tributes they received, are accurately described. At the same time, the personal side of the Curies' lives is well enlightened. This highly stimulating narrative, replete with anecdotes and conversations, is further enhanced with handsome pen drawings and a detailed index.

211. Schloneger, Florence. <u>Sara's Trek</u>. Newton, KS: Faith and Life, 1981. 105 p. Grades 5-10.
A story of the suffering and endurance of the Mennonites during the Second World War. Trusting the Nazis more than the Russians, for the Russians had taken away their farms and divided them into collectives and had taken their men into concentration camps, the Russian Mennonites flee to Wulka, Poland. In January 1945, when the Russian army begins to advance southward, they begin their journey again. Like other typical refugees, the Friesen family put their belongings on a small wagon pulled by a scrawny horse, with Sara's brother Franz in the driver's seat and Papa, Mama, and her older sister Marga following on foot. In the confusion Sara and her friend Liese get separated from the family. Her trek, during which she experiences not only cold, fear, worry, hunger, and daring escapes, but also companionship and compassion, takes her to a children's home in Ansbach, Germany. She is reunited with her family in Hattorf, where Papa dies of tuberculosis. Finally, with the help of the Mennonite Central Committee, the family arrives by train in a German Refugee Camp, and in 1948 they are among those fortunate families who pass the medical test for a journey to Canada. Full of hope for a life without constant fear, Mama expresses her gratitude: "Truly God has been with us."

212. Seroff, Victor. <u>Frédéric Chopin</u>. New York: Macmillan, 1964. 118 p. Grades 6-10.
This most readable biography of the Polish composer Frédéric Chopin was written by a concert pianist who left his native Russia at the age of eighteen to live in Vienna, where he gained a thorough knowledge of Chopin while studying under a pupil of one of the composer's own students. Although the author covers much of the same ground as other Chopin biographers, Seroff places special emphasis on the composer's affection for his homeland. When Frédéric completed his studies at the Warsaw Conservatory at the age of twenty, he was already famous for his compositions of concertos, waltzes, mazurkas, and polonaises. His recitals were reviewed

favorably, and in 1830 he gave his first public concert
at the Warsaw national theater. As he prepared to leave
for Vienna during the same year, he was approached by a
group   of   young   people,   his   friends   from   the
conservatory, who pressed a small container of Polish
soil into his hands. In his life, and especially in his
works, Frédéric remained totally loyal to his homeland.
Some nineteen years later, when he was buried in Paris,
this handful of soil was placed over his coffin as a
symbol of his faithfulness to Poland. In this well
written biography the author gives justice to Chopin's
accomplishments. Moreover, he portrays Chopin as fully
human. Sympathetic insights into Frédéric's childhood,
life under the constant shadow of illness, and stories
of his love for Kostancya Gladkowska, Countess Delphine
Potocka, and the novelist George Sand are vividly and
realistically interlaced with accounts of his muscial
accomplishments. Historical information concerning the
period is also included to help the reader understand
and appreciate the complexity of Chopin's personality
and his extraordinary inspirations and achievements.
Good quality photographs and pencil sketches accompany
the biography.

213. Serraillier, Ian. Silver Sword. Illus. C. Walter
Hodges. New York: Macmillan, 1959. 187 p. Grades 5-10.
A novel about the Balick family living in Warsaw first
published in England in 1956. Based on facts, the book
describes the tragic events which take place at the
beginning of World War II. First, their house and all
their possessions are destroyed. Then the parents are
taken away by the Nazis. The father is sent to a
prison, from which he later escapes to Switzerland,
while his Swiss wife is exiled to a concentration camp.
Moments before their house is blown up, the three
children, Ruth, Edek and Bronia, escape over the
rooftops. Temporarily they make their home in a bombed
cellar in war-torn Warsaw and keep themselves alive by
searching for and smuggling scraps of food among the
ruins. While hiding, as well as on their hazardous
journey to Switzerland, where they hope to be reunited
with their parents, they are guided by thirteen-year-old
Ruth, the oldest of the three. She faces numerous
difficulties with love, courage, and determination. She
is a reassuring mother to little Bronia; she finds her
brother Edek, who is arrested, and takes care of another
orphan, little Jan, who joins them on their journey.
With the help of the Russians, British, Americans, and
even some Germans they finally reach Switzerland. In
the end, it is Jan who is instrumental in bringing the
family together with the help of a symbolic treasure --
a small silver sword. Written in a vivid, fast-moving
style, the novel has memorable characters and a
suspenseful plot. For its excellenc in literature the
book recieved The Boys' Club Award in 1960, the Spring
Book Festival Award in 1959, and a special commendation

from the English Carnegie Medal Committee in 1957.

214. Singer, Isaac Bashevis.   A Day of Pleasure: Stories of a Boy Growing Up in Warsaw. Trans. Channah Kleinerman-Goldstein and others. Illus. Roman Vishniac. New York: Farrar, Straus and Giroux, 1969. 227 p. Grades 5 and up.
    A collection of nineteen autobiographical stories depicting the first fourteen years of Singer's life before and during World War I. Fourteen of these stories have originally appeared in a book of Singer's memoirs, while five appear in this book for the first time. Each story is a masterpiece. In the part entitled "A Day of Pleasure," the author reminisces over his experience of indescribable joy when he, as a small boy, earns a whole ruble. He thinks that with so much money he can find pleasures everywhere and decides for once to indulge in all those wonderful things he has never had a chance to enjoy. He takes several droshky rides around Warsaw and buys candy and fruit. When he parts with his last groschen, however, he feels terribly guilty for gorging himself, for not giving anything to the poor, and for all the lying he has done to avoid suspicion. The collection offers a beautifully drawn picture of the time and the social conditions of Polish Jews; it also offers other insights into the hearts and minds of men, both into the good and evil among them. As portrayed, young Isaac Singer has an immensely inquisitive mind, a rich imagination, a good heart, a yearning for knowledge, and a keen sense of humor. Carefully selected, expressive photographs add greatly to the appeal and the deep meaning of the stories. The book received the National Book Award for 1970.

215. Singer, Isaac Bashevis.   Joseph and Koza, or the Sacrifice of the Vistula. Trans. author and Elizabeth Shub. Illus. Symeon Shimin. New York: Farrar, Straus and Giroux, 1970. 38 p. Grades 3-6.
    The masterfully illustrated story gives a vivid account of the most powerful Polish pagan tribe, Mozovia, and tells about their strong beliefs in warlocks, witches, and in other evil powers, and about their conversion to a belief in one God. To pacify the evil spirits of the river Vistula, the most beautiful maiden is sacrificed each year. As the tragic sacrificial ceremony for the chieftain's daughter Koza is underway, a wandering Jewish goldsmith by the name of Joseph appears. He proves to the pagan Polish tribe God's mighty powers and saves Koza from her death and the country from human sacrifices. A beautiful picture book in a large format with superb oversized line drawings.

216. Skurzynski, Gloria.   Manwolf. New York: Houghton Mifflin, Clarion, 1981. 177 p. Grades 7-12.
    A very sympathetic and touching novel set in the Middle Ages, the book describes the social setting of the times with extreme clarity: the educated nobility, the

landowners, and the superstitious and poor serfs. The
story begins as Pan Reinman, a nobleman who always keeps
his face covered with a leather mask, asks Danusha's
master if he can take her as a servant on his trip to
Vienna. He is overcome by her beauty, and makes love to
her, after which he is remorseful. Despite the fact
that she has fallen in love with him, he sends her back
to her master. She gives birth to a child who, like his
father, is afflicted with a skin disease. The serfs
abuse the child Adam and deride his mother, calling her
a devil-lover, and forcing her and the boy to seek
seclusion in a monastery. When Queen Jadwiga comes to
the monestary, the boy begs her to cure him. When she
sees his face she is so frightened that she faints.
Adam is put in prison for casting a spell on the queen.
After weeks of torture he is freed by a friend of Pan
Reinman and reunited for the first time with his father.
The story sweeps the reader away into the time of noble
knights and despised serfs. Their impoverished and
destitute state, along with the superstitiousness this
created, is admirably brought out by the author. An
epilogue explains Adam's disease, of which there are
only seventy recorded cases in history! A very touching
book.

217. Slobodkin, Florence and Louis Slobodkin. Sarah
Somebody. Illus. author. New York: Vanguard, 1969. 71 p.
Grades 3-5.
  Sarah's family lives in a small Polish-Jewish village
around the turn of the century. Since Mama is busy with
the housework and her six children, Grandma, who lives
half a mile down the road, comes for a visit almost
every day. She is ninety years old and has lived in
Poland her entire life. She remembers Poland in the
days when she was ruled by kings. She also remembers
wars and the Russian rule of Poland. The rulers,
however, do not make too much difference to her family,
because they have always been poor. Although their men
spent much of their time studying the holy books, the
women have had no opportunity for education. All of her
life Grandma wished she could read, and even now in her
old age she would at least like to know how to write her
own name. Sarah's opportunity to become somebody comes
when Miss Chesnov, who studied in Warsaw, returns to the
village and teaches a small group of girls to read and
write for only four gulden a month. When Sarah writes
Grandma's name on a piece of paper, the old lady's
lifelong wish seems to be fulfilled. This simply
written story is accompanied by delicate sepia
illustrations which deepen the reader's affection for
Sarah and her family.

218. Stiles, Martha Bennett. Darkness over the Land. New
York: Dial, 1966. 269 p. Grades 6-10.
  Mark thinks he has always been German. In the fall of
1939, he is nine years old and lives with the Elend

family in the suburb of München. He attends school, but
is not considered a good student. He does not remember
things from the past the way other students do, and he
frequently says the wrong things. His classmates, Adolf
and Gregor suggest that he never repeat in school what
he hears at home; they further advise him when he is
called on to only say what he has heard the teacher say.
Mark's world is frightening and confusing. His teachers
accuse Jews, Poles, and Catholics of atrocities against
Hitler's Germany. Mark wants to believe in the Leader
and cannot wait to become old enough to join the Nazi
youth group. On the other hand, during the next five
years, he witnesses the brutality of the Third Reich and
becomes somewhat involved in the underground student
movement. The end of the war brings a shocking
discovery for Mark. Through an uncle, Mr. Przybylowicz
from Stanislawow, Poland, Mark finds out that he is a
Pole by birth and that his parents were killed by German
soldiers the first day of the war. His mother died
protecting him from enemy fire, but German medics picked
him up and took him to the seminary nearby. With the
help of Gottfried Elend, a seminarian, little Mark
became Mark Elend. His uncle wants to take him to
America, but by now Mark is old enough to think
independently, to understand the intricacies of the
human heart, and to make his own decisions. An
engrossing story with a vivid portrayal of the
indescribable misery of World War II.

219. Suhl, Yuri. On the Other Side of the Gate. New York:
Franklin Watts, 1975. 149 p. Grades 7-9.
This World War II story set in the Jewish Warsaw Ghetto,
is centered around a young couple, Hershel and Lena
Bregman, who are forced from their home by the Nazis
into the walled section of Warsaw. Like half a million
other Jews in confinement they experience hunger,
disease, and the constant fear of being deported to gas
chambers or to forced labor camps. Unlike most others,
Hershel and Lena are faced with another grave problem.
Knowing full well that pregnancies are against ghetto
regulations, they are expecting a child. Not only do
they have to conceal the birth of the baby boy to the
people around them, with the exception of a few trusted
relatives and friends, but they also have to keep the
baby David in hiding, which proves to be an extremely
trying task. For the young parents the most difficult
situation arises when their name is announced as having
been selected for transportation to another
concentration camp. They decide that their infant son
must be sent secretly out of the ghetto. Because of the
deadly danger present to anyone who shelters Jews in the
city, it is almost impossible to find a compassionate
individual willing to accept the infant. A Catholic
family is finally persuaded to take part in the effort
to rescue little David and to adopt him. The story
conveys most effectively the unique atmosphere of the

tragic historic period, as well as the irrepressibility
of the human will to survive.

220. Sullivan, George.   Pope John Paul II: The People's
Pope. New York: Walker, 1984. 137 p. Grades 5-9.
   The life and achievements of Pope John Paul II are
described in this biography. In two chapters the author
reviews his childhood in Wadowice, his youthful years
during World War II in Cracow, his work and his
underground activities, his secret meetings with other
Polish youths, his decision to enter the seminary, and
his ordination to the priesthood. The following three
chapters chronicle Karol Wojtyla's work as a parish
priest, a bishop, and as a cardinal. The rest of the
book, which is about one half of the biography,
discusses his accomplishments as pope and head of the
Roman Catholic Church. Included are good accounts of
John Paul's world travels, his visits to Mexico, Poland,
Turkey, Brazil, France, West Germany, Switzerland,
Spain, to ten African nations, to the countries in South
America and Central America, and to the United States.
His visitations of his native Poland, keeping alive the
ideals of personal freedom and bringing new hope and a
spiritual lift to his countrymen, is described with
special warmth and perception. Of particular interest
to non-Catholics and those not familiar with Catholicism
is the pertinent background information included in the
book, concerning such topics as the belief of Catholics
in the infallibility of the pope in regard to faith and
morals, his authority in governing the church, his
Vatican governmental responsibilities, the papal
election procedures, the turmoil within the Church, the
meaning of religious freedom, and the position of the
American Catholic Church. The political and historical
situation in Poland during the period of Karol Wojtyla's
childhood is also reviewed. The well-written biography
is illustrated with over two dozen photographs; sources,
however, are not given.

221. Szambelan-Strevinski, Christine. Dark Hour of Noon.
New York: Lippincott, 1982. 215 p. Grades 5-10.
   The story of twelve-year-old Trina, who, inspired by a
fairy tale about the sleeping knights of Poland, forms a
group named The Gray Knights, which goes about raising
resistence to the Nazis who occupy their city. The
group begins by murdering an officer responsible for the
death of a neighborhood family, and continues by
derailing and destroying a train, bombing staph cars,
and poisoning officers. Trina is also used by her
father as a messenger for the Polish Resistance. As
such, she finds herself in Warsaw on August 7, 1944,
when at the same time the Poles there rise in an attempt
to free their city. The role she and her friends play
in the revolt is graphically depicted. Overall, the
book is slightly too sensational to be believable. In
any case, the outrages of war which might lead a group

of twelve-year-olds to acts of murder and destruction
are not adequately treated by the author. The book
could give young readers a very incorrect impression of
what is and is not justifiable. These considerations
aside, the book is extremely fast-paced and
action-packed. It moves very quickly and is easy to
read.

222. Thomas, Henry. Copernicus. New York: Messner, 1960.
192 p. Grades 5-8.
An inspirational biography of the versatile sixteenth
century Polish astronomer, Nicholas Copernicus, who, in
order to help mankind, decides early in his life to
study both medicine and religion. Educated at Polish
and Italian universities, Copernicus practices medicine,
serves as a church official, successfully defends the
Allenstein castle against the Teutonic Knights, and
serves on the Council of German States. His greatest
interest, however, is astronomy. His fascination with
the mystery of the world leads him to the study of the
universe and the movements of the heavenly bodies. In
spite of living in the dreaded shadow of the
Inquisition, he persists with his research and
establishes his heliocentric notion of the universe.
His thoughts are completely revolutionary for a world
that, for thirteen centuries believed the Ptolemaic
theory, which maintains that the heavenly bodies move
around a motionless earth. It takes Copernicus thirty
dedicated years of study and experimentation, with only
the crudest intruments, to assemble and describe his
theories in a book which is published fourteen years
after its completion. Just a few hours before his
death, the book is delivered to him. The author of the
biography brings to life in a simple language and a
vivid style the political conditions, the social
atmosphere, and especially the prevalent way of thinking
during the turbulent years in which Copernicus lived.

223. Veglahn, Nancy. Dance of the Planets: The Universe
of Nicolaus Copernicus. Illus. George Ulrich. New York:
Coward, McCann and Geoghegan, 1979. 63 p. Grades 4-8.
Although the teaching of ancient writers - that the
earth moves around the sun, instead of vice versa - is
known to a few fifteenth century scientists, most
astronomers of the period accept the theory of Ptolemy,
a second century geographer, who believed that the earth
was the center of the universe and had no motion. At
the University of Cracow where young Nicolaus and his
brother Andreas study from 1491 to 1493, it is not
prudent to challenge the Ptolemaic plan of the universe.
Nicolaus Copernicus, however, has an inquiring mind and
cannot accept scientific facts based on tradition alone.
The author presents Copernicus' enthusiasm for
investigation and inquiry at the University of Cracow
and later at the Universities of Bologna and Padua
logically, and does so in a lively, readable style. He

ably summarizes the development of the Copernicus'
theories of the universe, his deeply felt need to convey
this knowledge to others, and his decision to write down
his findings. A glossary of scientific terms, a table
of identification of scientists and philosophers of the
period which are mentioned in the biography, as well as
a selected bibliography of sources are appended. Neatly
drawn black and white illustrations are completely
suitable for the convincingly written biography of the
great astronomer.

224. Waterton, Betty. <u>Petranella</u>. Illus. Ann Blades. New
York: Vanguard Press, 1980. N. pag. Grades 1-3.
When Petranella's father reads a letter from Uncle Gus
in America to the family, telling them that he acquired
a homestead somewhere in Wisconsin and inviting them to
join him, Petranella is delighted. She would gladly
leave the large city, which is perpetually blanketed
with a cloud of gray smoke which chokes the trees and
whithers the flowers growing in the window boxes. On a
homestead she could have a swing and chickens and a
garden with flowers. She almost changes her mind,
however, when she finds out that Grandma, because of her
age, will not be able to go with them to the new land.
With joy and gratitude, Petranella accepts from her a
small muslin bag filled with flower seeds to plant
around their new home. The journey by ship across the
ocean proves to be most difficult as are the hours of
waiting until they reach land, where her father has to
fill out a multitude of forms and papers. The hardest
trial for Petranella, however, is the loss of the small
bag of seeds she had been carrying in her pinafore.
Amidst the confusion, when the oxcart filled with their
belongings breaks its shaft and tips, Petranella
momentarily forgets her bag of seeds and cannot locate
them later. Petranella's sadness turns into joy several
weeks after their arrival to their homestead. She
discovers by surprise that the forgotten seeds have
sprouted beside the country road in Wisconsin. This
touching, deftly told story of an immigrant family is
enhanced with equally artful, full-page watercolors.

225. Wheeler, Opal. <u>Frédéric Chopin, Son of Poland: Early
Years</u>. Illus. Christine Price. New York: Dutton, 1948.
156 p. Grades 3-6.
A lively fictional account of the nineteenth century
composer's early life. The book traces various episodes
in Chopin's early childhood: his birth to his Polish
mother and French-born father, a schoolmaster in the
village of Zelazowa Wola, the coming of several
musicians on horseback to play Polish folksongs to the
little infant, his christening ceremony in the old stone
church of Brochau, and his family's move to Warsaw and
their warm family relationships. Brought to life are
other important events of young Frédéric's life: his
early fascination with music, his ability to play

waltzes, mazurkas, and minuets at the age of four, his piano lessons with Adalbert Zwyny, and the boy's own compositions at the age of six. The biography describes Frédéric's years of study at the Lyceum and at the Warsaw Conservatory, and it concludes with his successful concert in Vienna at the age of nineteen. The book contains excerpts from some of Chopin's compositions, preludes, waltzes and mazurkas. The story conveys the political and social atmosphere of the period and Frédéric's love for simple things in nature and for the music of the Polish country folk. Chopin's musical genius shines through all the important events of his early life. Black and white spirited drawings are faithful to the atmosphere of the story.

226. Wheeler, Opal. Frédéric Chopin, Son of Poland: Later Years. Illus. Christine Price. New York: Dutton, 1949. 155 p. Grades 3-6.
A continuation of Frédéric Chopin's biography. It begins with his farewell from Warsaw, his friends, his parents, and his three sisters before he goes to Vienna to give concerts and to have his compositions published. Somewhat disappointed for not being accepted there as warmly as when he gave his first concert Chopin decides to leave Vienna. Because of the attempted but unsuccessful Polish uprising against the Russians, Warsaw is placed under strict military rule. Therefore, Chopin is unable to return to his home city, but goes to Paris instead. With the exception of several trips to England, Scotland, and the island of Majorca, he remains in France until his death. The French, especially Romantic poets, novelists, artists, and musicians, adore his genius and graciousness. Chopin's premature death at the age of 39 due to tuberculosis is mourned by everyone. The bibliography describes most perceptively Chopin's relationship with the novelist Baroness Dudevant, as well as his relationship with his family, friends, his audiences, and his homeland. His musical compositions are well appraised. His ballads, scherzos, nocturnes, polonaises, and waltzes, in which Chopin expresses his longing for his homeland, are represented as masterpieces of poetic beauty. In them it appears as though the nation weeps and chants for those who fell in the wars for freedom. Samples of the master's music are given.

227. Wojciechowska, Maia. Till the Break of Day. New York: Harcourt Brace Jovanovich, 1972. 156 p. Grades 6-12.
The story of the author's twelfth to fifteenth years her experiences during World War II in Poland, her family's escape to France, where Maia and her older brother Zbyczek feel compelled to daringly and ingeniously resist the Nazis, her family's flight to Lisbon and London, and finally their embarkation for the United States. In spite of the author's justifiable aversion

to the Nazi's atrocities, she is not blind to the goodness of the other German people. Maia speaks of a young German soldier who begs her forgiveness for what his countrymen have done and risks his life in helping her family to escape from Nazi occupied France. To Maia the young man looks like and has the soul of a poet, and she would have fallen madly in love with him were he not a German. The story contains many psychologically sound insights into the heart and mind of an adolescent girl who is growing to maturity during the war and amidst much confusion. In addition, it is an excellent portrayal of the political atmosphere of the period, beginning with the German invasion of Poland in 1939 and ending three years later when Maia writes a blistering letter to Roosevelt and Churchill for delaying the invasion of Europe.

228. Wolfe, Rinna. The Singing Pope: The Story of Pope John Paul II. New York: Seabury. 1980. 120 p. Grades 4-8.
A vivid account of the life of Pope John Paul II, beginning with his early years in Wadowice and Krakow before World War II. In addition to highlighting the main events of his childhood, the author describes the political, social, and economic conditions in Poland during the early and middle decades of the twentieth century. Especially well presented are young Karol's student years just before and during the Nazi occupation. His will to continue his education secretly by attending underground university classes and his determination to keep Polish pride alive by establishing the underground acting group called Rhapsody Theater are perceptively described. Also outlined are Karol's training for the priesthood, his work in the factory, his constant battles with the Communist authorities when he becomes a priest, his creative and productive dedication to the Polish youth and Polish workers, his appointment as bishop and archbishop of Krakow and a few years later as cardinal, and of course his election to the papacy. The biography ends with the events of the 1980's and with a short, but effective appraisal of his life. In addition to these main events, the author tells a story of Karol Wojtyla as a man, his love for humanity, his interests in acting, sports, and music, and his unsurpassed courage in carrying out his mission as a world religious leader. A pronunciation guide, an explanation of his shield design, and photographs of him and those associated with him accompany the biography.

229. Wuorio, Eva-Lis. Code: Polonaise. New York: Holt Rinehart and Winston, 1971. 198 p. Grades 6-12.
Set in 1941, in the second year of the Nazi occupation of Poland, this story is about a band of orphan children, Jan, Wanda, Stas, Powel and their friends living in Warsaw. In order to stay alive the children seek shelter in half-ruined buildings, changing places

from time to time. The children struggle desperately to survive. They use all of their resourcefulness in their search for food and the most necessary clothing. In addition, they collaborate with the Polish underground by printing and distributing a dissident newspaper for the Polish children. Although facing the constant danger of being apprehended, imprisoned and executed, they neither waver in their friendship nor in their determination to serve their patriotic cause. When the youngest member of the gang, three-year-old Powel, becomes dangerously ill, Jan and Wanda escape across the border and flee through Hungary and Yugoslavia to England for help. Sustained by the deeply moving, nationalistic music of Frederic Chopin, exemplified in the Polonaise Militaire, a symbol of Polish resistance and of the Pole's hope for peace, but outlawed in Poland by the German government, the children eventually reach their destination, and the story ends on a positive note. An absorbing, moving story based on the author's memoirs, her interviews with refugees during the Second World War, and on Polish government documents.

230. Ziemian,   Joseph.   The Cigarette Sellers of Three Crosses Square. Trans. Janina David.   New York: Avon, 1977.   140 p. Grades 6 and up.
A stirring story about a band of Jewish children who, through their own ingenuity, courage, and care for each other,   and   with   the   help   of   various   Polish   people, survive the Holocaust of World War II.   Prior to the German occupation, the Warsaw Jewish community was the largest   of   its   kind   in   Europe.   In   November   1940 hundreds of thousands of Jews are segregated from the Polish population by being placed in a ghetto surrounded by walls and barbed wire.   When hunger begins to increase, food has to be smuggled in from the Polish or Aryan side of Warsaw.   This is done by a band of children who risk their lives daily by stealing across the barbed wires.   After most of the inhabitants of the ghetto are sent into extermination camps, some of these children remain in the non-Jewish section of the city. They stay alive by begging, singing Polish songs in trams and on street corners, by occasional labor, and by selling cigarettes on the Three Crosses Square.   Forced to conceal their true identity, they sleep in the damp cellars of various ruined buildings, in cemetery tombs, under bridges, and occasionally in the attics of Poles. This powerful, moving story is written on the basis of personal notes of the author's involvement in the Jewish Resistance Movement.   The book was first published in 1970 by the Lerner Publication Company. Photographs of children on the streets of Warsaw, as well as those of them in later years, add reality to the story and faith in the strength of human spirit.

231. Zyskind, Sara. Stolen Years. Trans. Margarit Inbar. Minneapolis: Lerner, 1981. 289 p. Grades 6-9.

A superbly written account of the author's experiences between the years 1939 and 1945. A Jew in Poland, Sara becomes terrified of the Nazis after their invasion. She and her family are immediately reduced to poverty in the fenced-off Jewish slum in Lodz. The story dramatically builds as this eleven-year-old girl is forced to continually undergo more strenuous trials. Her mother dies soon after the occupation. She is forced to earn her own living and later to support her father, who suffers from malnutrition. When he finally passes away, she is driven to attempt running out of the ghetto in hopes that a Nazi guardsman will shoot her. Throughout, she is supported by her family and by close friends at work. Inspired by the difficulties she faced in feeding her dying father from her own miniscule rations, she suggests that each of her co-workers donate a spoonful of soup to enable the dying mother of her friend to live. After her father's death, she is deported to a "country-work camp," which is actually the death camp Auschwitz. Per chance, she sees a friend and manages to sneak into her line and out of the one headed for the gas chambers. She is sent to a work camp where she and her four "sisters" work for 12 hours a day under constant terror and supervision. She is finally freed by the Red Army, but upon returning home realizes that there is no one left - all have perished. In an epilogue, the author then summarizes her post-war flight to Israel. The book is a most vivid and powerful description of the terror and ruthlessness unleashed by the Nazis against the Polish Jews. The author's superb writing does justice to a most fascinating topic, and one which needs to be studied and remembered.

OTHER FICTION

232. Adler, David A. <u>The Children of Chelm</u>. Illus. Arthur Friedman. New York: Bonim, 1972. 32 p. Grades K-3.
The three preposterous stories in this book are taking place in Chelm, Poland, a town where Jews have been suffering, but not from any kind of persecution. Rather, it is their own foolishness which haunts them. In Chelm, children have to bathe in the river, and they hate it. The city council members argue for seven days and seven nights and finally decide that children do not have to take their baths one at a time. They can take "a whole year's worth all at once...fifty short baths, one after another." The only time the town of Chelm is beautiful is on the day it snows. Since the snow covers their muddy, torn-up roads, they do not need to be repaired. In order not to ruin the smooth, white blanket, the children must not walk to and from school. The wise men of Chelm carry them back and forth on their shoulders. When the people of Chelm decide to build a school, they go to the top of the mountain and lug the heavy stones down, four people to one stone. Watching

their heavy labor, a little girl suggests that it would be easier to roll them down. Admitting that she is right, the men of Chelm carry the stones back to the top of the mountain, which proves to be hard work. But rolling them back down is very easy! Written in a simple, conversational style and illustrated with black and white drawings emphasizing the exaggerations and foolishness of the people of Chelm.

233. Banks, Lynne Reid. The Writing on the Wall. New York: Harper and Row, 1981. 244 p. Grades 6-12.
Narrated by sixteen year old Tracy, this is the captivating story of a girl growing up and finding out the hard way who her true friends really are. Tracy lives with her brothers and sisters in England. Their parents are immigrants. Her mother is Irish, her father Polish. During World War II he served in the Polish resistance movement in Ander's army. Now he owns a Polish delicatessen shop, selling all kinds of sausages and breads. In Tracy's opinion he has a brain, but no ear for languages. Sometimes she is a bit ashamed of the way he speaks, especially in front of her friends. It is no wonder they tease her and say that she is "up the Pole." Dad is much older than Mom. Tracy is aware of other differences between them, but it is only after some nearly tragic incidents during her sixteenth year that she fully realizes how dissimilar they actually are. When Tracy is caught smuggling drugs, Dad hurries to her, holds her in his arms, and listens to her story. In a remarkably gentle way he makes her realize the cause of her problem and misery. Most of all, he believes what she tells him. Mom, on the other hand, thinks only in terms of the family's disgrace. It is no wonder that Tracy picks up Dad's ways when dealing with other people, and not only his ways, but even his accent!

234. Chase, Mary Ellen. A Journey to Boston. New York: Norton, 1965. 114 p. Grades 5-8.
With competency and affection the author presents a story of Polish immigrants living along the Connecticut River in Western Massachusetts in a valley claimed by them to be one of the brightest, sunniest lands in all the world. Based on fact, the book is a portrayal of their hard work, their aspirations, their veneration of the old country, and their love for America. While describing their simple, colorful lives on the farms, the author contrasts this with a story concerning a tragic event during October of 1963, when two farmers who were good friends picked up a ten-year old boy, Ramon, on the way from Boston where they sold their produce, and of Ramon's death in a traffic accident. The touching story of the homeless boy, a grandson of Polish immigrants, which includes insights into the lives of his separated parents gives the book an element of somber realism within the picturesque ethnic setting.

Written in an easy flowing style with sentiments of
admiration for the Polish-Americans who, with their
strong personalities, vitality and hard work, add
brightness to the Connecticut Valley.

235. De Angeli, Marguerite. Up the Hill. Illus. author.
New York: Doubleday, 1942. 88 p. Grades 4-6.
The book offers a sympathetic look into the life of a
Polish-American family in a small Pennsylvania mining
town. The pleasant narrative centers around the little
girl Aniela and her older brother, Tadek, and portrays
the rich Polish culture and its delightful customs.
These give a tone to Aniela' and Tadek's simple, yet
colorful life, for the richness of the lof they feel for
each other, and for their love of the country of their
ancestors, as well as for America. Tadek wants to
become an artist, but it is a long climb upward. He
works in the mine where he drives Rossie the mine mule,
and in the evenings, when he is home, he draws and
paints. Although his mother wants him to become an
artist more than anything else, his father feels that
there is no money in painting, and that he should
continue working in the mines. Events, like Aniela's
Christmas wish, Tadek's painting of a mural in the
church, as well as Mama's willingness to work in the
factory in order to support Tadek while at school, bring
him closer to the realization of his dreams. Drawings
in color and black and white and double-page end papers
are very effective in supporting the story's theme and
its warm atmosphere. A pronunciation guide to the
Polish terms and names is appended.

236. Eichelberger, Rosa. Bronko. Illus. Hedley Rainnie.
New York: Morrow, 1955. 192 p. Grades 4-8.
After years of loneliness, fear, and hunger in a
concentration camp within war-torn Poland, Bronko is
finally on his way to being reunited with his mother,
whom he has not seen since the bombing of Warsaw over
eight years ago. He is twelve years old when he boards
the ship carrying displaced persons to New York.
Although he looks forward to meeting his mother and to
life in a free country, he also experiences fear,
confusion, and uncertainty. When he sees the Statue of
Liberty in the distance, however, he becomes reassured.
His heart fills with warmth, joy, and a new zest for
life. The bulk of the story deals with Bronko's
adjustment to the perplexities of urban life in New
York, his initial misconceptions about the severity of
school regulations and the role of the police, and his
longing to become part of a youthful gang. Bronko's
victories over his fears and the friendships he makes
with the neighboring boys, Rory, Winnie and even with
notorious Sizzle, a member of the Space Pilots gang, are
perceptively described. An insightful portrayal of the
adjustment a young person must make in America, the
story is told with much adventure, suspense, and

appreciation for the ideals of democracy.

237.   Estes, Eleanor.   The Hundred Dresses.   Illus. Louis
Slobodkin. New York: Harcourt, Brace and World, 1944.   80
p. Grades 3-6.
    Wanda Petronski, the daughter of a Polish immigrant,
does not have any friends. She comes to school alone
and goes home alone. This does not mean that the girls
in her class do not talk to her. They wait for her
after school and tease her because she lives with her
father and brother up on Boggins Heights, which to them
is a place only good enough for picking wild flowers;
they tease her because of her strange name and because
she always wears the same faded blue dress to school,
although she claims to have a hundred more at home.
Wanda tells them that they are made of silk and velvet
of all colors and that they are all lined up in her
closet. And they actually are! With her special
talents, Wanda has designed a hundred dresses for a
special exhibit in school. To the surprise of her
classmates she wins first prize, but is not there to
receive it. Her father has written a note to the
teacher explaining that they have moved to a city where
there are plenty of people with funny names. This
simple, perceptively written story reveals, without
moralizing, the prejudices immigrants often face. A
moving story, most effective impressionistic pictures,
and an attractive layout made this a Newbery Honor Book
in 1944.

238. Glasgow, Aline.   The Pair of Shoes.   Illus. Symeon
Shimin. New York: Dial, 1971. 48 p. Grades 3-6.
    To be without shoes is the hardest thing for Jacob, the
eldest   in   the   family.   In   the   opinion   of   the
thirteen-year-old boy approaching his Bar Mitzvah, a man
is not a man unless he walks in shoes. Shoes, however,
are hard to come by, and the only pair in the family is
shared by all three children. During a family crisis in
which his sister Dubbie badly twists her ankle while
wearing the shoes, Jacob realizes the true meaning of
manhood when it becomes clear to him that the virtues of
courage, self-sacrifice, and concern for others are
worth more than owning one's own pair of shoes.
Shimin's distinguished drawings highlight the simply
written, deeply moving story of a poor Jewish family in
late nineteenth century Poland.

239. Hautzig, Esther.   A Gift for Mama.   Illus. Donna
Diamond. New York: Viking, 1981. 56 p. Grades 3-6.
    When Mama was growing up, all the birthday and Hanukkah
presents were handmade at home, never purchased in the
store. Now she wants her daughter Sara to continue the
family tradition. Papa and Mama just love all the gifts
Sara has made so far for their birthdays, anniversaries,
and Hanukkahs. For this Mother's Day, too, Sara is
expected to make a gift. But this time Sara decides not

to follow the family custom. She is determined to buy
Mama a gift. She knows exactly what she will get her.
It is a pair of black satin slippers, trimmed with blue
leather, that would perfectly complement the robe Papa
gave her for her last birthday. Sara sees the beautiful
slippers in the window of the Bata shoe store, but she
does not know how she will get the nine zlotys necessary
to purchase them. She decides to earn the money by
mending socks, fixing runners in stockings, making elbow
patches, and turning shirt collars for the university
students who are friends of her Aunt Margola. When
Mother's Day arrives, Sara's gift astonishes everyone,
especially Mama. In her eyes it is just as good to earn
money to buy a gift as it is to make a gift. A deftly
written story, the book portrays a loving Jewish family
living in Vilno during the 1930's and is complemented
with gently drawn black and white illustrations.

240. Kelly, Eric P.   The Christmas Nightingale: Three
Christmas Stories from Poland. Illus. Marguerite De Angeli.
New York: Macmillan, 1932. 73 p. Grades 4-8.
    The title story is about an incident which takes place
in the cottage of a charcoal burner on Christmas Eve
sometime during the days of King Kasimir. The humble
cottage stands in the very center of the huge Forest of
Lubel. As the charcoal burner sits around the open
fireplace with his wife, and their two sons and a
daughter, he hears a faint knock at the door. When the
father opens it there stands a poor lad about five or
six years old nearly frozen stiff. "The Christ Child,"
the youngest, Elzbieta, thinks. The boy cannot speak;
his lips move but no sound comes from them. He is
warmly accepted into the family. Although he appears to
be of gentle birth, for several years his identity
cannot be established. Before he learns how to speak
again, however, he begins to sing the songs of the
birds, which he can reproduce almost to perfection.
Most of all, he delights the charcoal burner's family
with the sweet, powerful music of the nightingale.
Years later on another Christmas Eve, it is this song, a
gentle burst of melody, that brings the lad back home
into the embrace of his own mother. The story "In Clean
Hay" tells about the traditional Christmas puppet show
taking place in Krakow; "Anetka's Carol" is about a
little girl who regains her sight on Christmas Eve.
Black and white illustrations complement the old,
idyllic tone of the stories.

241. Kelly, Eric P. In Clean Hay. Illus. Maud and Miska
Petersham. New York: Macmillan, 1953. 31 p. Grades 3-6.
    A delightful story about four children who, on Christmas
Eve, go to the city of Krakow to present their puppet
show. Antek the oldest, who is fifteen, his younger
brothers Stefan and Christopher, and their ten-year-old
sister Anusia have built a little theater on folding
legs.   Their mother has made dresses for the wooden

figurines in all kinds of colors. Producing a puppet
show is the children's chance of making a little money
for their books, tools, and clothes. Coming to the
marketplace, Anusia sings the Christmas carol, while
Christopher plays the violin, Antek makes the puppets
dance, and Stefan helps wherever needed. Anticipating
requests for several performances, they are suddenly
stopped after their first show by a dignitary wearing a
huge star. The manner in which the children give the
Christmas puppet show in the large Falcon Hall, and with
which they experience the true spirit of Christmas in
the home of a neighbor, makes this a most appealing
Christmas story. It would be difficult to imagine
drawings that would interpret the tale better than do
Petershams' authentic illustrations in gentle colors.

242. Krauze,   Andrzej.   What's So Special About Today.
Illus. author. New York: Lothrop, Lee and Shepard Books,
1984. N. pag. Grades K-2.
    Krauze's first children's book, originally published
outside his native Poland, offers an affectionate look
into a most unusual preparation for a child's birthday
party. With earnestness and joyous anticipation, all
the animals are made ready. T.T. Tortoise starts on his
journey before dawn, Granny Owl spends all night baking
a cake, Freddy Frog presses his suit, and Sarah Stork
polishes her long beak. Reggie Rabbit is out in the
garden picking his loveliest rose, and Twiggy Piggy
soaks in the bath longer than usual. Colonel Cockerel
pins all his medals on his bright green jacket, and
Abner Turkey decides to share his best cider with his
relatives and friends. Toby Dog refrains from fighting
with Caroline Cat, and Ellie Elephant and her son
rehearse their musical selections until they sound
perfectly harmonious. Written in brief questions, which
appear at the bottom of each amusingly funny
illustration, this is an exceedingly attractive book and
is an excellent choice for reading aloud to
preschoolers.

243. Lenski,   Lois.   We Live in the North: Short Stories.
Illus. author. Philadelphia, PA: Lippincott, 1965. 152 p.
Grades K-3.
    "Auto-Worker's Son," the first of three stories in this
collection, tells about a Polish family living several
decades ago in Hamtramck, an automobile manufacturing
center in Detroit. The houses in this all-Polish
neighborhood are painted white, the grass around their
houses is kept green, and beautiful flowers bloom in
their gardens. The simple narrative is centered around
a young boy, Joseph, whose dad works two miles from
their house at the Dodge auto plant. Scenes like the
creation of a cemetery for the animals, named "Peaceful
Paradise," where the children bury a dead bird, a
squirrel's tail, a turtle, and a goldfish, or the
family's reaction to Uncle Ed's Americanization of his

name are described with sensitivity and true
understanding. The black and white drawings capture the
warmth of the relationships in the closely-knit family,
the family's reverence for the Polish customs, and their
respect for America.

244. Lownsberry, Eloise. <u>Marta the Doll</u>. Illus. Marya
Werten. New York: Longmans, Green, 1946. 118 p. Grades
3-5.
On her nameday Hanka's heart-wish comes true. Her older
sister Marysia brings her a doll from the market, a big
doll with fair hair and blue eyes that open and shut.
From that moment on the home life on a farm in Poland,
the rich colorful festivities and customs, and the
friendships and relationships between people are
centered around Hanka and her doll. To Hanka, Marta the
Doll is just like any other member of the family. She
is very much alive and seems to be interested in Hanka's
activities at home, in the barn, in the fields, and in
the woods. As Hanka takes the doll to her favorite
places and shares with her her thoughts and feelings,
the simple traditional life in a Polish mountainous
village is revealed. Background information, notable
events and stories are skillfully woven into the warmly
human narrative. Delicately drawn illustrations with
Polish folkloric motifs are faithful to the text and to
the atmosphere of life on a Polish farm just before
World War II.

245. Mark, Michael. <u>Toba</u>. Illus. Neil Waldman.
Scarsdale, NY: Bradbury, 1984. 105 p. Grades 3-6.
Nine illustrated vignettes centered around a perceptive
ten-year-old girl named Toba and around her family
living in a Jewish village in Poland at the beginning of
the twentieth century. Toba is very fond of her dear
Papa, Reb Cohen, who was at one time the finest
dressmaker in Lenchintz, but who now, due to his
blindness, makes only shawls. Toba threads his needles
and helps Momma to sell the shawls at the Litvak fair on
every first Sunday during the summer months. On the
first day of the summer of her eleventh year, when Toba
is finally allowed to go alone to the stream in the
nearby forest, she finds a bird's egg in the moist
grass. Searching in vain for its mother, Toba brings
the precious egg home, places it into a wooden bowl,
which she sets in the warmest place in the house or in a
sunny spot outside. Never doubting that the beautiful
speckled egg is alive, Toba is bitterly disapponted when
Mr. Horowitz, the man who knows more about animals and
plants than anyone else in Poland, tells her that the
egg is diseased and that regardless of her keeping it
warm and safe, she would never bring it to life. The
book describes other events in Toba's life. If there is
any event, however, that Toba loves above all others,
including her birthday and Chanukah, it is the
eight-hour train ride to Kracow for their family

gathering. The sounds the engine makes, its roaring and
whistling, its screech before its stop, its violent
jerks when it starts again and of course, the distinct
aroma of the food Momma brings along, consisting of
meats, cabbage, bread, and fruits, are all unforgettable
experiences. Although a bit forced, the stories offer
sympathetic insight into the life of a young girl and
her relationships with her family.

246. Mayne, William. <u>The Mouse and the Egg</u>. Illus.
Krystyna Turska. New York: Greenwillow, 1980. N. pag.
Grades K-3.
A long-tailed mouse curls his tail, straightens it, ties
a knot in it, ties a second knot and a third, unties it,
and curls it around while Grandfather complains to
Grandmother about his monotonous breakfast - a brown
egg. Although Grandmother boils it one morning, fries
it the next, scrambles it the next, and whisks it with
milk the following day, Grandfather is tired of them
all. Believing that they should always be thankful for
what they have, Grandmother is dismayed and sends
Grandfather to the speckled hen to ask her to lay a
different sort of egg, which she promptly does. The
golden egg, however, can do nothing to satisfy
Grandfather's hunger. To the starving man a brown egg
with an ordinary shell, with the white under it and
the yellow yolk in the middle, appears to be a wonderful
treat again. He is sorry for complaining about his food
and gives thanks to Grandmother and to the Lord for
giving him the brown egg, warm and fresh with his tea
every morning. The narrative is enriched with
delightful borders containing Polish folklore motifs and
embellished with colorful, gently humorous, expressive
illustrations.

247. Porazinska, Janina. <u>In Voytus' Little House</u>. Illus.
Stanislaw Bobinski. Trans. Lucia Merecka Borski. New York:
Roy, 1944. 47 p. Grades 2-4.
Although grown-ups do not notice anything unusual in the
house, the boy Voytus sees and hears many of the
household objects coming to life. They fight and
rejoice, they hide from him, and they dance and scurry
around the house and the garden. His sister Yagusia's
rag doll keeps hiding herself in the wrong places. Once
she is found under a pile of brushwood quietly talking
to a rooster; then she slips noiselessly under the
table, whispering to the spiders. Just when little
Yagusia needs her sleep the most, the two rockers on the
yellow cradle quarrel, each wanting to rock in a
different way. Although the fireplace poker has only
one leg, and the broom has more than three hundred, they
make a most merry couple, together dancing a polka and
sweeping around the floor in circles. The good-hearted
corner argues with the bench next to the warm, clay
stove about which of them is more useful in the house.
An ugly stain on the wooden floor wants to sit there

forever. It refuses to budge when swept by a broom or a
duster, but it wails and runs away from a boiler, hot
out of the oven. Warmth and gaiety permeate the short
imaginary selections which are illustrated with simply
drawn humorous drawings.

248. Porazinska, Janina. My Village.   Illus. Stanislaw
Bobinski. Trans. Lucia Merecka Borski. New York: Roy,
1944. 46 p. Grades 2-4.
    This book about the author's village, reflecting the
peaceful beauty of life in the country, consists of a
series of vignettes written in a poetic, light style and
of softly drawn illustrations. There are rows of
cottages in the village with thatched roofs and painted
doors, surrounded by narrow gardens filled with
sunflowers and mallows. The path to the author's home
is sweet; it is lined with gayly colored wild flowers.
The road from her home, however, is bitter, for it is
overgrown with hawthorns and briars. In the early
morning, the sun comes timidly through the green foliage
and in the evening, in its sombre colored cloak, calls
to the moon to guard over the village in its absence.
Little Dorothy runs across the meadow to catch the
sinking sun in her bag. When she is resting in her
cradle, the old man Sleep murmurs softly, wishing her
silence and peace. A scarecrow stands by a cherry tree,
stretching his arms and catching the young sparrows, the
little thieves. Dark smoke whirls out of the chimney
with glad news of barley, pork, and sausage for dinner.
An old beggar passing through the village is rewarded by
kind-hearted people with pennies, bread, and butter.
While he is carrying his dinner, however, the sun warms
his bags, steals his butter, eats it up, and the old man
must go from house to house begging in the village.

249. Simon, Solomon. The Wise Men of Helm and Their Merry
Tales. Trans. Ben Bengal and David Simon. Illus. Lilian
Fischel. New York: Behrman, 1945. 135 p. Grades 5 and
up.
    Fourteen of the merriest and most unusual tales about
the Helmites, a Jewish people, who live hidden from the
world, deep in the forests of Poland. The world which
knows them considers them fools, but the people of Helm
believe themselves to be the wisest of all. They cannot
help it if foolish things are constantly happening to
them. Gimpel, the wisest man in all of Helm, believes
that the summer days are longer because they expand on
account of the heat and that they contract in the winter
because of the cold. Tired of carrying their grain to a
neighboring town to be milled, the Helmites decide that
Helm should have its own watermill. On Gimpel's
suggestion, they build it on the highest mountain peak
in order that it may be admired by people far and wide.
Completed, it is a sight to behold, but it does not
move, and the Helmites are convinced that the millstones
do not turn because the climate in Helm is not right for

the watermill.   After a series of other wonderfully
humorous misadventures, the Helmites decide to go into
the world and spread the wisdom of their cherished
heritage.   Interspersed throughout these stories are
bits of universal truths.   The illustrations in a soft
green color admirably reflect the characters and the
spirit of the wise men of Helm.

250. Singer, Isaac Bashevis.   Naftali the Storyteller and
His Horse, Sus and Other Stories.   Trans. Isaac B. Singer,
Joseph Singer, and Ruth Sohachner Finkel.   Illus. Margot
Zemach.   New York: Farrar, Straus and Giroux, 1976.   129 p.
Grades 4-8.
     Of these eight stories, two, "A Hanukkah Eve in Warsaw"
and "Growing Up," are autobiographical.   Three stories
deal with the hilarious fools of Chelm.   They include
"The Fools of Chelm and the Stupid Carp," in which a
carp is punished by drowning for slapping the community
leader across the face; "Lemel and Tzipa" which deals
with two fools who are frequently swindled by pranksters
and storekeepers, but who possess more love than all the
learned men in Chelm; and the story of Dalfunka, a
suburb community where rich men live forever.   Three of
the stories contain Jewish and Polish folktale elements.
The most touching is the title story about Naftali the
storyteller and his horse Sus.   As a young boy Naftali
loves stories and books and wants to become a bookseller
in spite of his parents' objections that there is no
money in the trade.   As a young man, Naftali builds
himself a wagon and loads it with the storybooks he has
collected over the years.   With his horse Sus, he rides
from town to town selling or giving away the books and
telling stories, because he who tells stories does not
live momentarily but as long as his stories of the world
and of human folly are kept alive.   These tales,
containing much humor, unbelievable exaggerations, joy,
wonder, and a lot of wisdom, are enlivened by expressive
line drawings.

251. Singer, Isaac Bashevis.   Stories for Children.   New
York: Farrar, Straus, Giroux, 1984.   338 p.   Grades 3-8.
     A superb collection of thirty-six stories, complete with
an author's introduction and a masterfully written
epilogue.   In it Singer discusses the conditions which
are present when he created his stories.   Focusing on a
theme in each story, he writes both passionately and
with a belief that he is the only one who can tell that
particular story.   He emphasizes that the writer must
base his roots firmly in his environment.   The more
solidly he is rooted in a specific area, the more he is
understood, not only on a national, but also on an
international level.   The stories gathered in this book
certainly reflect his theory.   His characters are
totally Jewish, and the little towns and settlements
where the stories take place are Jewish communities.
His stories are nonetheless translated into all of the

major languages of the world and are enjoyed by children and adults worldwide. Completely ignoring the idea that literature should convey a message, Singer's stories are so powerful, witty, and imaginative that they completely involve the reader as he ponders the underlying bits of wisdom and eternal truth. Some of the stories brought together in this volume have already appeared in other collections and in single editions. More than half of them, however, have not been published previously in book form. Although without illustrations, the book's format, with large print and wide margins, is most attractive. This time, the master storyteller has decided to speak to young readers the way he was spoken to when a child - in words only.

Romania

252. Arnott, Kathleen. Animal Folk Tales Around the World.
Illus. Bernadette Watts. New York: Walck, 1971. 252 p.
Grades 3-6.
    A handsomely illustrated collection of thirty-nine
    folktales from all parts of the world including
    Czechoslovakia,   Russia,   Hungary,   and   Romania.
    Typically, animals are often the heroes. "The Snake
    Prince" is a Romanian folktale. It involves a poor
    elderly couple who are very unhappy because they had no
    children. In his futile search for a son, the old man
    remembers his wife's words that a bird, a beast, or a
    fish would be better than nothing. He decides to take
    home a small snake that suddenly appears at his feet.
    Because of the man's affectionate care for him, the
    snake begins to speak and begs the old man to go to the
    King and ask for his daughter's hand in marriage. As
    expected, the King, who wants to have some fun with the
    old man, asks him to perform two impossible tasks before
    promising his daughter to the old man's "son." While
    the old man and the old woman sleep, the snake-son
    creates a huge field of ripe millet from a great forest.
    The following night he constructs a golden bridge
    extending from the palace to the old couple's cottage.
    Finally, after the princess and the snake prince are
    married and enter their magnificent house, which appears
    magically at the side of the golden bridge, the snake
    changes into a handsome young prince.

253. Manning-Sanders, Ruth.   A Book of Devils and Demons.
Illus. Robin Jacques. New York: Dutton, 1970. 126 p.
Grades 3-6.
    In the preface to the twelve stories dealing with devils
    and demons, the author indicates the ethnic origins of
    the tales.   Most of them originated in European
    countries. "Jack and the Hell Gate" and "Ironhead" are
    Hungarian tales, "The Little Red Mannikin" is from the

Carpathian region of Russia. "The Demon's Daughter"
originated in Transylvania, the largest region of
Romania, which is separated from the rest of Romania by
the Carpathian mountains and the Transylvanian Alps.
The demon's daughter is actually a beautiful girl who
was stolen from out of the world when she was a baby.
She learns the secret of her master's seemingly
invincible powers and is able to free a young prince
from out of the demon's clutches. In his great
distress, and having been tricked by the demon, the
prince's father, the king, had promised the evil one his
only son at the time of his birth. On his twenty-first
birthday the prince was seized by the demon and dragged
into his kingdom beyond the world. As soon as the
pretty girl caught a glimpse of the young man, strong,
handsome, and good-hearted, she fell in love with him.
In her attempt to save him, she risks the wrath of her
"father" by stealing his magic whip. With it she is
able to perform the seemingly impossible tasks which the
demon has requested of the prince. In their desperate
flight from the demon, who in his rage pursues them, the
girl changes herself and the young man five times into
animal forms or inanimate objects until the happy couple
finally reaches the end of the demon's kingdom and the
palace of the king, the prince's home. There is one
exquisite pen and ink drawing for each story.

254. Manning-Sanders, Ruth.   A Book of Dragons.   Illus.
Robin Jacques. New York: Dutton, 1965.   128 p.   Grades 4
and up.
There are kindly dragons, there are proud dragons, and
there are bad and savage dragons in the fourteen
folktales gathered from around the world. The
Macedonian story "Janni," the Slav story "The Prince
with the Golden Hand," and the Romanian story "Stan
Bolovan," all tell about evil dragons that have to be
either slain or outwitted. With the help of a magician,
Stan Bolovan and his wife beget over a hundred children,
but in their view not one too many. In his search for
food, Stan encounters a dragon, who every evening robs a
shepherd of his lambs and ewes. Stan is really
terrified at the mere thought of a dragon, but the
picture of his hundred children clamouring for food
makes him promise to the shepherd that in exchange for
some animals, he will get rid of the giant thief.
Boasting of his strength, he convinces the dragon that
he can crack his skull, throw a giant club into the
moon, dig up a spring, and eliminate trees from the
entire forest. In order to get rid of his threatening
company, the frightened dragon delivers sacks and sacks
of golden ducots to Bolovan's house. Rushing away from
the shouting of the hundred hungry children, the dragon
vows to himself that he will never come near Stan's
house or the shepherd's sheepfold again. One fine line
drawing per story highlights the vibrancy and humor of
each tale.

255. Manning-Sanders, Ruth. A Book of Giants. Illus. Robin Jacques. New York: Dutton, 1963. 125 p. Grades 3-6.

As the author explains in the preface to the collection, these stories about giants come from many countries, including Georgia, Russia, and Romania. "Prince Loaf," a Romanian tale, tells about a poor shepherd boy who delivers a giant from his agony by pulling out a pitchfork which was stuck in the underside of his two yard long foot. To reward the boy the giant gives him a belt to wear, a belt which makes him invisible. In addition, the giant invites him to a giant's dance in the forest and to the giant's banquet in the great golden hall down in the hole in the earth. Here the shepherd helps himself to a crusty loaf of bread, which later proves to have magical powers. Everytime he bites into it a golden coin appears in his mouth, but the loaf remains whole. The invisible belt and the giants' loaf completely change the kind shepherd's life. They even win him a princess as a wife, a princess whom he never stops loving, and therefore they both live happily ever after. The tales are handsomely illustrated with black and white drawings.

256. Manning-Sanders, Ruth. A Book of Sorcerers and Spells. Illus. Robin Jacques. New York: Dutton, 1974. 125 p. Grades 3-6.

"Sorcerer Kaldoon" is one of the twelve folktales included in this collection. It is an absorbing Transylvanian story. It tells of the great magical powers possessed by the sorcerer Kaldoon who showers a poor farmer and his wife with untold riches in order to obtain their only daughter, lovely Anna, in marriage. When the unwilling girl tries to escape the dreadful situation, three young men, sons of Anna's nurse, come to the rescue. Through their love, courage, and resourcefulness, they outmaneuver the evil sorcerer. In his storming rage over loosing Anna, Kaldoon bursts into flames and is completely consumed by fire, save a handful of grey ash. Two stories "Go I Know Not Whither and Fetch I Know Not What" and "The Three Swans" are Russian stories. They are both intriguing tales containing a full measure of magic, sorceries, and spells. Expressive black and white pen drawings appropriately portray the eeriness of the themes.

257. Protter, Erik. A Childrens' Treasury of Folk and Fairy Tales. Illus. Bertall et al. New York: Beaufort, 1982. 211 p. Grades 4-10.

An anthology of European folk and fairy tales, fables, and poems edited and adapted by Erik Protter and illustrated with black and white drawings by artists native to the countries from which the tales originated. They are arranged according to broad geographical regions. The section entitled "From Lithuania, Russia, Rumania, Bohemia, and Slovakia" contains ten stories.

"The Czar's General and the Clever Peasant" is a
Lithuanian folktale in which a witty humble peasant
outsmarts a haughty general. "The Czar's Frog Daughter"
is a Russian story from the Afanasiev collection. "The
Tale of the Pig" is from Caucasia. "The Peasant and the
Waterman" and "How One Should Carve a Goose" are
versions of two of Tolstoy's humorous stories. Three
stories are from Czechoslovakia: "Kristina and the
Devil" and "The Greedy Taylor" are Bohemian, while
"Radonejd" is a Slovak story. "Ivan and His Knapsack"
is a Romanian legend in which Ivan, a good old soldier,
has encounters with the Lord, St. Peter, Death, and with
the Devil. His adventures take him to heaven and to
hell, and he is guilty of a series of pranks at the
expense of Father Death. A valuable collection for
storytellers.

258. Purnell, Idella and John M. Weatherwax. Why the Bee
Is Busy and Other Rumanian Fairy Tales Told to Little Marcu
by Baba Maritza. Illus. Helen Smith. New York: Macmillan,
1930. 134 p. Grades 3-5.
Little Marcu lives in the country in a house with a high
peaked, red tile roof. As in the homes of other
peasants a square clay oven with benches against its two
walls lies in the corner of the largest room. It is by
this oven during the winter, and under a large willow
tree in front of their house during the summer evenings,
that the grandmother, Baba Maritza, tells her
grandchildren fairy tales. Through her stories, the
mysteries of nature are revealed to the children. They
explain why the tortoise has a round back, how the
sparrow hawk won his freedom, why the lark wears a crown
and why it flies up and down, why the bee is busy and
the spider sullen, why the woodpecker has a long nose,
why everyone loves nightingales, why the cuckoo never
sings in winter, why the hornets live in houses made of
old cardboard, and how an insignificant little gnat
helps the gypsy man Cuza to be on time at his wedding.
Brightly colored full-page illustrations as well as
delicate pen drawings and silhouttes add a joyous
Romanian spirit to the stories.

259. Rudolph, Marguerita.   The Magic Egg and Other Folk-
stories of Rumania. Illus. Wallace Tripp. Boston: Little,
Brown, 1971. 71 p. Grades 2-5.
Six amusing animal tales are here retold in a clear,
  direct style. The cover story, "The Magic Egg," is
partly a cumulative tale in which a magic hen's egg, a
lobster, a cat, a mouse, a rooster, and a goat outsmart
a fox and help a kindly old couple out of their poverty.
Four other stories: "The Tufty Hen," "The Proud Goat,"
"The Partridge, the Fox and the Hound," and "How the Fox
and the Hedgehog became Friends" contain encounters
between benevolent, but clever animals and their eternal
enemy, the cunning fox. The only story lacking a fox as
one of the characters is the "Brave Rabbit and the Bug

with Golden Wings." In this story the trickster is an old big bear just awakening from his winter sleep. A small bug who has been befriended by a conceited young rabbit saves the rabbit's life from the gluttonous bear. The numerous pen-and-ink illustrations with soft green and brown watercolor add expressive details to the characters of the stories.

260. Ure, Jean. <u>Rumanian Folk Tales</u>. Illus. Charles Mozley. New York: Watts, 1961. 194 p. Grades 4-10.
Originally published in England in 1960 under the title <u>Pacala and Tandala and Other Rumanian Folk-Tales</u>,   the book is a compilation of thirty-five stories. They were told originally by the individuals listed in "The Story-Tellers" section at the end of the book. These stories were recorded in Romanian at the end of the nineteenth and at the beginning of the twentieth century as told by the common people. According to the author's notes the compilation is a faithful translation and not a retelling of the original stories. Even more so than the folk literature of other nations, these stories reflect the divided and stormy history of Romania. From the third to the twelfth century, waves of invaders from the north and east overran the Roman province of Dacia, the ancient territory of today's Romania. Some of the Slavs, who knew much about farming settled in villages among the Romanians. Folk tales about boyars like "Poor Man's Clever Daughter," "The Boyar and the Gypsy," and others reflect the life of the people during this period.   The fifty year reign of Moldavia's national hero Stephen the Great, who bravely fought the Turks on the side of the peasants during the second half of the fifteenth century, is remembered in the "Old Man's Tale of Prince Stephan." After the Romanians were converted to Christianity in the nineth century, some folktales were given Christian characters.   "A Story of Three Brothers" tells about three orphan brothers who were taught how to live by the good Lord and Saint Peter as they walked on the earth. Other tales teach lessons of simple wisdom. In "The Story of an Egg" Neculai finds out that his wife Maria cannot keep a secret. In the "Proper Way to Lay at the Table" a simple peasant teaches a conceited soldier humility and proper table manners. Black and white pen-and-ink drawings add an amusingly humorous touch.

TRADITIONAL LITERATURE: SINGLE EDITIONS

261. <u>The Enchanted Pig: Rumanian Fairy Tale</u>. Illus. Jacques Tardi. Mankato, Minnesota: Creative Education, 1984. N. pag. Grades 3-5.
In a book hidden in a room, which the three daughters of the king enter against the wishes of their father, it is written that the eldest will marry a prince from the East, the second a prince from the West, and the

youngest a pig from the North. As the prophecy is
fulfilled for her older sisters, the youngest Princess
grows progressively more concerned each day. Then, in
time, it happens. An enormous pig from the North
appears at the palace and asks the King for the hand of
his youngest daughter. Noticing that the behavior of
this pig is unlike that of other pigs, the King advises
his daughter to submit to her fate, which she obediently
does. Arriving at his dwelling after their marriage,
the Princess soon notices that, although he remains a
pig during the day, her husband changes into a handsome
prince during the night. Trying to keep her husband in
human form, the princess follows the advice of a wicked
witch and fastens a piece of thread tightly around his
foot while he is asleep. He awakes horrified, and she
soon realizes what she has done. Just three days before
the spell was to be broken and he was to return to his
princely human form, he is now forced to continue to
suffer because of her impulsive act. He disappears over
nine seas and nine continents, and in her three year
search for him, she wears out three pairs of iron shoes
and blunts a steel staff. Completely worn out with
weariness and hunger, she finally finds him, and, in
great joy, they both return to their kingdom. There is
little grace in the writing style of the narrative, and
the book is marred by gaudy cartoon-like illustrations.

262. Ross, Tony. <u>The Enchanted Pig: An Old Rumanian Tale</u>.
Illus. author. New York: Bedrick, 1983. (Distributed by
Harper and Row.) N. pag. Grades K-3.
While the eldest daughter of a king marries the Lord of
the East, and the next marries the Lord of the West, the
youngest sister has to marry a pig who claims to be the
Lord of the North. On the wedding day the pig changes
into a handsome prince. No wonder the little princess
falls in love with him and is very happy. As soon as
the morning comes, however, her husband turns into a pig
again! Acting on the instructions of a magical bird,
the following night, the princess ties a cord to his
feet and tries to hold on to him. As she pulls the cord
a bit too tight, the pig awakes with a roar and runs
away squealing that he will not be found until she wears
out three pairs of iron boots in search of him. Aided
by the magic bird, the princess looks for her husband on
the moon, questions the North Wind about him, and asks
the Sun King about his whereabouts. After a year, when
the soles of her third pair of iron boots are completely
gone, she returns to earth and finds the pig in a high
tower in a strange land. She has to build a ladder to
be able to reach him. In her love, the little princess
does not hesitate to cut off one of her own fingers to
make the last rung on the ladder. As soon as she kisses
her pig, the spell is broken, and the pig turns into the
most handsome prince in the land. Richly illustrated in
deep watercolors.

263. Van Woerkom, Dorothy. <u>Alexandra the Rock-Eater: An</u>
<u>Old Rumanian Tale Retold</u>. Illus. Rosekrans Hoffman. New
York: Knopf, 1978. N. pag. Grades 1-5.
    When Igor and his wife Alexandra wish for dozens and
    dozens of children, they receive a hundred of them.
    They love them all, but the children soon eat all their
    turnips, all their honey, all their fruit, and drink
    their milk until their only cow is dry. Alexandra
    decides that she must go out into the world to find more
    food. In exchange for some of his animals, the spunky
    woman promises a shepherd to rid him of a young dragon
    who is snatching his sheep and cows. Alexandra outwits
    the dragon by making him believe that she can squeeze
    buttermilk from stones, put out the light of the moon,
    dig up the river, and remove trees from the whole
    forest. Clever Alexandra even makes him carry home the
    sacks of gold which are given to her by the young dragon
    and his mother. Told in a lively humorous style, the
    story is illustrated with colorful, amusing paintings.

          HISTORICAL FICTION - BIOGRAPHY - AUTOBIOGRAPHY

264. Burchard, S.H. <u>Nadia Comaneci</u>. Sport Stars Series.
New York: Harcourt Brace Jovanovich, 1977. 64 p. Grades
2-5.
    The daughter of an automobile mechanic and a hospital
    nurse, Nadia lived with her parents and her younger
    brother Adrian in a small modern town located in the
    foothills of the Carpathian Mountains. Athletic
    programs were an important part of children's education
    when Nadia attended school. Her talents and love of
    gymnastics were discovered by the coaches of a special
    sport high school when Nadia was still in kindergarten.
    Nadia began her intensive training with a group of the
    best women gymnasts from Romania. At the age of seven
    she was the youngest girl to participate in the Romanian
    National Championships. Because of her talents,
    courage, and seriousness, her training team soon
    included a choreographer, a pianist, a doctor, and a
    masseur. By the time she was eleven years old, Nadia
    won the 1973 National Championship and the Tournament of
    Friendship in Moscow. At the age of fourteen she became
    the youngest champion of Europe. Nadia was not quite
    fifteen when she participated in the Olympics in
    Montreal, Canada in 1976. She was the first Olympic
    gymnast ever to receive a perfect score. Nadia returned
    to her exuberant countrymen with three gold medals, one
    bronze medal, and seven perfect scores. A large-print,
    simply written biography, the book is accompanied by
    numerous good quality photographs. It should be
    especially useful for sport lovers with average and
    below average reading ability.

265. Ileana, Princess of Romania. <u>I Live Again</u>. New York:
Rinehart, 1951. 374 p. Grades 7 and up.

Ileana, the youngest daughter of King Ferdinand, and Queen Marie of Romania, tells a touching story of her life, from the time she was a child before World War I, through the dark and stormy days of World War II, to the beginning of her new life in the United States. As she stresses in her notes, the autobiography is her personal story. She never intended it to be a political or historical work. Convinced that the struggle for freedom is one of the most important issues in the world, and passionately devoted to her mother country and to its centuries-old struggle for independence, Princess Ileana describes her life as typical of life during a period of heightened national stress and misery. Although she gives a superb account of the historical events which she personally witnessed and explains the facts necessary to set the framework for her reminiscences, the strength of the work lies in her deeply human story, her devotion to her parents and family, her strong sense of duty, her deep faith, her concern for those in need, her ability to see issues fairly, without resentment or hatred, and her strong, poignant fight for survival. During the war, pregnant with her sixth child, she drives the other five children eight hundred miles through Romania, Hungary, and Austria. Exiled from her people in 1948, she finally settles in the United States, after short stops in several European countries and Argentina. Selling her precious, jeweled diadem, a gift from her mother, the Queen, in order to pay her debts and to bring her children from Argentina, she bravely begins a new life in a New England town, confident that her positive attitude and the absolute faith which had sustained her in the past will be her strength in the future.

266. Kluger, Ruth and Peggy Mann. _The Secret Ship_. Garden City, New York: Doubleday, 1978. 136 p. Grades 4-8.
This story is adapted from an episode taken from _The Last Escape: The Launching of the Largest Secret Rescue Movement of All Time_, which was written by Peggy Mann on the basis of taped interviews with Ruth Kluger, as well as others, and published in 1973. _The Secret Ship_ is an emotional story about Ruth Kluger's role in the illegal rescue of European Jews on the ship "Hilda," which was intended to sail from the icebound port of Balchik, Romania to Palestine. Ruth Kluger was born in Romania, moved to Palestine at the age of nineteen, and returned to Romania five years later as the only female member of the Mossad, a secret organization established to move Jews from the Nazi-occupied countries. Balchik, a village port on the Black Sea where the ship Hilda, with over seven hundred men and women aboard, waited, was far away from Bucharest, where Ruth Kluger was staying during the winter of 1939. In order to aid the endangered ship, Ruth had to go to the village which was completely cut off from the rest of the country, especially during winter. Half frozen, Ruth traveled in

by an old car to Danube, east on the river ferry, and
finally by horse and sleigh on a single lane road, full
of snow and ice. The Secret Ship is a fast moving,
thoughtful story of Ruth Kluger's heroic efforts to save
human lives. It is filled with suspenseful incidents
and enough historical and geographical inserts to
provide a good understanding of the tragic events which
occurred during World War II.

267. Miller, Elizabeth Cleveland. Young Trajan.   Illus.
Maud and Miska Petersham.   Garden City, New Jersey:
Doubleday, Doran, 1931. 232 p. Grades 6-9.
Frosina, a young Romanian girl, lives with her family at
the south of the Carpathian Mountains in the valley of
the Prahova River. The oldest of four children, Frosina
is sent to the school at Breasa to learn new designs in
weaving and embroidery, so that she may be able to help
her   impoverished   parents   with   earnings   from   her
handiworks. The young girl is unhappy with her parents'
decision. She is fond of her sisters, Margarita and
Maria, and loves her baby brother Josif. She does not
want to leave her home in the beautiful valley, with the
whitewashed cottages where she knew all her neighbors.
Slowly, with the help of other girls her age at the
Scoala   Industriala,   she   manages   to   get   over   her
homesickness, and gradually begins to enjoy every aspect
of her new life. She learns complicated sewing and rug
weaving techniques, makes many new friendships, and
enjoys new ways of recreation, especially dancing "hora"
to the sound of gypsy fiddlers. When Frosina meets
Trajan, a handsome, clever, courageous young man from
Breasa, she becomes involved in his work, in the
struggle for peasant rights against the injustices of
landowners. With the personable story of Frosina, her
friendship with Trajan, and their falling in love, the
novel offers an impressive picture of the gloomy
economic condition of the Romanian peasants before World
War II and their first efforts to revolt. The book also
gives a colorful sketch of Romanian folk customs and
traditions. This is a well-written, perceptive story
against an interesting historical background.

268. Peck, Anne Merriman and Enid Johnson. Young Americans
from Many Lands.   Illus. Anne Merriman Peck.   Chicago:
Whitman, 1935. 273 p. Grades 3-6.
The intent of the nine stories presented in this
collection is to show the variety of childrens' lives
that existed in the United States prior to World War II.
Due to the preservation of native languages and original
customs by various national groups, children living in
ethnic communities shared in the colorful heritage of
their parents while they participated in the American
way of life.   The story "Gypsy Nura" relates the
experiences of a nine-year-old Romanian Gypsy girl and
those of her family and friends. As they did in the old
world, her family travels from place to place, singing,

dancing, playing their fiddles and drums, and showing their skillful bear Binko in country fairs and circuses. Binko dances, scuffles around on a pair of roller skates to the sound of tambourines, and wrestles with his master. Sitting in a tent, wearing a bright red dress and a necklace of gold coins, Nura's mother tells fortunes to the young and old. Before the winter arrives, the family rents a store in Chicago, where mother sets up a place by the large window to tell fortunes and to sell medicinal herbs. To make some money, Nura and her brother, Liubo, play music and dance in the nearby Romanian cafe. They even go to school. But when the warm weather comes, the gypsy family hits the road again. The story "Jan and Marenka, Young Czechs" is a lively account of the colorful, warm life of Czech family living in a Czech neighborhood in the United States. Even the school Jan and Marenka attends offers courses in the Czech language and in the geography and history of their homeland. The stories in this collection are appropriately illustrated in black and white as well as in color.

269. Seuberlich, Hertha. <u>Annuzza: A Girl of Romania</u>. Trans. Stella Humphries. Illus. Gerhard Pallasch. New York: Rand McNally, 1962. 198 p. Grades 5-10.
First published in German, this novel written in the first person by Annuzza, a sixteen-year-old sympathetic, intelligent girl, who lives with her family in a Romanian village in the foothills of the Carpathian mountains before World War II. The story begins with the memorable events in her eleventh year and tells of her struggles to grow up over the next five years. Annuzza is proud of her home in the country; she enjoys participating in the old, rich traditions of the villagers. Most of all, she loves the large maize field where she is able to hide and read or daydream. In her house Annuzza is not allowed to study. She is destined to become a farmer's wife someday. Studying is considered a waste of time; it infuriates her parents. Because of Annuzza's insistence, and with the help of her teacher, her talents are discovered, and it is decided that she is to go to town to study. After four years of doing what she always wanted, of living a life imbedded in study, of establishing new friendships and of experiencing the joys and disappointments of new relationships, Annuzza must make another decision. As she longs for more education, she struggles with the thought of returning home, to the country, where she could become a teacher in the village school. The novel presents an excellent portrait of Romanian village life and the unique character of the Romanian peasant. The treatment of Annuzza's problems and of her relationships is realistic, and the bits of wisdom imparted from Drago, the mountain shepherd, Father Stanescu, the village priest, and her teacher, Mr. Marignu, are gems - simple and deeply true. The map of Romania and

the   black-and-white   drawings   are   an   appropriate
accompaniment to a very good story. The book was given
the Lewis Carrol Shelf Award in its year.

270. Winlow,   Clara   Vostrovsky.   Our Little Roumanian
Cousin.   Illus. Charles E. Meister.   The Little Cousin
Series.   Boston: Page, 1917. 113 p. Grades 3-6.
The boy Jonitza lives with his family in a comfortable
house in the city of Galati, a port on the lower part of
the Danube River in the southern province of Moldavia.
Somewhat below the hill on which their house is
situated, Jonitza can see the lower part of town with
its business buildings, mills and gigantic warehouses
for grain, which is exported from Romania on ships along
the Danube River. In their free time Jonitza and his
friends make trips to the nearby marsh where they amuse
themselves by trying to recognize a variety of ducks
living there. They also visit the lower part of town,
where groups of young peasants in their gayly
embroidered national costumes dance their sacred Pyrrhic
Dance, a dance that came to Romania from its Roman
predecessors. Through a month long trip that Jonitza
takes with his mother to the farm in the foothills of
the Carpathian Mountains, much of the colorful life of
the Romanian country folk, as well as highlights from
Romanian history, are brought to life. In a pleasant,
storytelling style, the primitive peasant houses with
their turf-covered roofs, some with flowers painted on
their walls to let others know that a maiden lives
there, the preparation of simple meals, like "mamaliga,"
a cold corn meal mush, the celebrations of various
holidays, especially mystery-filled St. George's Day or
the Witch's Sabbath as it was called, the friendship
Jonitza establishes with his country "cousins," and the
stories with which these young people amused themselves
are depicted. Told in a simple, informal style, and
illustrated   with   several   high   quality   sepia
illustrations.

Yugoslavia

TRADITIONAL LITERATURE: COLLECTIONS

271. Berlić-Mažuranić, Ivana. <u>Croatian Tales of Long Ago</u>.
Trans. F.S. Copeland. Illus. Vladimir Kirin. London:
Allen, 1924. 259 p. Grades 4-8.
   Four fairy tales, each consisting of several chapters
written in a simple fashion, but nonetheless with great
skill and a sense for the dramatic and fantastic. The
original Slav names are translated into English so as to
convey a suitable impression. The main characters in
the story "How Quest Sought the Truth" are the
grandfather Witting, his three grandsons Bluster,
Careful, and Quest, and the supernatural beings, All
Rosy, a source of light pictured as a beautiful youth,
Rampogusto, the ruler of evil forces in the world, and a
host of nasty goblins under his authority. Through
briskly-moving episodes the story clearly brings out the
themes of goodness, reverence for old age, ways of
finding the truth, the importance of listening to the
instincts of one's heart, and a belief in a final reward
for a virtuous life. The other three stories tell of
the interactions of humans with such beings as the
Dawn-Maiden, who sails the seas in the early mornings in
her boat of gold; the mighty Sea King, who reigns in the
depths of the waters; the beautiful Sea-Maidens, half
woman and half fish; Reygach, a simple giant, the
Vataress Fairies, the enchanted snakes; and various home
spirits that live around and haunt the hearths of
peoples houses. Handsomely printed and illustrated with
splendidly composed impressionistic paintings, the book
is a rare, old treasure.

272. Ćurčija-Prodanović, Nada. <u>Heroes of Serbia: Folk
<u>Ballads</u>. Illus. Dušan Ristić. New York: Walck, 1964. 178
p. Grades 5 and up.
   Four epic cycles of ballads first collected by the
internationally known nineteenth century Serbian
folkloric scholar Vuk Karadžić. Created by anonymous

poets and sung by bards to the accompaniment of the
"gusle," these ballads kept the Serbian spirit for
freedom alive during the gloomy centuries of Turkish
despotism. Retold in prose, they still sing of the
glory and greatness as well as of the decline of the
Serbian kingdom, its tragic defeat at the Field of
Kossovo, of the legendary hero, Kralyevich Marko, of the
Serbian knights and outlaws, and of their century-long
struggle against the Turks. Through their tragic
elements and through their depth and eloquence, the
ballads can be compared favorably with the most famous
tragedies of world literature. The greatest European
romantic poets, such as Goethe and Merimee and folk
artists of the highest repute, such as the Brothers
Grimm, translated some of these ballads into German and
French. Distinguished illustrations and ornaments
resemble the strong, beautiful fresco paintings on the
walls of old Serbian architecture. An author's note and
a glossary of Serbian terms are appended.

273. Ćurčija-Prodanović, Nada. **Yugoslav Folk-Tales**.
Illus. Joan Kiddell-Monroe. New York: Walck, 1960. 210 p.
Grades 4 and up.
　　Twenty-nine amusing Serbian tales, fables, and humorous
vignettes based primarily on folklore originally
collected by Vuk Stefanović Karadžić and Jaša
Prodanović. The stories offer a delightful blend of
unforced humor, silliness, irony, gentleness, sadness,
and above all, bits of truth. The stories contain
animal characters, such as a cock, who with his friends,
the fox, the wolf, and the bees under his wings,
outsmarts the Tsar himself. There is a dog that
outmaneuvers a wolf, and a talking colt that saves a
young boy from his cruel stepmother. Other characters
include wise and foolish tzars, kings and queens, old
women and young maidens, beautiful princesses and
handsome princes, poor villagers, cowherds and shepherds, gypsies, travelers and soldiers, wise men and
fools, even saints, like Saint Sava, the patron of
Serbs, and the devil himself. There are enchanting
fairies; there is a frog-wife, a swan-girl and magic
objects, such as a magic ring that brings a poor soldier
the Tsar's daughter for his wife, and a vine which gives
a pail of wine every hour. Illustrations in color as
well as in black-and-white are perfect for the mood of
the stories.

274. Fenner, Phyllis R. **Time to Laugh: Funny Tales from
Here and There**. Illus. Henry C. Pitz. New York: Knopf,
1942. 240 p. Grades 4-8.
　　Twenty humorous stories selected from treasures of
folklore from around the world. The story about the
laughing prince is taken from Parker Fillmore's
collection of Yugoslav folktales. The protagonist is
Stefan, the youngest of three brothers, who, like his
oldest brother Mihailo, does not spend all of his time

reading books and does not always get the best bargains,
like his next brother, Jakov. He is, therefore, scorned
by both of them and not respected by his own father.
The only one who appreciates him and loves him dearly is
his little sister Militza. Stefan is kind and jolly and
always ready to tell her stories. When the Tsar of the
kingdom in which the three brothers live sends heralds
through the land to announce that anyone who can make
his melancholy daughter laugh will be awarded with three
bags of gold, it is Stefan, encouraged by Militsa, who
succeeds at the difficult task. Stefan's stories,
especially one in which he tells about his young days
when he was very, very old, amuse not only the Princess,
but also her father, the Tsar. It follows quite
naturally that Stefan and the Princess marry. Moreover,
in a very short time their castle and the entire country
change from a gloomy place into a place of laughter and
happiness. Even more importantly, the people of the
entire kingdom realize that they are working all the
harder and better because of their cheerfulness.

275. Fillmore, Parker. The Laughing Prince: A Book of
Yugoslav Fairy Tales and Folk Tales. Illus. Jay Van Everen.
New York: Harcourt, Brace, 1921. 286 p. Grades 4-8.
    A collection of fourteen tales, full of rich humor,
magic, extraordinary adventure, and a fascination with
the goodness and innocence of youth. In the title
story, "The Laughing Prince," the youngest of three
brothers, who, although neither studious nor clever like
his older two brothers, is kind and jolly, enjoys
plowing and harvesting, and has a wonderful way with
animals, is able to make a sad princess laugh and,
therefore, gains her hand in marriage. Similarly, in
the story "The Little Lame Fox," the youngest of three
brothers, who again is not as bright and clever as his
brothers but is honest and good hearted, is selected by
the Golden Maiden as her next husband and, unlike his
older brothers, lives a happy and prosperous life. The
third story also follows this pattern. A Princess, who
had been changed by a dragon into a peafowl, after her
enchantment is broken, selects the youngest, most
faithful, and most humble son of the tsar as her
husband. "Nightingale in the Mosque" tells about the
Sultan's youngest son, who, with truth in his mouth and
courage in his eyes, is privileged to marry the Flower
of the World. In the story "The Vilas' Spring," the
younger brother, who is always ready to share what he
has and believes that good is stronger than evil,
marries a princess and is made heir to the kingdom. The
origins of the stories are not given.

276. Haslip, Joan. Fairy Tales from the Balkans. Illus.
Dodo Adler. London, England: Collins, 1933. 150 p. Grades
5-8.
    A compilation of nine stories which supposedly
originated in the various republics of Yugoslavia, Bul-

garia, and the other Balkan countries. In one of the
stories, the grateful ghost of a dead man repays a good
deed to a young peasant by helping him to establish a
prosperous business and by removing the enchantment from
the beautiful maiden whom the peasant has selected to be
his wife. In the story about the lame fox, the youngest
of three brothers, who is considered a simpleton, shows
special kindness to a starving fox by sharing his entire
lunch with her. In her gratitude, the fox helps the
kind-hearted lad in finding not only a vine which pours
out buckets of wine, a golden horse, and a golden apple
tree, but also a lovely princess with skin as white as
ivory and curls of gold. A deed of mercy by a simple
shepherd to a poisonous snake is again richly rewarded
by the rarest of gifts, an understanding of the language
of the animals. Goodness of heart figures prominently
in the other stories as well. For being gentle and
considerate to a small frog in distress, the youngest of
three princes receives a fairy for his bride and
inherits his father's kingdom. Several stories,
especially the one about the lovely tsarena, have an
unmistakenly Russian influence. They contain characters
frequently appearing in Russian tales, such as Baba Yaga
and Tsar Ivan. The well-told stories are illustrated
with black-and-white drawings as well as with color
plates.

277. Kavčič, Vladimir. The Golden Bird: Folk Tales from
Slovenia. Trans. Jan Dekker and Helen Lenček. Illus. Mae
Gerhard. New York: World. 1969. 156 p. Grades 3-8.
   Eighteen folktales selected from nineteenth-century
sources, altered only slightly to make them more
attractive to children. In the past, these stories
lived among the peasants and shepherds, among the
hunters and beekeepers, and among the spinners and
weavers. They fully reflect the bygone times of
Slovenian people who in their hardships always believed
that good would triumph over evil, that the poor would
eventually find the good luck which would free them from
constant worries, and that the evil feudal lords would
somehow recognize their wickedness, and be punished, or
become compassionate toward their subjects. The animal
tales in the collection include such favorites as "The
Golden Bird." "The Grateful Rooster," "Five Musicians,"
"How the Squirrel Got Married" and "The Lucky Cat."
Most tales contain much robust wit and humor. A cook
saves his master, the miller, from the wrath of the king
when he wittingly answers concerning the number of stars
in the sky, the distance from the earth to heaven, the
worth of his kingdom and the subject of his thinking. A
good-natured blacksmith outsmarts the devil himself, and
the youngest of three brothers gets the best of the
bargain when he outmaneuvers his rich master. Smoothly
translated and effectively illustrated in clear pen and
ink drawings.

278. Mijatovies, Elodie (Lawton). <u>Serbian Folk Lore</u>.
Trans. Csedomille Mijatovies. Popular Tales. New York:
Blom, 1964. 316 p. Grades 5 and up.
   A superb collection of twenty-six stories first
published in England in 1874. According to W. Denton,
who wrote the introduction, the stories were selected
and translated from two sources. Most come from the
Serbian folktales originally collected by Vuk Stefanović
Karadžić on the urging of Jacob Grimm and published in
Vienna in 1853. Others are taken from Bosnian folktales
that were first collected by the Society for the Young
Bosnia and published in Croatia in 1870. In Serbia
these tales were told mostly by older women at strictly
women's gatherings while spinning or during the summer
evenings under the crown of a large tree. When men
related the same themes, they did so in the form of
poetry to the monotonous music of the gusle. Some of
the tales in this collection have counterparts with
similar themes in Grimm's collection of German tales and
in Afanasyev's Russian tales. Examples include "Who
Asks Little, Gets Much," "The Wise Girl," "The
Golden-Fleeced Ram," "The Golden Apple Tree," "Lying for
a Wager," and the "Snake's Gift: Language of Animals."
There are several delightful legends in the collection,
one of the most clever being "The Legend of St. George,"
in which the great saint, with much patience and
ingenuity, converts the Trojan people.

279. Petrovitch, Woislav Maxim. <u>Hero Tales and Legends of</u>
<u>the Serbians</u>. Illus. William Sewell and Gilbert James.
London: Harrap, 1914. 394 p. Grades 6 and up.
   There is a wealth of folkloric materials gathered in
this volume under fifteen chapters. In the first two
chapters the author provides an excellent frame of
reference by explaining the historical and biographical
data which played an essential role in creating Serbian
epic poetry, its heroic ballads, and its lyric songs.
Moreover, the author discusses in a thorough, but clear
and succinct style, the Serbian national customs and the
superstitious beliefs of the people. The influence of
paganism, with its worship of the natural powers, as
well as the effect of Christianity on the oral
literature of the early historical periods, is
explained. Most of the heroic ballads that were
originally composed in verse, and were perpetuated in
their oral tradition in verse, were likewise first
written down in the Serbian language in verse. In this
translation, however, most appear in a beautiful, poetic
prose. The only exceptions are three ballads which come
from a collection translated in verse by the English
poet Sir John Browning and which were first published in
England in 1827. Sir Browning selected the ballads from
a collection gathered by the most known Serbian
folklorist, Vuk Stefanović Karadžić and translated them
with precision and faithfulness to their original
spirit. The themes of the ballads contained in the

collection include the admirable feats of the Serbian national heroes, especially their beloved Prince Marko, the good deeds of their monks and Christian saints, and the people's admiration for the gifts of nature.   In addition to the tales of heroes, the collection contains twenty spirited folktales and several pages of clever and witty anecdotes.   The ballads and folktales are illustrated   with   impressionistic   black-and-white drawings.   The book was reprinted by Kraus in 1972.

280. Rootham, Helen, trans.   Kosovo, Heroic Songs of the Serbs.   Boston: Houghton Mifflin, 1920.   90 p.   Grades 6 and up.
Nine epic poems in Serbian and English dealing with the heroes of the tragic battle on Kosovo (1389) in which Serbia lost its freedom.   Included are poems about the noble Tsar Lazar and the Tsaritsa Militsa, the old hero Jug Bogdan with his nine sons, whom the mother finds dead on the field of battle, and the beautiful Maiden of Kosovo comforting the bleeding heroes with cool water and red wine.   These epics admired by Goethe and Jacob Grimm are written in a simple picturesque language. They   reflect   the   poetical   genius   of   the   Serbian peasantry as well as the undying sorrow of the Serbian people, their unspeakable anguish, their strong faith, and their passionate love of freedom and justice.

281. Spicer, Dorothy Gladys.   Long Ago in Serbia.   Illus. Linda Ominsky.   Philadelphia: Westminster, 1968.   158 p. Grades 5-10.
The noted folklorist and art historian here selects and retells ten Serbian stories that impressed her during her travels through Yugoslavia.   In the story "The Shepherd with the Curious Wife," an honest shepherd, Timok, moved by compassion, saves a serpent from fire and receives as a reward a special gift, the ability to understand the speech of living creatures.   This gift brings him prosperity, his own pasturelands and flocks, bountiful crops, and a beautiful girl for a wife.   When his wife's curiosity almost causes a disaster, Timok's understanding of his rooster, who is boasting how he controls the inquisitiveness of hundreds of his wives, helps him to change his wife's heart, and they both enjoy happiness until they die at a ripe old age. Themes from other stories include: families with two or three brothers, of whom the youngest is the handsomest, the kindest, the smartest, and the most fortunate; a people's lust for power and wealth bringing woes to themselves; and explanations for natural phenomena, such as like why the stones at the edge of the field will never have a chance to sustain the hungry and comfort the sad and will never grow or be fruitful.   Lively, conversational text and folk-style drawings enhance the spirit of the stories.

TRADITIONAL LITERATURE: SINGLE EDITIONS

282. Ginsburg, Mirra. How the Sun Was Brought Back to the Sky . Illus. Jose Aruego and Ariane Dewey. New York: Macmillan, 1975. N. pag. Grades K-3.

Adapted from a Slovenian folktale, this luxuriously colored cumulative picture story tells of five worried chicks and some of their animal friends and of their long journey to find out why the sun has disappeared. A snake in a vegetable patch, a magpie on a fence, a rabbit in a furrow, and a duck by a brook are of no help to the chicks, as they ask for directions to the sun's home. The hedgehog in the hollow, however, surely knows the way. He guides the small band to the top of the mountain, on a white cloud to the silver moon, and from there to the sun's palace. The animals help the great star to get rid of gray clouds until the sky appears clean, fresh and golden once again. Vibrant watercolors add an amusing touch to the simple text and impart an atmosphere of child-like wonder, curiosity, and friendship.

283. Levstik, Fran. Martin Krpan. Trans. F.S. Copeland. Illus. Tone Kralj. Ljubljana, Slovenia: Mladinska Knjiga, 1960. N. pag. Grades 4 and up.

First written in 1858 in the original Slovenian for publication in a journal, this beloved tall tale is accompanied by thirty superb paintings by one of the most respected Slovenian artist, Tone Kralj. The narrative and colorful illustrations vividly portray the story of a Slovenian peasant Martin Krpan, who, with his ingenious wit and superhuman strength saves Vienna from the terrible giant, Brdavs. Brdavs challenges all the champions of the Austrian empire to a single combat and slays everyone who accepts the challenge, including the Emperor's son. As a last resort, the Emperor sends a large coach to Slovenia to bring Martin to the palace. While selecting weapons in the royal armory from a collection of sabres, swords, steel breast plates, and helmets, Martin crushes one after another in his hands. Making his own butcher ax and a club, he proceeds with the selection of a horse. Since he is unable to find one that cannot be dragged over the threshold by its tail, Martin fights and defeats Brdavs on his little mare. Written in the lively, robust language of a Slovenian peasant and with an unmatched humor, the story has been published in many editions and, over the years, has been translated into most European languages.

284. Mirković, Irene. The Greedy Shopkeeper. Illus. Harold Berson. New York: Harcourt, Brace Jovanovich, 1980. N. pag. Grades 2-4.

Translated and adapted from Serbian, this is a tale about a poor farmer named Ivo who comes to town to have his horse's harness repaired. While looking in a shop window, he trips and falls. Picking himself up, he

spots a merchant's purse under a cobblestone. At that
moment, a town cryer comes through the narrow street,
shouting that Raffik, the merchant, is offering a gold
coin to the finder of his lost money pouch. Being an
honest man, Ivo immediately takes the purse to Raffik's
shop. The greedy Raffik, however, now has second
thoughts concerning the reward. Stealthily he takes one
of the ten golden coins from the pouch, slips it into
his pocket, and accuses Ivo of having already taken the
reward. Insisting that he has never opened the purse,
Ivo is dragged to the court. In his kindness and
wisdom, the judge decides that if there are only nine
coins in the purse, it surely cannot belong to Raffik.
"An honest man is a rich man," concludes the judge and
hands the wallet with the nine golden coins to Ivo.
Soft sepia drawings accented with aqua, the color of the
end papers, perfectly convey the character of the
Serbian town and the wit of the story.

285. Sawyer, Ruth. <u>This Is the Christmas: A Serbian Folk-
tale</u>. Boston: Horn Book, 1945. N. pag. Grades 3-6.
The Serbian villagers, although honest and hard-working,
do not like Gypsies. They consider them thieves and
tricksters who should be excluded from their midst.
When a little blind Gypsy boy is found on a cliff high
over the river after a storm one summer day, Father
Janovich quickly decides that he is one of the "Cigani,"
and should not be taken into their home. Mother
Janovich, however, thinks that it is the will of God for
them to keep him. As the boy, Marko, gets older, the
Janovich's set him to tend their sheep. Kept separately
from the family, Marko sleeps in the pasture, playing
sweetly to his lambs on his self-made pipe, calling the
birds from the woods and caring for the other small
creatures with care and tenderness. Only in extremely
cold weather is Marko allowed to sleep in the house. As
a "Cigan" he is excluded from all merrymaking and from
all of the festivals, even from the joy and beauty of
the Christmas celebration. On his twelfth Christmas
Eve, however, when his immense desire to be with the
valley-folk in church, worshiping the Little King, is
denied to him, he brings into his shed a wounded
ewe-lamb. After binding her broken leg with strips from
his tunic, Marko, along with the lamb, kneels on the
straw and prays that they be accepted and treated as are
the other boys in the family and the village. The
midnight service over, the people are amazed to see a
dazzling light shining over the valley, coming from the
shed on Janovich's farm. Coming to the farmyard, they
find the blind boy and the lamb kneeling on the straw,
with the boy Christ lying next to them. Filled with awe
and humility the valley-folk finally realize how blind
they have been to the goodness of the gypsy boy.

286. Valjavec, Matija, and Cene Vipotnik. <u>The Magic Ring:
A Picture Story from Yugoslavia</u>. Illus. Marlenka Stupica.

Cleveland, Oh: World, 1968. N. pag. Grades 2-4.
   A Slovenian folk tale, first written down in verse by
Matija Valjavec, a nineteenth century collector of folk
literature. In 1957, it was written in prose by Cene
Vipotnik and published in Slovenian in Ljubljana. The
story is about a poor shepherd who lives with his mother
in a cottage in the mountains. The boy gathers dried
sticks for firewood and then sells them in the village.
With the money he receives, he is able to buy bread for
himself and his mother. The mother is rightfully upset
when on three consecutive days, instead of bread, the
shepherd brings home a puppy, a cat, and a small ring.
The kind-hearted boy had exchanged his coins for the
animals, rescuing them from some boys who had been cruel
to them. The little ring, which was given to the boy by
a grateful snake, proves to have magical powers.
Everytime he taps it with his finger, twelve obedient
knights appear before him, asking for his orders. The
magic ring provides the boy, his mother, the cat, and
the dog with everything they need. It also helps him to
accomplish the impossible tasks imposed on him by the
emperor in order to win his beautiful daughter in
marriage. When the magic ring is stolen from the young
man by a wicked Maharajah from the East, the cat and the
dog come to the rescue. Elegant colorful illustrations
by one of the best illustrators of children's books
enhance the gentle magic and the ethnic flavor contained
in this authentic folk tale. Marlenka Stupica received
the prestigious Fran Levstik Award in 1958 for her
excellent illustrations.

HISTORICAL FICTION AND BIOGRAPHY

287. Adamic, Louis. <u>Grandsons: A Story of American Lives</u>.
New York: Harper, 1935. 370 p. Grades 7 and up.
   They met toward the end of World War I in a rest zone
somewhere west of the Meuse-Argonne Front: the
narrator, a twenty-one-year-old immigrant, who had
arrived in America three years before the war started,
from Slovenia, at that time a province of Austria, and
twenty year old sergeant, Peter Gale, whose grandfather
had come from Slovenia in the 1870's. After they
exchange their knowledge about the old country, Peter
emphasizes the fact that his grandfather, Anton Gale,
was killed in the Haymarket riot, which was part of the
labor strikes in Chicago in 1886. Nine years later,
when the two men meet again in the United States and
become friends, Peter elaborates on the role his
grandfather played in the riot and relates not only the
story of his own life, but also the story of Anton
Gale's other two grandsons, Peter's brother Andrew and
his cousin Jack Gale. Peter becomes a reporter, a
perceptive writer, but a somewhat unstable and neurotic
individual due to a war injury. Andrew, "a fugitive
from inner inferiority," acquires an anarchistic atti-

tude toward the world and, in his ambition for money and power, becomes a gangster. Their cousin, Jack Gale, a laborer, and his wife Mildred, become involved in Marxist revolutionary activities. A captivating story of three grandsons and of America, written with an instinct for the dramatic and the colorful, and with a definite inclination toward the leftist movements of the 1930's.

288. Archer, Jules. <u>Red Rebel: Tito of Yugoslavia</u>. New York: Messner, 1968. 190 p. Grades 6-10.

Tito was born in 1892, as Josip Broz, in the mountain village of Kumrovec just to the north of Zagreb, the capital of Croatia, which then belonged to Austria-Hungary. He was the seventh of fifteen children born to his Croatian father, Franyo Broz, and Slovenian mother, Marija. While his father drank heavily, his mother worked incessantly in order to feed her family. As a young boy, Josip attended the village two-room elementary school for four years. He also worked in the fields and helped with the primitive household chores. Being tough and athletic, he was often selected to lead the village boys' raids on fruit orchards and to fight against boys from other villages. When Josip was fourteen, he was considered old enough to support himself. He was sent to the town of Sisak to work as a waiter. Bored because the job did not offer him any learning experiences, he apprenticed himself to a locksmith. After four years, while attempting his first metalworking job, he wandered restlessly through the cities of Austria-Hungary, coming into contact with the radical socialist movements. In 1914, when World War I broke out, Josip was sent as a soldier of Austria-Hungary to the Russian front. Captured by the Russians, Josip learned their language, studied Marx and Lenin, and upon his release from prison in 1917, joined the Communist Party. In 1920, Josip returned to Croatia, which became a part of Yugoslavia after the war, and helped to organize the Yugoslav Communist party. He was imprisoned, released, and sought after. While trying to keep away from the police, he assumed the name of Tito. The major part of the biography, which deals with the establishment of Tito's power and his leadership of Yugoslavia, is written interestingly, but it seems one-sided and lacks the careful research of historical facts expected in a serious biography.

289. Davies, Ellen Chivers. <u>A Boy in Serbia</u>. New York: Crowell, 1920. 164 p. Grades 4-6.

Speaking in the first person through a young boy, Milosav Stoyanovitch, the author describes in short vignettes the simple village life of the Serbian peasants during the first decades of the twentieth century. From his earliest days he remembers his mischief, his weakness for sweet things, and his fondness for climbing apple trees and nut trees; fruits always tasted better when he had to climb for them. Like the other children in the village, Milo had to take the family's pigs to the oak forest before he was old enough to go to school and see to it that they found enough acorns to keep them satisfied. Often he would meet other children there, taking their goats and pigs to the feeding grounds. Since their four-footed charges carried bells around their necks, it was not particularly difficult to keep them from straying away. If the sun was not too hot, the young swineherds and goatherds engaged in games or played their simple merry tunes on their pipes made of reeds. With profound love for his country and his people, the author describes in a simple, flowing style other aspects of the child's world, including the first day in school, the celebration of the Serbian national festivals, one of the greatest being St. Sava's Day, rich Serbian folklore, the people's beliefs and religious observances, and the memorable familial events. The narratives are accompanied by black and white photographs.

290. Feuerlicht, Roberta Strauss. The Desperate Act: The Assassination of Franz Ferdinand at Sarajevo. New York: McGraw-Hill, 1968. 176 p. Grades 7 and up.
The book describes the assassination of Franz Ferdinand in Sarajevo on June 28, 1914, an act which triggered World War I. More than just tracing the movements, motives, and acts of the six assassins involved in the plot, however, the book surveys the entire history of Serbia, revealing the mood of the Serbians at that time, the historical elements which contributed to the Serbian view of the world, especially of Austria, and why such an assassination attempt was likely. It describes previous assassination plots, most of which ended in failure, but which inspired this one. The placement and movements of the six assassins are plotted and their mistakes analyzed. Maps help greatly in this area. Finally, the reason for their success, and the ensuing course of events are explained. The trial of the plotters is also covered. Only a small part of the book deals with the actual planning and carrying out of the mission. Rather, the book takes a deeper view of this engrossing topic, assassination and assassination attempts, and brings out what is interesting in such historical events: the coincidences, the ironies, and the mistakes of both law enforcement officials and of the criminals themselves. One obtains a feel for the amateurishness of the assassins and the despair felt throughout Serbia that leads six teenagers, who had never seen or met each other, to seek the life of Franz Ferdinand. Black and white photographs and maps are extremely interesting and helpful.

291. Franchere, Ruth. Tito of Yugoslavia. New York: Mac-millan, 1970. 184 p. Grades 6-10.

A biography of the postwar leader of Yugoslavia, covering mostly Josip Broz's childhood, the events of his youth that shaped his belief in Communism, the role he played in augmenting the Communist Party of Yugoslavia, and his leadership in the partisan movement during World War II. Only a small section of the narrative is devoted to the twenty-five years of Tito's government of Yugoslavia, covering the period between World War II and 1970, the year the book was published. The author vividly portrays Tito's childhood, describes many interesting events, such as the trading of the family's dog Polak for firewood, Josip's and his friends' games in the old castle, Cesargrad, and Josip's apprenticeship to the locksmith Nikola Karas. Josip's love of reading and learning and his patriotic feeling of brotherhood toward his people and the people of other Slavic countries are also reflected in the parts covering the early years of his life. The author explains that when Josip served in the Austrian army, he vowed that he would rather use deception than allow himself to be caught. He followed this motto in his undercover work and in times of strife during both World Wars as well as during the difficult inter-war period. Like Archer's biography of Tito, this work seems to be an oversimplified account of Tito's life, his accomplishments, and the role he played before and after World War II. Some historical facts regarding his opposition, the free elections during the postwar period, and the initial response of the people to the Communist form of government have little objectivity.

292. Holberg, Ruth Langland. Michael and the Captain. Illus. Sandra James. New York: Crowell, 1944. 114 p. Grades 4-10.

An adventure story about a Serbian boy living at the beginning of the seventeenth century when the Balkan countries were under Turkish occupation. In those days, very young boys were taken by force from their parents to be raised in Turkey as Janizaries, soldiers in an elite guard of Turkish troops, who would later fight side by side with Turks against their own countrymen, often plundering the country of their birth. They were expertly trained in both Islam as well as in Turkish warfare. When his family finds out that Michael may be kidnapped by the Turks, they send him away. In Walachia (today's southern region of Romania) he comes in contact with Captain John Smith, an Englishman who ably and courageously fights with the East European nations against the Turks. Michael and the Captain live an adventurous life together, and are eventually captured and serve as slaves to the Khan of Mongolia. In the end Michael returns to his old home in Serbia. A fittingly illustrated, stirring story as well as a vivid portrayal of the Serbian way of life and of Eastern Europe under the Turks.

293. Judson, Clara Ingram. <u>Petar's Treasure: They Came from Dalmatia</u>. They Came From Series. Boston: Houghton Mifflin, 1945. 186 p. Grades 4-6.

A part of the "They Came From" series, this is a story of the Petrovich family coming from the island of Brac, in the Adriatic Sea off the coast of Dalmatia. The father comes to America first; the others follow later. They settle in Biloxi, Mississippi, where they all work at shrimp and oyster fishing and in the canning factory. Petar, the oldest boy, is the hero. He has honest ambitions and wants to earn enough money to enable his mother to remain out of the factories and his father to afford his own land. He hears of pirate treasure buried on an island in the Gulf. When the chance comes for Petar to go to the island to dig for it, he finds only rusty kettles which, when cleaned, turn out to be made of copper and are quite valuable. It is a touching story of an immigrant family, warm and colorful in the description of Dalmatian customs and festivities as well as in their desire to become part of America.

294. Kay, Mara. <u>The Burning Candle</u>. New York: Lothrop, Lee, and Shepard, 1968. 159 p. Grades 6-9.

This moving and emotional story takes place soon after World War II. It begins on the Yugoslav religious feast of Slava, which Zora and her family strictly observe against the will of the Communist Party. On this day, Zora shelters and saves a run-away loyalist, Steven, by hiding him in the mountains. Together they plan to escape with the aid of friends. She is to receive a letter, notifying them of the day his friends leave for Italy. In the meantime, her conscience is troubled, as her neighbor is arrested for "liking the king," having been turned in, as Zora later finds out, by one of her schoolmates. Furthermore, she is afraid that her brother, a party member, is spying on Steven and her. Milan, her brother, has been asked to spy on them; but, knowing full-well the consequences, he decides to leave the party, and, although he is promptly sent to a work camp, he feels that for the first time he can call his life truly "his." Zora works to set Steven free, and can herself escape if she will write a composition for a scholarship competition. The topic, however, is "Slava, and Other Superstitions, Enemies of the People." Her response to this question enables her also to consider her life as truly "hers." The book captures the reader from the very beginning and holds his attention throughout. It is, however, rather extreme in its political views.

295. Madison, Winifred. <u>Call Me Danica</u>. New York: Four Winds, 1977. 203 p. Grades 4-8.

Ever since her family received their first postcard from Uncle Ivo and Aunt Nevenka, who live in Vancouver, Canada, twelve-year-old Danica has wanted to live there. She has always loved the village of Kalovar, which was slightly more than an hour's travel from Zagreb, the capital of Croatia, where she has lived with her parents, her older sister, Mirjana, and her younger brother, Marko. The postcard from Vancouver, however, showing the wonderful city with its shops, bridges, high buildings bathed in golden lights and reflected in the shimmering waters of the ocean, strongly attracts her. To Danica's father, on the other hand, leaving their homeland is out of the question. Their ancestors have lived in Kalovar since the sixteenth century and they belong here. Besides, when something is far away, it always seems brighter and better, but life is never easy and is pretty much the same everywhere. When Tata, Danica's father, dies suddenly, toward the end of the year, the family's financial situation becomes desperate. Mama finally gives in. In his letters Uncle Ivo tells them of the job he has found for Mama and of the place he and Aunt Nevenka have prepared for them to live in. It is extremely difficult for the family to sell their village inn, but leaving their country, their animals, and their friends is an even sadder experience. With Mama's determination to give the family a new opportunity, and with Danica's enthusiasm about going to Vancouver, the family endures the heart-breaking farewell, the initial hardship in adjusting to the new customs, to their work, school and to these people, who hold values so different from their own. In her own voice Danica tells a good story of the life in Croatia and of the experiences the immigrants encountered in Canada, the country of their adoption.

296. Mann, Peggy and Katica Prusina. A Present for Yanya.
Illus. Douglas Gorsline. New York: Random House, 1975.
119 p. Grades 3-6.
Based on the childhood experiences of Katica Prusina, who lived in Yugoslavia in the years following World War II, this is the story of a poor Bosnian girl living in Slavonia who helps her impoverished family with the work that Mama does not have time to do. Papa, who was injured in a prison camp, is still unable to get out of bed, and during the summertime her older brothers, Marko and Ivo, hire themselves to farmers to earn a few dinars. On her first trip to the market with Mama to sell their cabbage, herbs, and eggs, Yanya spots a most beautiful doll in a shop window, a doll with black curly hair, large blue eyes, long lashes, and dressed in a red silk dress with lace at the cuffs. Although it seems impossible to Yanya, who does not own even a pair of shoes, that she would ever have enough money to buy the lovely French doll, somehow she feels that someday she will own her. And she does. With patience, courage, much ingenuity, and determination she eventually earns five thousand dinars and bargains for the doll. With her, Yanya's bleak world fills with excitement and contentment. Uncluttered pencil illustrations add a pleasant touch to the simply written story and

effectively portray the cultural atmosphere of post-war Slavonia.

297. Pupin, Michael.   <u>From Immigrant to Inventor</u>.   New York: Scribner, 1923.   396 p.   Grades 6 and up.
A superbly written autobiography of the Serbian-born American physicist who made significant discoveries leading to great progress in the development of a long-distance telephone system, of radio transmission networks, and of telegraphy. The first few chapters, in which Pupin vividly describes his birthplace and his proud Serbian heritage, have an especially charming touch. In simple language Pupin explains how his native town, Idvor, enjoyed special status for more than a century under the Austro-Hungarian authorities as a military frontier of Austria against the Turkish invasions. For their heroic defense of the Austrian Empire, the Serbs of Idvor received a written guarantee of spiritual, economic, and political autonomy. As Pupin warmly remembers from his childhood, the Serbs of Idvor were faithful to their old customs and gathered frequently during the long winter evenings in one of their houses, exchanging words of wisdom and telling stories and singing songs about their heroic struggles against the Turks and their brave fights in the Napoleonic Wars. In the author's opinion, the cultivation of these and the other old traditions was the cornerstone of the spiritual strength of his people and was, perhaps, one of the most important elements of his idealism as a young immigrant and as an American scientist. The chapters in which Pupin discusses what he has brought to America and the hardships a greenhorn faces offer a most sensitive and insightful picture of the life of a teenage immigrant. For this distinguished autobiography, Pupin recieved the 1924 Pulitzer Prize.

298. Shapiro, Irwin.   <u>Joe Magarac and His U.S.A. Citizenship Papers.</u> Illus. James Daugherty.   Pittsburgh, PA: U Pittsburgh P, 1979.   58 p.   Grades 4-8.
A tall tale about the greatest steelman that ever was, Joe Magarac. He is big and strong and works like a magarac (meaning donkey in Serbo-Croatian). Born on an ore mountain somewhere in Croatia, Joe arrives in the United States and meets his cousin Steve Mestrovich, who helps him find a job in the Braddock steel mill. Joe Magarac works in an open-hearth furnace, throwing in ore, scrap, and limestone, and making rails better and faster than anyone else. His superintendent thinks Joe will need a thousand dollars to get his U.S.A. citizenship papers. Papers for a big man cost more, he tells him. Joe Magarac wants to work day and night to make double money for the papers. He goes to Homestead mill and asks for a job, not telling anyone he has a job in Braddock. After that he works day shifts at one mill and night shifts at the other. Joe Magarac eventually gets his citizenship, but not the way one would expect.

Written in a strong, humorous style, the story is a superb metaphor reflecting the plight of "greenhorns" and the contribution immigrant laborers made to the wealth of the United States. Black and white vigorous drawings match the story perfectly. For its imaginative contribution to children's literature the author of the book received the Julia Ellsworth Ford Award when the book was first published in 1948.

299. Upjohn, Anna Milo. Friends in Strange Garments. Illus. author. New York: Houghton Mifflin, 1927. 148 p. Grades 3-6.

The author, a volunteer relief worker in Europe during World War I and associated with the American Junior Red Cross after the war, traveled widely while gathering material for these stories and seems to be eminently competent in portraying the life of children in other lands. As is emphasized in the introduction, it is the intent of the stories to demonstrate "the likeness of heart" among the children of the world, in spite of the differences in the surroundings in which they live. Of the sixteen stories gathered in this book, three take place in Yugoslavia (one in Macedonia, one in Montenegro, and one in Serbia), two in Albania; two in Czechoslovakia; and one in each of the countries of Bulgaria, Romania, and Poland. In the story "Draga's Entrance Examination," the author gives a glimpse into the school life of Macedonian children and skillfully weaves into the narrative descriptions of Macedonian national costumes, food, and historical events and personalities, such as Serbian Prince Marko, who chose not to tell a lie, even though his adherence to truth cost him his crown. "Mirko and Marko" were two Montenegrin pigs, beloved playfellows to the girl Zorka. In the story "Kosovo Day," a girl, born in America of Serbian parents, takes part in the colorful celebration of the memorable historical battle between the Serbs and the Turks. The stories, with their artfully-executed illustrations, are a vivid evocation of times and places between the two World Wars.

300. Winlow, Clara Vostrovsky. Our Little Servian Cousin. Illus. John Goss. The Little Cousin Series. Boston: L.C. Pate, 1913. 101 p. Grades 3-5.

To an eight-year-old Serbian girl, Militza, it seems totally unjust that she is not told the secret that was discussed by her older brother Dushan and three of his companions behind the cattle-shed. Pleading with him and promising him absolute secrecy is of no avail. Like everyone else, he thinks that if little girls get too wise, they tend to get in trouble. Little girls, indeed, are expected to be involved in completely different tasks than boys. When not in school, Militza is learning to spin, weave, embroider, and knit. She also helps in the garden and sometimes she tends the flocks. She is taught to be modest and diligent and is not to try to match herself against boys. The life of her brother Dushan, on the other hand, is much freer. Besides assisting his father in getting fruit and vegetables ready for the market, he takes the family sheep and pigs to the pasture, where he also plays with his friends or engages in playing the simple musical instrument called "svirala." In addition to colorful description about the lives of Serbian children at the turn of the century, the author skillfully weaves into the narrative the people's most loved folktales and legends, the meaning and the joy of their national festivities, and the cultural and historical events of the period, especially the approaching Balkan wars and the intensified Serbian national distrust of the Habsburg authorities. Illustrated with high quality full-page plates in tint.

OTHER FICTION

301. Berlić-Mažuranić, Ivana and Lorna Wood. The Brave Adventures of Lapitch. Trans. Theresa Mravintz and Branko Brusar. Illus. Herold Berson. New York: Walck, 1972. 137 p. Grades 3-6.
  Lapitch is a twelve-year-old apprentice to a shoemaker. He is small for his age, but usually as cheerful as a bird. His master is Scowler, a tall, frightful man with thick hair, long mustaches, and a deep growling voice. Evidently, his heartlessness is due to the great sorrow he experienced several years ago. While selling shoes at a fair, his three-year-old daughter Maritsa got lost in a crowd and vanished. The same misfortune, on the other hand, has left his wife even kinder and sweeter. While Master Scowler allows Lapitch only hard, stale bread, Mistress Scowler smuggles him pieces of fresh bread whenever her husband is not watching. On one occasion, blinded in his anger over his own mistake in cutting a pair of boots too small for a rich gentleman's son, the master beats Lapitch with the boots and orders his wife to burn them. Not knowing the cause of his master's wickedness until the end of the story, Lapitch decides to run away. In the middle of night he walks stealthily out of his master's workshop and begins his seven-day adventurous journey. On the way he helps an old tired milkman to deliver milk, finds a couple of geese lost by a poor boy Marko in a swamp, helps farm laborers with their work, discovers the thieves who stole his shiny boots, laborers' tools, and the farmer's ham, and best of all, befriends a girl, left in a strange town by a group of circus performers. In the end, when the children, through unexpected twists and turns, return to the Scowlers, the girl is recognized as Maritsa. To Lapitch, with such a happy ending, everything appears to be well, even his master's cruelty. Had Master Scowler not been so hard-hearted, Lapitch would not have run away and Maritsa would not

have been found! Amusingly affectionate line drawings
enhance the appeal of a well-told story.

302. Ćurčija-Prodanović, Nada. Ballerina. Illus. by Dušan
Ristic. New York: Criterion, 1964. 255 p. Grades 5-8.
   A sixteen year old high school student, Lana, has
completed five years of study at the Ballet School at
Skopje. Wishing to advance in her training, she enters
the State Ballet School in Belgrade. If she passes her
test, she will be the eighth student in the sixth form.
As she exercises with the other girls, first at the
barre, then in the center of the room performing
adagios, valses, and finally point-work, the teacher,
Miss Nina, is pleased. Although Lana is accepted with
kindness by all her high school teachers (the girls
attend regular high school courses in the afternoon),
her classmates give her the cold shoulder. Lana feels
isolated and unwanted. Most of the girls become
especially resentful of her after she is singled out by
a visiting ballet expert from England as being highly
gifted, hard working, and beautiful. In spite of Lana's
efforts to suppress her happiness, the cold atmosphere
surrounding her continues and is hard for her to bear.
A good portion of the book deals with Lana's improving
relationships with her adolescent classmates. She feels
some good will coming toward her after she is caught
with some other girls chatting in the dressing room
instead of attending an important class and receives,
with the rest of the group an appropriate punishment.
However, with the exception of Katia, who soon offers
her friendship, the girls do not accept her fully until
a tragic train accident, in which Lana loses the toes on
her right foot. The story ends on a positive note.
Through tremendous effort and determination, Lana
returns to the ballet and her classmates share in her
pride and happiness when she is selected to dance the
white butterfly in the performance "The Papillons" and
to become a member of the Ballet Theater the following
fall. Somewhat slow moving and burdened with an
overabundance of details regarding the ballet school,
the story offers good insight into the life of the youth
in post-war Yugoslavia.

303. Cankar, Ivan. The Bailiff Yerney. Trans. Sidonie
Yeras and H.C. Sewell Grant. Illus. Nora Lavrin. London:
Pushkin, 1946. 105 p. Grades 7 and up.
   When the novel was first published in its original
Slovenian in 1907, it was immediately acclaimed as a
profound literary work and was soon translated into
several major languages. With it, the author, Ivan
Cankar, brought to light the tragedy, the soul and the
conscience of the small Slovenian nation, which was at
that time a part of the Austrian empire. The story is
about a peasant, Yerney, and his search for justice.
For forty years Yerney works for his master. He builds
houses, he ploughs and sows, he harvests crops, and he

mows and thrashes. He calls for God's blessings upon the land, and he soaks the land with the sweat of his brow. Now that his master is dead his young son takes over, and Yerney, the bailiff, is asked to pack his bundle and leave. Believing to the end that he can find justice, Yerney seeks affirmation of his beliefs of the fairness of human and divine laws from the village mayor, a band of children, a group of peasants, several justices in Ljubljana, a priest, even from a court in Vienna. Invariably, he receives the same discouraging response that the servant must do what his master tells him to do. Yerney's tragedy seems to be a tragedy not only of many Slovenian peasants, but also of the Slovenian nation as a whole. Superb illustrations add drama and depth to the poignant story of the bailiff Yerney.

304. Catherall, Arthur. <u>Yugoslav Mystery</u>. New York: Lothrop, Lee and Shepard, 1962. 158 p. Grades 4-8.
Fourteen-year-old Josef Piri and his grandfather, Stepan, have worked together for the past four years. They live on a small island in the Adriatic Sea and make their living by fishing for sardines. As they are sculling along one summer night on their twenty-foot boat waiting for just the right moment to drop and draw in the net, they are interrupted by four men in a big sea-going launch pretending to be of the Yugoslav police force. They seem to be looking for an escaped convict. In reality, however, they are members of the outlawed Ustashis group looking for a man from the island whom they have kept as a prisoner and who has jumped into the sea from their launch. The man had fought during the war with the Yugoslav Partisans. Known to the islanders as the Eagle, he disappeared at the end of the war. Distrustful, Josef and his grandfather volunteer no information. From the few words they exchange with the four men, they both suspect that the person they are looking for might be Josef's father. Although politically biased, the adventurous story of the father's escape and his final return home makes for most captivating reading.

305. Cervon, Jacqueline. <u>The Day the Earth Shook</u>. Trans. John B. Brown. East Rutherford, NY: Coward, 1969. 186 p. Grades 5-10.
Set in Yugoslavia, partly in Croatia and partly in Macedonia, this is an absorbing, moving novel of four young Frenchmen traveling to Greece through Yugoslavia. As they camp in a small village on the Adriatic coast, a native boy, Filip Miravic, saves Cecile from a poisonous adder. This begins a friendship which takes them to the distant city of Skopje, where Filip wants to attend a technical school, and where, in July, 1963, all five become immersed in the rescue operations during the earthquake nightmare. The story is powerfully and dramatically written and is rich in background of people

and places.

306. Gidal, Tim and Sonia Gidal. <u>My Village in Yugoslavia</u>.
Illus. Tim Gidal. My Village Series. New York: Pantheon,
1957. 74 p. Grades 3-7.
A part of "My Village" series, this partly fictionalized
story is told in first-person by the Macedonian boy,
Stotye. It gives a detailed account of the activities
which take place in a rugged mountain village, with
references to the important events in the history of the
country. Through Stotye we learn about life in the
village, its centuries-old customs and national
costumes, and its food; we also learn of the occupations
and recreational activities of the villagers. It is a
fresh, vivid, sympathetic portrayal of the hero and his
family and friends. The volume has sixty candid black
and white photographs taken by Tim Gidal. There is also
a glossary of foreign words and a sketch of the village
with the surrounding mountain areas.

307. Held, Kurt. <u>The Outsiders of Uskoken Castle</u>. Trans.
Lynn Aubry. New York: Doubleday, 1967. 353 p. Grades
6-10.
Branko's mother, a poor factory worker in Senj, has just
been buried. His father, a violin player, is somewhere
on the road playing in resort towns along the Adriatic
coast, and the boy does not know if he will ever return.
So Branko is homeless and without any means of support.
Hungry and lonely, he roams through the market and makes
his rounds of the stands filled with fish and produce.
On an impulse, he picks up a fish that has accidently
fallen into the gutter without anyone noticing it. At
the moment he is about to tuck it under his shirt,
however, he feels a heavy hand on his shoulders. The
rich farmer, Karaman, has called the police. Accused of
thievery, Branko is imprisoned, but escapes with the
help of Zora, a girl of his age, also an orphan, who
witnesses the sad incident in the marketplace. Zora is
a member of a small band of homeless children who call
themselves Uskoki after a group of dissidents, who, in
the distant past, fought for the rights of the poor
peasants. She takes Branko to the half-ruined Uskoken
castle, where he is initiated into the gang. Although
the four boys and Zora steal fruit and chickens for
survival and swear vengeance against the boys of
well-to-do parents, they manage to retain their basic
honesty, sincerity, and respect for the poor. In the
end, decent and concerned individuals are found in Senj,
who offer the orphans their homes and their care. First
published in German, this adventurous, well-written
story reflecting the social conditions of pre-World War
II Yugoslavia has since been translated into several
languages.

308. Hope-Simpson, Jacynth. <u>Black Madonna</u>. New York:
Nelson, 1976. 139 p. Grades 6-12.

Stephen and Robert attend the same high school in Yorkshire, England. Robert, who wants to become a physical education teacher, belongs to a small group of enthusiasts who climb mountains and explore underground caves. Stephen hopes to go to the university in the fall to study Russian. His engineer father has just left for Yugoslavia, where he is a consultant for the installation of a hydroelectric plant, and wants Stephen to join him there. Knowing that the southeastern part of Yugoslavia has quantities of limestone, which means the presence of underground rivers and many opportunities for caving, Robert is quickly persuaded to join Stephen on his trip. The boys drive an old car and camp along the way through Western Europe and Yugoslavia to Belgrade and on to the southernmost point, the Lake Ohrid near the Greek border. They get acquainted with the peasants' way of life in the countryside, get in touch with a culture different than their own, and establish firm friendships with some most colorful individuals. It is not until Robert finds an icon of a black Madonna in a dark cave, however, that their extraordinary adventure begins. Robert, Stephen, and their Serbian friend, Zoe, become involved in the courageous struggle against foreign art smugglers for a 700-year-old icon. The story is quick-paced and filled with suspense, and the dangers the group encounters are convincingly described.

309. Hutterer, Franz. <u>Trouble for Tomas</u>. Trans. Joyce Emerson. Illus. Irene Schreiber. New York: Schreiber, 1959. 121 p. Grades 4-6.
Ten-year-old Tomas lives with his mother, a younger sister, Anka, and their donkey, Yascha, in a small house at the end of a village on the Danube River. Yascha has been with the family for five years. The donkey has carried sacks and baskets filled with wood, produce, fish, and other heavy burdens. Since his father's death two years ago, Tomas has tried to earn money with Yascha. Every Friday he goes to a neighboring town with his friend Marko to sell fish. Yascha is most content when he's with Tomas and never refuses to carry the loads he puts on him. He is as great a friend to him as he is Marko or George, the village boys. When he hears that his mother is under pressure to sell Yascha to the money lender, who wants the donkey for his own son, Tomas is devastated. First he tries to hide Yascha on a little island in the Danube. After the beloved donkey is found and taken, he and his friends try every way to rescue him. Their opportunity comes when Tomas finds and returns two bears, who disappeared from the visiting circus. The series of events through which Tomas regains his donkey are filled with determination, love, and adventure. Graceful pen drawings complement the perceptively told story.

310. Kušan, Ivan. <u>Koko and the Ghosts</u>. Trans. Drenka
Willen. Illus. Paul Galdone. New York: Harcourt, Brace
and World, 1966. 215 p. Grades 5-8.
  For a long time the Milich family wanted to move from
Green Hill into town, but apartments there were very
difficult to get. This time they were lucky. One of
their friends' aunt, Miss Rosa, told them about the
death of an old man who owned an apartment in the same
building. Like his parents and his younger sister Mary,
thirteen-year-old boy Koko enjoys living in the
comfortable apartment. Most of all, however, he enjoys
the friendships he soon establishes. He is especially
fond of Zlatko, who is a year older than he, and whom he
finds imaginative and resourceful. Sitting on the grass
in a junk yard across the street from Zlatko's house,
the two boys share their secrets and the stories of
their adventures, real and highly imaginative. Wanting
to reveal a special secret to his friend, Zlatko
proposes that he and Koko become blood brothers by
dropping three drops of blood into each other's cut
fingers. By consenting bravely to this physical bond,
Koko and his friend promise to do whatever they can for
each other and share all of their secrets. This pledge
is the beginning of a mysterious adventure for the two
boys. Neither of them is convinced that ghosts exist,
but searching for a secret tunnel under an old shed and
actually seeing a tall white figure moving across the
yard one evening changes their beliefs. These episodes,
as well as such strange, frightening occurances as a
threatening letter, the disappearance of some electrical
fuses, and the cutting of the wires from the apartment
building, set the two boys on their way to a most
surprising discovery. A well constructed story with an
intriquing plot written in a crisp, broadly humorous
style and illustrated with amusingly effective drawings.

311. Kušan, Ivan. <u>The Mystery of Green Hill</u>. Illus.
Kermit Adler. Trans. Michael B. Petrovich. New York:
Harcourt, Brace, and World, 1962. 286 p. Grades 4-8.
  This dramatic detective venture is set in the village of
Green Hill in southwestern Yugoslavia soon after World
War II. Five boys, ages eleven to fifteen, Koko, Tom,
Blacky, Cockroach, and Bozo try to discover who is
poisoning their watchdogs, emptying their chicken coops,
driving away their pigs, and stealing their possessions,
such as laundry hung up to dry and outdoor water pumps.
Mrs. Milich, Koko's mother, thinks that it is the work
of a gang. She and Koko go to the police. But the
militia is short-staffed and cannot help. The war had
ended only a month or so before and they have their
hands full with more important matters than chasing
chicken thieves. The boys decide to find out for
themselves who the robbers are. They have to plan
carefully, boldly, and cautiously. Among others, Isaac,
the old solitary woodcutter, and his blind dog are
suspected. In the end, however, it is Isaac who helps

them find the thieves and who saves the boys from deadly danger.   The   story   contains   much   action,   surprising turns,   and   a   dramatic,   unexpected   ending.   An explanation of the main characters giving their ages, grades they attend, their physical characteristics, and their main traits, is helpful.

312.   Kusan,   Ivan.   <u>The Mystery of the Stolen Paintings</u>. Trans. Drenka Willen.   Illus. Charles Robinson.   New York: Harcourt Brace Jovanovich, 1975.   256 p.   Grades 5-8.
Koko still thinks it is all a dream.   A couple of weeks ago his best friend's father called Koko's parents to ask if Koko would go to Paris with his son Zlatko.   The boys would stay there as guests of Zlatko's uncle, who is a painter.   In preparation for the exciting trip, Koko, under Zlatko's tutelage, studies French daily and listens to Zlatko's stories about the glories of Paris as well as about its dangers.   Koko has never been on a plane before.   By the time he and Zlatko reach Paris, his ears are buzzing, and he feels quite dizzy.   Meeting Zlatko's uncle in the huge arrivals building, Zlatko wants to go to the city immediately to show Koko its attractions.   But Uncle Pokle, as he is called in France, other ideas.   Coming to his apartment he leads the boys to the attic.   With four keys, each of which is taken from a different hiding place, Uncle Pokle unlocks the attic room.   By removing a triple curtain, he shows the boys a painting of a lovely young woman smiling at them mysteriously.   Zlatko recognizes it   immediately   as   Mona   Lisa.   Believing   that   the painting is the same one he saw a year ago in the Louvre, Zlatko is stunned.   Uncle Pokle tells the boys not to reveal his secret to anyone, not telling them that he has been commissioned to paint a copy of the priceless painting to be used in the filming of a movie about the theft of the painting.   Although expecting adventure in Paris, neither of the boys ever had thoughts of being involved in the theft of two Mona Lisas and of experiencing such dangers while there. Soon after the uncle's painting mysteriously disappears from the attic, Koko is kidnapped, but escapes, with Zlatko's help.   The chase after the villains, which ends in a complete surprise, includes many close calls, unexpected   twists,   and   escalating   suspense.   The full-page line drawings reinforce the action, drama, and humor of the story.

313.   Maksimović, Desanka.   <u>The Shaggy Little Dog</u>.   Illus. Józef Wilkón.   Winchester, MA: Faber and Faber, 1983.   N. pag.   Preschool - Grade 2.
Written by a prize-winning poet in her native Yugoslavia and amusingly illustrated in charcoal and crayon by a Polish artist, this is an affectionate story about a playful   stray   dog.   He   comes   from   nowhere   and   just stays.   He romps around the farmyard, races after the ducks,   and   chases   after   butterflies,   bees,   and

ladybirds. With soft howling he sympathizes with those
who are ill in the house and keeps those who appear to
be lonely company. He barks with pleasure when he sees
children at play or older folk happily together. But
just when everyone begins to love him, the little dog
leaves. A natural selection for a nursery school group.

314. Pellowski, Anne. <u>Have You Seen a Comet? Children's
Art and Writing from Around the World</u>. New York: John Day,
1971. 120 p. Grades 2-12.
A delightful collection of poems, stories, and vignettes
written by children from various parts of the world
ranging in age from those in the primary grades to those
in high school. It was the goal of the compiler to
include works by children from all members of the United
Nations, but, of course, not all responded positively
and in time. Most of the writings appear in their
original language, as well as in their English
translation. Of the sixty-one selections grouped under
such broad subject headings as "God Is There," "To Be,"
"I Speak Your Name With Respect," "Walking Down the
Street," "Was It a Dream," and "Peace Is the Fruit of
the Garden," five pieces are from the children of
Yugoslavia, three from the children of Poland, and three
from the children of Czechoslovakia. The five writings
by Yugoslav teenagers, three poems and two short essays,
were originally written in the Serbo-Croatian language.
The poems, written in a light verse, express the beauty
of spring, the meaning of a young tree's whisper in the
woods, and the sad thought of a fallen hero on a moonlit
winter night. The prose selections deal with such
themes as the wedding customs in Yugoslavia and the
mystery of life. High quality full-page reproductions
of selected children's paintings held in the
international collection of children's art at UNICEF's
Information Center on Children's Cultures accompany the
beautiful literary selections.

315. Župančič, Oton. <u>A Selection of Poems</u>. Trans. A.
Lenarčič and others. Ed., introd. Janko Lavrin. Ljubljana:
Državna Založba Slovenije, 1960. 51 p. Grades 6 and up.
Translated selections from the works of one of the
greatest Slovenian poets of all times. Rooted in his
native soil, especially in the regions of Bela Krajina
(White Carniola) bordering on Croatia, Župančič's
impressionistic poems presented in this collection
contain patriotic themes. "Girl of Bela Krajina"
expresses a yearning for a beloved who works in a
foreign land. Similarly, in the fragment from one of
the best known poems, "Meditation," the poet portrays
the fate of the Slovenian people. They should be
gathered in the fields beneath the picturesque mountains
of Triglav and Karavanke, but in reality often find
themselves beyond the reach of vision among the steel
furnaces and in the mines of America and Westphalia.
Other poems, including "The Waterfall," "The Lake," "In

the Evening," "The Ailing Roses," and "A Night Psalm,"
mirror universal themes, such as the poet's deep
feelings of his love, faith, and yearning for peace,
against the splendor of natural phenomena. Smoothly
translated by six individuals, the collection represents
a small bouquet of Župančič's melodic verses from a
field of unsurpassed lyric poetry.

Author, Translator, and Illustrator Index

Numbers below refer to entries, not pages.

Title Index

Numbers below refer to entries, not pages.

Subject Index

Numbers below refer to entries, not pages.

About the Author

FRANCES F. POVSIC is Associate Professor and Head of the Curriculum Resource Center in the University Library at Bowling Green State University. Slovenian by birth, she has studied and worked in both the United States and Europe. Her articles have appeared in journals such as *Booklist*, *The Reading Teacher*, *Journal of Reading*, and *College Research Libraries*, and in the publications of the Educational Resources Information Center.